THE REPRESENTATION OF MEN IN THE ENGLISH GOTHIC NOVEL 1762-1820

Front cover:
Illustration from Thomas Rowlandson's *Dance of Death* (1815) "The Duel".

THE REPRESENTATION OF MEN IN THE ENGLISH GOTHIC NOVEL 1762-1820

Kate E. Behr

Studies in British Literature
Volume 69

The Edwin Mellen Press
Lewiston•Queenston•Lampeter

Library of Congress Cataloging-in-Publication Data

Behr, Kate E., 1964-
   The representation of men in the English Gothic novel, 1762-1820 / Kate E. Behr.
      p. cm. -- (Studies in British literature ; v. 69)
   Includes bibliographical references and index.
   ISBN 0-7734-7016-6
      1. Horror tales, English--History and criticism. 2. English fiction--18th
   century--History and criticism. 3. English fiction--19th century--History and criticism. 4.
   Gothic revival (Literature)--Great Britain. 5. Men in literature. I. Title. II. Series.

   PR858.T3 B54 2002
   823'.087209352041--dc21

                                                                    2002067869

This is volume 69 in the continuing series
Studies in British Literature
Volume 69 ISBN 0-7734-7016-6
SBL Series ISBN 0-88946-927-X

A CIP catalog record for this book is available from the British Library

The Edwin Mellen Press   The Edwin Mellen Press
        Box 450   Box 67
   Lewiston, New York   Queenston, Ontario
    USA 14092-0450   CANADA L0S 1L0

                The Edwin Mellen Press, Ltd.
                Lampeter, Ceredigion, Wales
                UNITED KINGDOM SA48 8LT

              Printed in the United States of America

To my parents

TABLE OF CONTENTS

Preface

The feminist literary criticism of the 1970s and 1980s assured a new importance for Gothic fiction. Ever since becoming popular at the end of the eighteenth century, it had suffered, in canonical terms, from being thought lightweight and sensationalist; leisure reading -- women's reading. Its ready adaptability, both in the nineteenth and twentieth centuries, to new forms of romantic and melodramatic plots did nothing to help its image. But in the last quarter century, its significance to both literary history and theories of fictional composition and consumption has been increasingly recognized.

In the first place, the rediscovery of large numbers of women writers of Gothic fiction has greatly increased our knowledge of their role within a growing literary marketplace, responding to demand but also self-consciously experimenting with the form as soon as conventions started to become established. If the names of Ann Radcliffe, Charlotte Smith, and Mary Shelley had remained relatively well known, a host of other authors -- such as Charlotte Dacre, Sophia Lee, Eliza Parsons and Regina Maria Roche -- have been reexamined, and our sense of the possibilities of the genre greatly extended. Acknowledging and exploring the connections between popular fiction and the volatile politics -- both national and international -- of the late eighteenth and early nineteenth centuries has enabled us to gain an understanding of the ideological connections between imaginative narrative and contemporary issues concerning justice and liberty, imprisonment and freedom. An important aspect of the political dimensions of the novels is, without doubt, the ways in which they engage contemporary debates about the role of women. The publication of Mary Wollstonecraft's *A Vindication of the Rights of Women* (1792) and of the work ascribed to Mary Hays, *An Appeal to the Men of Great Britain in Behalf of Women* (1798), are just the most obvious part of the feminist context in which the emotions and desires of Gothic fiction's women must be placed. Moreover, current discussion of the genre has not limited itself to the issues of representation or the internal structuring of the novel, but has paid increasing attention to the position of the reader swept up in the text. Popularly, even notoriously, this reader was habitually figured as female. Plenty of contemporary comment expressed anxiety, real or faked, about the excitement that this writing might awaken in women readers, and more recent critics have considered both what these anxieties reveal about conservative views concerning women in the society of the time, and what, indeed, may most have appealed to women readers about these novels. Understanding the dynamics of the marketplace adds considerably to our understanding of what is at stake in both the preparation and devouring of Gothic fiction.

Recent years have witnessed a broadening and deepening of the concerns of gender based criticism: issues of performativity; the place of queer theory, and -- of the greatest importance for this study -- the need to pay close attention to constructions of masculinity. If -- as Simone de Beauvoir so succinctly put it, in terms which underpin so much of the feminist criticism of the second half of the twentieth century -- women are not born, but made, the same may be said to be true of men. It is, of course, far more accurate to speak of 'masculinities' rather than 'masculinity', since, like femininity, the concept is a changeable and adaptive one, dependent on the cultural moment to give it meaning. Contexts determine the ways in which such characteristics as heroism, violence and villainy are construed as masculine or associated with particular types of masculinity; the ways in which behaviors and attitudes, bodily appearance and habits of speech are given gendered connotations. If Gothic fictions tend towards a reliance on stereotypes -- one of the criticisms which has regularly been leveled against them -- then they are especially well positioned as cultural barometers, revealing some ideological norms of their period.

One of the great strengths of this study is that Professor Behr has given us a full sense of the mobile social and literary world within which, and against which, the masculinities of Gothic fiction take shape. Gothic men have a tendency to appear as Manichean doubles, heroes and villains: those that fall somewhere in the middle -- a passive, enfeebled father, for example -- are to be pitied, or disapproved of, rather than representing some kind of golden mean. The exceptions to this tendency for types of men to be placed in polar opposition to one another are bandits, robbers, servants, demons, and devils, and Kate Behr writes about these important representatives of various outsider classes with a compelling energy. A central tenet of her argument, however, is that those literary masculinities which are developed within the pages of Gothic fiction need to be placed in relation to other forms of prose writing which were becoming popular among a rapidly growing middle-class. We must take into account both aspirational and critical stances towards the behavior -- real or assumed -- of aristocrat and gentry. To this end, it becomes important to look outside the pages of novels, and Kate Behr does a wonderful job of aligning the men of Gothic fiction, whether improbably perfect or scandalously wicked, with the values promoted in the pages of conduct manuals, designed for those who knew perfectly well that one was not necessarily born a 'gentleman', but one could try and make oneself into a 'perfect' one. This self-construction was often predicated on opposing active forms of masculinity with an assumed passive femininity -- precisely the dynamics which Wollstonecraft and others set out to denaturalize. The strategies of Gothic fiction are necessarily more complicated: the exertion of a villain for reprehensible ends instantly calls into question any equation of active masculinity with virtue; can turn a woman's resistance into a form of resolute action in its own right, and ensures that one promotes the importance of the ends to which characteristics celebrated as 'masculine' are put, rather than the mere possession of these characteristics in the first place.

This book began its life as an Oxford doctoral thesis, which I had the greatest pleasure in supervising. Kate Behr's research quickly stopped me taking the men of Gothic fiction for granted, and made me look deeper into the cultural context that fed into their stereotyping. More than that, her enthusiastic excavation of numerous texts which lay far outside the scope of the extant canon not only strengthened her arguments concerning stereotypes and the many small but telling variations which were played on them, but I owe her a great debt for having introduced me to a large number of novels which were new to me, and which greatly increased my knowledge of, and interest in, the genre. The popularity of Gothic fiction stimulated a number of writers whose works are only just starting to be re-read and re-evaluated for what they contribute to our comprehension of literary, social and gender history. Kate Behr's book contributes significantly to the field.

Kate Flint
Department of English
Rutgers: The State University of New Jersey, New Brunswick

Acknowledgments

No work appears unaided, and there are many people and institutions to whom I owe grateful thanks.

For the financial support that enabled me to spend three years at Oxford working on Gothic men, I would like to thank the British Academy, and Pembroke College, Oxford. For supervising, reading, advising, suffering, and finally writing the preface to the manuscript, I am very grateful to Dr. Kate Flint. I would also like to thank the English Department at Iona College, who gave me a course remission when I really needed it in order to work on revising the manuscript. Some of those whom I would like to acknowledge died before the manuscript ever reached this stage, but grateful thanks are still felt and owed to Dr. Frances Stephens and Dr. David Fleeman. Memory eternal! Finally, I would like to express my appreciation and affection for my husband, and sons, Felix and Rufus, without (to paraphrase P.G. Wodehouse) whose enduring love and support the manuscript might have been finished in half the time.

Introduction

Criticism of the Gothic has typically either considered the male characters as negligible elements of the Gothic formula, or has grouped them together as a single, powerful element. Men are perceived *en masse* as the threatening patriarchal society, surrounding and dominating the heroine, who has long been considered as the most important character type of the Gothic romance.

The engravers who prepared the frontispieces for the Minerva Press' most famous Gothic romances chose to illustrate striking moments in the story, featuring a threatened or isolated woman, often depicted in a state of unconscious dishevelment.[1] The most exciting moments in the tale are also often the most static, frozen moments of terror, supporting the idea that the Gothic is composed of specific set pieces, and thus the women represented are passive. They are the still, focal point of the picture and the focus of emotion for the reader.

They are also stereotypes – every heroine is clearly marked out by her beauty, her youth, her exemplary moral character, and her helplessness. However, the active male characters surrounding the supine heroine are the focus of this study. They too follow recognisable patterns of character and role, consistently fulfilling a certain function or role within the plot. There is always a hero, there must always be a villain who oppresses or obstructs (otherwise there is no story), and there is a supporting cast of male friends, rivals, parents, servants, and officials. From 1764, when Walpole self-consciously wrote that he was creating a new genre – 'an attempt to blend the two kinds of romance, the ancient and the modern' – to 1820 (and later), the reader of the Gothic novel might confidently expect to encounter a certain cast of characters involved in certain types of

---

[1] Dorothy Blakey, *The Minerva Press 1790-1820* (Oxford: Oxford University Press, 1939), 89-94.

relationship that could only be played out in certain surroundings.[2] Walpole established the formula: a castle or ruin (with dungeons, vaults, and a secret passage to the chapel); a guilty tyrant; a suspected history of blood spilt; supernatural manifestations; a nobly-born hero; a suffering but morally intrepid heroine; fear; subterranean adventures; and a mystery connected with birth and inheritance. These conditions influenced the creation of character and this set the trend for succeeding novelists. Gothic novels were concerned, from their very inception, with the devastating effects of uncontrolled passions, and this necessarily formed a pattern of tyrants and victims – power and submission followed by the inexorable workings of divine retribution. The characters thus play roles within the formula of the Gothic novel that are reproduced across the whole spectrum of the genre. To this extent they are stereotypes.

Males appearing in Gothic novels, however, do not simply fulfil stereotyped roles within the Gothic formula (as hero, father and villain, for example) but are also stereotyped *characters*. One does not encounter different male characters who are cast in the villain's role, for example; but rather similar characters cast in similar roles. Thus one may argue that there is a Gothic formula of character as well as of role and situation.

One function of this study, then, is to reveal, by examining a wide variety of texts, the specific male character stereotype which a reader might typically expect to encounter in a certain role or situation. By first locating these stereotypes and examining not only the repeated pattern of their representation but the way in which these representations are manipulated, we arrive at an understanding of the Gothic formula. This method of approach develops within the inevitable circle of any inquiry; an examination of the function of a particular stock character

---

[2] Horace Walpole, *The Castle of Otranto, A Gothic Story* (1764; repr. from 1798 text, Oxford: Oxford University Press, ed. and intro. W.S. Lewis, notes, J.W. Reed Jr., 1982), 7.

(individual text by individual text) leads back to a wider understanding not only of these stock characters, but also of the formula itself.

This method also applies to the organisation of the chapters. Before considering stock figures individually, the genres of fantasy, horror and romance are examined and their influence on the creation or representation of male stereotypes in the Gothic novel is considered. Then, in order to establish the ideal patterns of behaviour for the hero, we turn to contemporary conduct books; it is in this chapter that the importance of the female stereotype in relation to that of the male becomes apparent. Having established what the contemporary ideals for masculine behaviour were, the next chapter considers actual representations of the hero figure as an idealised stereotype of masculinity. The father is what the hero eventually becomes, and so the following chapter considers the representation of the father figure, which reflects back onto the figure of the hero and more generally the stereotype of masculine activity which both embody. The villain figure (the only male figure to have received any substantial critical attention) is opposed both to the hero and the 'good' father; he is often represented as perverting both the role of the father and the positive activity associated with the idealised stereotype of masculinity. Thus, as a negative image of both hero and father, he is the next stock figure to be considered. The stereotype of masculinity is then further scrutinised in a chapter on the victim figure, which examines the importance of the female victim, and also suggests that the stereotype of masculinity itself can be viewed as a form of victimisation within the Gothic formula. The final chapter examines the stock male characters of servants, bandits and spectres or demons, whose representation within the romances reinforces our understanding of the roles that major characters play in the Gothic formula.

In establishing the sources of the stereotypes used in the Gothic romances, it has been necessary to investigate other contemporary literature to discover whether the values and expectations of an eighteenth-century reader contributed to the creation of character and formula, or whether the Gothic itself created and imposed expectations for the reader. These are not necessarily antithetical hypotheses: both solutions proved to be possible. Some figures, like those of hero and father, were supported by the evidence of other types of eighteenth-century literature, while the villain figure proved to have literary antecedents, and the wicked monk was almost a Gothic invention.

Though other types of literature proved to be important evidence for the sources or representation of various stereotypes, the most important sources of all have obviously been the Gothic romances themselves. In attempting an accurate examination of a part of the Gothic formula, I have not made any value judgements or created definitive divisions between different types of Gothic. This is not to say, however, that my choices either of date parameters or of texts are random ones.

My attitude towards the selection of novels from which to draw the material for an examination of stereotypes, and the dates within which these novels fall, is inclusive rather than exclusive. An examination of stereotypes and formula must include the earliest Gothic novels, the most 'serious' Gothic novels and the 'market-Gothics.' These last are, perhaps, the most exciting sources of evidence for the representation of stereotype and the workings of formula. Texts like George Walker's *The Haunted Castle*, or *The Three Spaniards* and W.H. Ireland's *Gondez the Monk* present a crude working of Gothic formula and blatant (in Ireland's case, exuberant) stereotypes.[3]

The choice of texts to be studied did, however, require some rudimentary definition of what, for the purposes of this study, is considered to be Gothic. Some authors and texts virtually chose themselves – no assessment of the Gothic would be complete without some reference to the well-known authors of the

---

[3] George Walker, *The Haunted Castle*, 2 vols. (London: Minerva Press, 1794) and *The Three Spaniards*, 3 vols. (London: Walker, Hurst, 1800). W.H. Ireland, *Gondez the Monk*, 4 vols. (London: Longman, Hurst, Rees and Orme, 1805).

genre, Walpole, Radcliffe, Lewis, Mary Shelley, and Maturin. The choice of lesser-known authors was rather more difficult, but the texts chosen fulfilled two basic criteria: first, that they should have most of the Gothic 'trappings'; and second, that there should be instances of either the supernatural, the apparent supernatural, or passions raised to a height at which they acquired a supernatural force.

The choice of date parameters (1762-1820) within which to study as wide a variety of Gothic material as possible was entirely pragmatic. Although most assessments of the Gothic novel begin in 1764 with the publication of *The Castle of Otranto*, 1762 was preferable as the year in which Thomas Leland's *Longsword, Earl of Salisbury: An Historical Romance* appeared, ushering the figure of Reginhald the wicked monk onto the literary scene. The year 1820 is similarly a publication date and convenient endpoint. Maturin's *Melmoth the Wander* appeared in 1820 and was received as a revival of a dying genre.[4] Of course, the publication of *Melmoth the Wanderer* does not mark the end of the Gothic as a literary mode – many studies have been done on the Gothicism of Dickens or Charlotte Brontë, for example – but, after *Melmoth*, critics have discussed either Gothicism or a Gothic root for non-realist texts, not the Gothic itself.

The dominant impression of a Gothic romance has been of a tableau whose centre of attraction is a sacrificial victim, female and senseless, hair and dress in equal but charming disarray. This study draws attention to the active but critically unseen participants hovering around the central figure. It shows how writers have represented and used the identity of the powerful figure holding the knife, the rescuer in the background and the assembled group of watchers who are allowing – even encouraging – the rite to take place.

---

[4] Elizabeth Napier, *The Failure of Gothic: Problems of Disjunction in an Eighteenth-Century Literary Form* (Oxford: Clarendon Press, 1987), xii-xiii.

1

The Gothic Formula and the Critics

I. The Formula

Gothic fiction is formula fiction:

The world of the gothic novelist bore no relation to reality. The air was thick with the smell of putrefying corpses on lonely gibbets, and picturesquely ruined castles were inhabited by bats and mad nuns. Generations of virtuous but insipid heroines languished in dark and dreary dungeons from which they were rescued by impeccable heroes, while a fitful moon shone through a break in the clouds after the storm with which so many of these novels opened. It was almost a convention of such tales that the hero should be cheated out of his rightful inheritance by some moustached and scheming relative who had first murdered the boy's parents. A secret closet was opened, and the ghosts of the murdered ones shocked the villain into discomfiture. The rightful heir was restored to his estates, having first rescued his beloved from the unwelcome attentions of the villain.[1]

This list is not a definition. These conventions and appurtenances describe part of a 'Gothic' formula, but do not define the term 'Gothic.' Despite the intense critical discussions of the last few decades, many of which have tried to classify the elusive atmosphere peculiar to 'Gothic' fiction by analysing it according to various critical, ideological stances, no simple definition has been posited and universally accepted. We are left with lists of specific stock elements, like the one above, coupled with various late twentieth-century interpretations of a reader's probable expectations of and emotional reactions to the text.[2] In the end, the for-

---

[1] Victor E. Neuberg, *Popular Literature: A History and Guide* (Middlesex: Pelican, 1977), 151. Despite the arch tone, this summary of conventions indicates not only how the Gothic is popularly understood, but also highlights the major themes, motifs and settings. Cf. Chris Baldick (ed.), *The Oxford Book of Gothic Tales* (Oxford: Oxford University Press, 1990), xvi, for a similar list.

[2] Cf. David Richter, whose argument is based on his observation that critics commonly treat the Gothic more as a myth, as a collection of conventions or as a story to be told, reporting important events, but rarely, if ever, treat it historically, considering the context and background. *The Progress of Romance: Literary Historiography and the Gothic Novel* (Columbus, OH: Ohio State University Press, 1996), 21.

mula always seems to triumph over individual interpretations of its elements in combination.

Whatever else is understood by the term 'Gothic,' the above list indicates that the following stock elements are definitely part of our popular understanding of the formula. These elements are the setting – typically archaic, isolated and illuminated by dramatic weather conditions; the interaction of stock character types – villain, hero and heroine; the presence of the supernatural and the eventual disclosure of a secret. This study focuses on one expression of the formula – the representation of stock male characters. Examining the representation of men within a large number of Gothic romances establishes repeated patterns that reveal the formula for the literary characterisation and role of 'Gothic' men. At the same time, this aspect of the formula is placed within a contemporary, literary/cultural context, tracing a nexus of influences, or histories, that helped to create the stock characters peopling the world of the Gothic romance.

Concentrating on the conventions of the Gothic romance might be considered a reactionary stance, a reversion to the focus on appurtenances adopted by the earliest twentieth-century critics of the Gothic.[3] These early works are limited in scope, providing a compendium of devices but little more. Later criticism, seeking to establish the Gothic as a 'serious' genre, used psychoanalysis to demonstrate how this type of fiction might reveal unconscious desires and repressed social anxieties.[4] More recent work has tended to re-evaluate the conventions them-

---

[3] Eino Railo, for example, considered stock characters as important components of Gothic fiction and gave them individual chapters in his study of the links between the Gothic and the Romantic in *The Haunted Castle: A Study of the Elements of English Romanticism* (London: Routledge, 1927). Other early twentieth-century critics writing on the Gothic novel, Montague Summers, *The Gothic Quest: A History of the Gothic Novel* (London: Fortune Press, 1938), and Edith Birkhead, *The Tale of Terror: A Study of the Gothic Romance* (London: Constable, 1921), produced works largely consisting of enthusiastic lists of stock devices or, in Edith Birkhead's case, of plot summaries.

[4] E.g. Robert Hume, 'Gothic versus Romantic: a Revaluation of the Gothic Novel', *PLMA* lxxxiv (March 1969), Robert Kiely, *The Romantic Novel in England* (Cambridge: Harvard University Press, 1972), and Masao Miyoshi, *The Divided Self: A Perspective on the Literature of the Victorians* (New York: New York University Press, 1969). See also Fred Botting, *Gothic* (London & New York: Routledge, 1996), 17-20.

selves, and here the most influential study is Eve Kosofsky Sedgwick's *The Coherence of Gothic Conventions* (1980).[5] It is an assimilative, thematic study in which 'surface' conventions are not examined as indicators of psychological depth – as would have been popular in the mid-twentieth century – but, tending towards a more post-modern perspective, are considered as the essential structure by which the world of the Gothic romance is to be comprehended. In stressing the coherence of Gothic conventions and the presence of a formula, Sedgwick was reacting against 'Gothic' criticism that either uses the conventions of the Gothic formula as signifiers of depth or dismisses them as top-dressing.[6] Two different, critical approaches to Gothic appurtenances are apparent: in one camp are found those critics (like Sedgwick and Napier) who focus on the signs or the conventions of the Gothic, and in the other are located those who focus on what these signs signify. In other words, there are critics who consider the Gothic as formula, and there are critics who concede the presence of certain frivolous and repetitive trappings but assert that the 'Gothic' exists beyond and despite them.[7]

Beyond her, perhaps questionable, assertion that Gothic conventions are unified, Sedgwick makes two points about the Gothic formula which have a bearing on this study. First, she justly observes that 'The formula for the Gothic novel functions at the level of particular more or less obligatory scenes,' which suggests that the formula stabilises the Gothic and also indicates that relationships between

---

[5] Eve Kosofsky Sedgwick, *The Coherence of Gothic Conventions* (1980; repr. London: Methuen, 1986).

[6] Elizabeth Napier, who also asserted that Gothic fiction is essentially formulaic, though denying that there is any formal coherence to the Gothic novel, takes a similar position. *The Failure of Gothic: Problems of Disjunction in an Eighteenth-Century Literary Form* (Oxford: Clarendon Press, 1987), 29. Napier reacted specifically against Robert D. Hume's influential article, 'Gothic versus Romantic,' in which one of his stated objects was 'to suggest that the Gothic novel is more than a collection of ghost-story devices' 282.

[7] Although I have stated this critical position in extreme terms, critics who adopt the 'depth psychology' approach do dismiss the appurtenances of the Gothic as mere trappings. Masao Miyoshi, for example, refers to 'the incidental trappings of the Gothic,' *The Divided Self*, 10.

characters follow recognisable and repeatable patterns.[8] Characters and their relationships are stereotyped. If one accepts Sedgwick's (and Napier's) contention that the formula of the Gothic romance is found in repeated stereotypical relationships or in the recurrence of certain set pieces, then an examination of formula must be focused on these stereotypes and recurring scenes, rather than on the plot which, although it does stimulate the reader's interest and excite the reader's curiosity, exists primarily to bring these characters into their predestined relationships within the Gothic formula. Therefore, the focus of this investigation is on the sources and representations of male character stereotypes as they appear in the set pieces that constitute the Gothic formula.

Sedgwick's second point is that the scope of the novel is not necessarily limited by the formula:

> The second remarkable thing about the Gothic formula, mitigating its narrowness, is the range of tone and focus possible within it. Granted that the novel contains a hero and heroine, either one can hold the writer's attention, sometimes to the almost complete neglect of the other [...]. Again, the novels' obligatory villains, though almost always of the same generation and displaying the same physiognomy, can be just a cursory adjunct to the plot, like Clara Reeve's Lord Lovel, or can be the animating center of the novel, like Ambrosio.[9]

Sedgwick suggests that the formula can be manipulated to achieve different effects, highlighting a starting point for further investigation. This present study also considers points at which the basic stereotypes are manipulated, extended, or reinforced, testing and demonstrating the prevalence of the Gothic formula, as applied to character rather than theme. In order to demonstrate the existence and coherence of this part of the Gothic formula, it was necessary to examine a wide variety of works, ranging from those still in print to those which have sunk into obscurity.

---

[8] Sedgwick, *Gothic Conventions*, 10. Cf. Napier, *The Failure of Gothic*, 29, in which she asserts that the reader's enjoyment and the stability of the genre can both be traced to the repetition of conventional scenes and events.

[9] Sedgwick, *Gothic Conventions*, 10-11.

Whether well known or deservedly obscure, Gothic texts are slippery, resisting classification and definition. Despite the suggestion that Gothic criticism falls into only two groups, there are, of course, many attitudes or ideologies that have shaped and distinguished the approaches and the conclusions of individual critics. The dominant critical approaches of the latter half of the twentieth century have tried to elevate the Gothic in various ways – all of them using the Gothic to represent a conscious or unconscious index of contemporary anxieties about gender, class, or self. Thus the Gothic has acquired universal, popular significance as feminist literature, as a reflection of revolutionary ideas and anxieties about them, and as either a Romantic precursor or Romantic underbelly, revealing the darker side of Romanticism. Without necessarily being aligned with any of these approaches, this study has certainly benefited from the complex of insights that they offer, and a brief survey of their approaches is both appropriate and necessary.

II. The Gothic and the Romantic

'Romantic' critics of the Gothic like Masao Miyoshi, Elizabeth MacAndrew, Robert Keily and R.D. Hume have placed the Gothic in the context of its literary relationship to the Romantic Movement.[10] Thus, their focus is upon those elements in the Gothic that seem most in tune with 'Romantic' themes and preoccupations – a focus upon the individual, upon the mind, and upon the imagination.[11] There is certainly a valid connection between the Gothic and Romanticism when Romanticism is considered in terms of a late eighteenth/early nineteenth-century

---

[10] Miyoshi, *Divided Self*, 3-45. Elizabeth MacAndrew, *The Gothic Tradition in Fiction* (New York: Columbia University Press, 1979). Robert Keily, *The Romantic Novel in England*, and Hume, 'Gothic versus Romantic', 282-90.

[11] R.D. Hume, for example, concluded that the reader of both Gothic and romantic writings becomes absorbed with the individual because he/she is constantly confronting internal states of being, and so both Gothic and Romantic writing are focused on and preoccupied with the mind. 'Gothic versus Romantic', 288-9. Cf. David Simpson's analysis which, while indicating that the term itself cannot be easily defined, does suggest that a focus on the individual self is a valid component of Romantic writing. 'Romanticism, criticism and theory', in Stuart Curran (ed.), *The Cambridge Companion to British Romanticism* (Cambridge: Cambridge University Press, 1993), 10.

period label without any other prescriptive characteristics.[12] There are also, however, aesthetic as well as temporal connections between the Gothic and other forms of Romantic writing. Theories of the sublime, for example, which located the sublime sensation in the individual response rather than regarding it as an integral attribute of the object viewed, have been applied to Gothic and Romantic writing alike.[13]

There are, then, evident connections between the Gothic and the Romantic: when considered chronologically and when considered aesthetically or thematically. However, there are some drawbacks to focusing exclusively on the Gothic/Romantic connection – feeling is privileged over formula and the villain-hero dominates. Critics who view the Gothic as a Romantic precursor have concentrated increasingly on the psychological depths that they perceive in the Gothic novel. They have exploited the Gothic as an expression of the perversities of human nature: 'Gothic fiction gives shape to concepts of the place of evil in the human mind.'[14] They have suggested (and this is reminiscent of the awesome obscurity that Burke identified as an essential part of the sublime) that Gothic novelists were attempting to name the unnameable, bringing darker reality nearer to consciousness.[15] If these critics discuss characterisation at all, therefore, it is typically to concentrate attention on the fascinating qualities of the villain-hero:

> It is often said that in Gothic fiction there are either no believable characters at all or else there is one so monstrously absorbent as to make the form seem

---

[12] In essence, this is the 'Romantic' definition given by David Simpson, 'Romanticism, criticism and theory', 1.

[13] For a further discussion of the sublime and its connection to the representation of male character see

[14] MacAndrew, *Gothic Tradition*, 3. Hume similarly states that the Gothic novel could be viewed as a psychological investigation of evil. 'Gothic versus Romantic', 287.

[15] The phrase 'this nameless mode of naming the unnameable' was used by Mary Shelley, when commenting on the typographical blank denoting the monster's name on the playbill of Peake's *Presumption: or the Fate of Frankenstein*. Betty T. Bennett (ed.), *The Letters of Mary Wollstonecraft Shelley*, 3 vols. (Baltimore and London: Johns Hopkins University Press, 1980-1988), i. 378.

a kind of obscene exhibitionism. There is nothing between the cipher and the creature of gargantuan potency in an empty world.[16]

Robert Kiely's central point, that the Gothic villain can be a developed character (albeit over-developed) while other characters are generically empty stereotypes, is as misleading as his assumption that this observation is a critical given. For the figure of the villain, though subject to some interesting variations in representation, is as much a stereotype as the other stock characters within the Gothic formula. Perhaps more importantly, and Kiely's comment does indicate this, the villain figure is frequently represented as an intensification and perversion of the ideal active male stereotype presented in the figure of the hero.

Another consequence of treating the Gothic as a Romantic precursor showing many embryonic Romantic themes, is that not only do all characters save the villain fade into insignificance, but so does the Gothic itself. It becomes valued only for those works that seem to demonstrate 'serious' psychological interests and pre-Romantic themes. In his reply to Robert Platzner, R.D. Hume makes this point very clearly:

> My "superficial catalogue" of its characteristics is an attempt to differentiate serious Gothic writing from what J.M.S. Tompkins calls "market-Gothics" – surely a necessary prelude to suggesting that Gothic writing be considered along with the works of the greatest "Romantic" poets.[17]

Given that Hume wanted to establish the literary importance of the Gothic, his distinction between 'serious' and 'market-Gothics' is understandable. Unfortunately, this distinction prevents any wider understanding of the Gothic or the Gothic formula. A close reading of the 'market-Gothics' is vital to an understanding of the Gothic genre as a whole, particularly to an understanding of the Gothic formula and its stereotypes which, though more crude perhaps than those found in

---

[16] Kiely, *Romantic Novel in England*, 115-16. Cf. MacAndrew who similarly describes typically Gothic characters as simplified embodiments of ideas. *Gothic Tradition*, 12.

[17] Platzner, 'A Rejoinder', 268.

'serious' works, are nevertheless present in 'market-Gothics' in a clearly apparent form.

III. The Female Gothic

Not all critics who have explored the Gothic in terms of psychological depth or the surfacing of repressed emotions have focused on either the villain-hero or the Gothic/Romantic relationship. Just as Sedgwick and Napier reacted against a specific mode of criticism that denied the importance of the formula, this study too was undertaken partly as a reaction against a prevalent critical stance that sees the Gothic only as an expression of female experience, written by, for and about women.[18] Therefore, although the primary purpose is an examination of male stereotypes, this study also considers the grounds on which the Gothic genre has been associated with women, and has been given the epithet 'female.'

Since 1976, the year in which the term 'Female Gothic' entered the critical vocabulary, the Gothic genre – once neglected, despised and dismissed – has been reinterpreted, discovered to be a genre with particular and very close associations with the female – also neglected, despised and dismissed.[19] However, when Ellen Moers first coined the term 'Female Gothic' in *The New York Review of Books* before developing it into a chapter of her book *Literary Women*, it was based simply on gender and genre. She wrote:

> What I mean by Female Gothic is easily defined: the work that women writers have done in the literary mode that, since the eighteenth century, we have called the Gothic. But what I mean – or what anybody else means – by the "Gothic" is not so easily stated except that it has to do with fear.[20]

Given this definition, one has to agree that there is indeed a Female Gothic – and a female version of any other genre that one cares to name. Despite, however, the

---

[18] For a discussion indicating how the heroine becomes the focus of attention see Bette B. Roberts, *The Gothic Romance: Its Appeal to Women Writers and Readers in Late Eighteenth-Century England* (New York: Arno Press, 1980), 228.

[19] Cf. Dale Spender, *Mothers of the Novel* (London: Pandora Press, 1986), 243.

potential variety suggested by 'the work that women have done in the literary mode,' Moers's chapter welds the 'Female Gothic' into a single, coherent tradition stretching from the eighteenth century to the present day. The basis for this tradition is the expression of female experience, which forms a consistent part of Moers's argument. In her introduction, she categorically denied the existence of a particularly female style whilst the effect of the book is to promote the idea of continuing and accessible female thematics. To this end Moers discussed Mary Shelley's *Frankenstein* as a female birth myth, and Emily Brontë's *Wuthering Heights* and Christina Rossetti's *Goblin Market* as further fantasies (or perversities) of childhood, eventually identifying 'Female Gothic' as the literature of the monster, with its fearful roots in the nursery and the liberating cruelties of girlhood. The Gothic property of fear is thus linked to female experience, creating the Female Gothic.

It is a fascinating reading but, perhaps significantly, the texts on which Moers concentrated (with the exception of *Frankenstein* which, however, appeared in its revised version in 1831) all date from the mid-nineteenth century – at least fifty years after the inception of the Gothic genre. The examples selected by Moers suggest, therefore, that the Female Gothic expressing female anxiety, at least in her terms, is a late development. The only eighteenth-century practitioner that Moers mentioned in the Female Gothic chapter (and that briefly) is Ann Radcliffe, whose works certainly express the anxiety of the heroine in threatening situations. In a later chapter Moers suggested that Ann Radcliffe trafficked 'in real female fears', the loss of respectability, and the very real restraint present in girlhood and later in marriage that might lead to actual imprisonment for the eighteenth-century bride. The first brief mention of Ann Radcliffe's contribution to the Female Gothic is, however, much more significant than Moers herself realised. Mrs. Radcliffe's contribution to the Gothic, as identified by Moers, is both

---

[20] Ellen Moers, *Literary Women* (New York, 1976; repr. London: The Women's Press, 1986), 90.

structural and thematic – it lies in the creation of a central figure, 'a young woman who is simultaneously persecuted victim and courageous heroine.'[21] Moers has correctly identified the importance of the female; however, as this present study will show, the female victim/heroine figure was always a key element of the formula of the early Gothic romances, including those predating Mrs. Radcliffe. Thus, one can assert that there *is* a valid classification of the Gothic novel as 'female,' but it is a classification that includes the earliest examples *and* works written by men.

The gender basis of Moers's original definition, however, associated not only female writers with the Gothic but also the female condition with fear. The assumption that female writers use the Gothic to express a peculiarly female experience of fear (or, as Sedgwick suggested, both hysteria and paranoia) is a natural extension of Moers's definition.[22] But fear of what?

Some critics suggest that the fear inherent in the Gothic genre *per se* is concerned in the Female Gothic specifically with female identity, and with what the heroine might become – the mother.[23] This interpretation of the Female Gothic with its potential doubling of mother and heroine (and potentially destructive relationship between them) suggests that the Female Gothic concretises the fear of the female self. This is what Moers earlier described as the 'self-disgust, the self-hatred and the impetus to self-destruction'; this is what she saw as the typically female action of giving '*visual* form to the fear of self' of holding 'anxiety up to the Gothic mirror of the imagination.'[24] Juliann Fleenor echoes the same fear in her introduction to *The Female Gothic*:

> It is essentially formless, except as a quest; it uses the traditional spatial symbolism of the ruined castle or an enclosed room to symbolise both the culture and the heroine; as a psychological form, it provokes various feelings of terror, anger, awe and sometimes self-fear and self-disgust directed toward

---

[21] Moers, *Literary Women*, 91.

[22] Sedgwick, *Gothic Conventions*, vi-x.

[23] See Tania Modleski, *Loving with a Vengeance: Mass-produced Fantasies for Women* (London: Methuen, 1984), 68.

[24] Moers, *Literary Women*, 107.

the female role, female sexuality, female physiology, and procreation.... It reflects a patriarchal paradigm that women are motherless yet fathered and that women are defective because they are not males.[25]

Like Moers and Modleski, Fleenor clearly saw the Female Gothic as a separate tradition, partaking of some of the symbolism of the Gothic, but identifiable by the sense of ambivalence towards the female self. The patriarchal paradigm to which she referred, however, is present in the earliest Gothic novels only in a limited and modified form. Both heroines and heroes are indeed motherless, yet, as we shall see, the formula of the Gothic romance demands that they be *fatherless* also. The good father figure establishes the paradigm of the 'good' father early in the novel and is then rendered impotent, forced into absence.[26]

The Gothic, whether written by men or women, can indeed take the form of an individual quest for identity: the birth-secret or the absent father which are prominent features of many Gothic romances almost guarantee the hero's or heroine's search for an identity and a family name. The reflection of a patriarchal paradigm or the presence of a quest for identity, then, is not enough to justify the appellation 'Female Gothic.' Nor, to be fair, did Fleenor assert that it was. Of her definition she said: 'Although most of these characteristics can apply in differing degrees to the Gothic as written by men, the use of the spatial imagery is different, especially with the feelings of self-fear and self-disgust.'[27] What differentiates 'male' Gothic from 'female' Gothic, then, according to Fleenor, is the expression of female anxieties, conveying protest, rage and terror in a conflict over female identity.

All this assumes a female readership. This is an assumption apparently made by many critics for whom Female Gothic seems to depend not only on a female

---

[25] Juliann Fleenor (ed.), *Female Gothic* (Montreal/London: Eden Press, 1983), 15.

[26] E.g. Radcliffe's St. Aubert, in Radcliffe, *The Mysteries of Udolpho* (1794; repr. Oxford: Oxford University Press, ed. and intro. Bonamy Dobrée, 1980); Regina Maria Roche's Clermont in *Clermont*, 4 vols. (1798; repr. London: A.K. Newman & Co., 1836); and Clifford, the adoptive father in Eliza Parsons, *The Mysterious Visit: A Novel, Founded on Facts*, 4 vols. (London: Hurst, Hatchard, Carpenter & Co., 1802). For a further discussion on the fate of the father figure see

author (beginning inevitably with the works of Ann Radcliffe, particularly *Mysteries*) but also a sympathetic female reader. Most work on the readership of the Female Gothic, by critics like Kay J. Mussell and Joanna Russ, has concentrated on Modern Gothic – the works of Victoria Holt and Susan Howatch for example.[28] Women almost exclusively read the Modern Female Gothic, and thus theories about female anxiety and female reassurance that seem to depend on woman to woman contact may be posited with some confidence. It is when the Female Gothic is considered generically and theories, formulated it seems about the Modern Female Gothic, are read backwards and applied to earlier works in order, perhaps, to establish an unbroken literary tradition, that assumptions about readership, and therefore about the Female Gothic as currently defined, can no longer be maintained.

Plenty of evidence exists demonstrating that the majority of early Gothic romances were written and read by women. Witness, for example, the dire warnings about the effects of reading romances in many conduct books of the period directed at women. Furthermore, satires on the genre like Eaton Stannard Barrett's *The Heroine* (1813) and, of course, Austen's *Northanger Abbey* (1818) concentrate on the comedy generated by the figures of young women who attempt to apply the standards of the Gothic romance to real life.[29] All this supports the popular stereotype of the female who closeted herself eagerly with the latest 'horrid' romance. Nevertheless, in the late eighteenth and early nineteenth centuries, more men than Henry Tilney or, less fictionally, Percy Shelley, Richard Brinsley Sheridan, Sir Walter Scott and the Marquis de Sade read Gothic romances. We cannot, therefore, assume an *exclusively* female readership for any of the earliest Gothic texts.

---

[27] Fleenor (ed.), *Female Gothic*, 15.

[28] Joanna Russ, 'Someone's Trying to Kill Me And I Think It's My Husband: The Modern Gothic', and Kay J. Mussell, 'But Why Do They Read Those Things?: The Female Audience and the Gothic Novel', in Fleenor (ed.), *The Female Gothic*, 31-56 and 57-68.

[29] Eaton Stannard Barrett, *The Heroine or Adventures of a Fair Romance Reader*, 3 vols. (London: Henry Colburn, 1813). Jane Austen, *Northanger Abbey* (London: John Murray, 1818).

While asserting that men also read the earlier Gothic romances, there is no attempt to deny or ignore the valuable points made by these critics about female anxiety generated within and by the texts. An exclusively female readership cannot be assumed, but neither can one assume that male and female readers had (or have) an identical response to the situations and emotional conflicts posed by the Gothic. Norman Holland and Leona F. Sherman's joint essay 'Gothic Possibilities' directly addresses this question of gender, reading and response.[30] Their analysis of differing male/female projections is based on woman's self-abnegating position within contemporary society. They suggest that women experienced a sense of both pleasure and menace from their reading of anxieties about penetration in Gothic romances because the pain of nothingness, or non-active identity demanded by social expectation, is painfully yet, paradoxically, satisfyingly filled by penetration. Men, they consider, identify with the female anxiety but the threat of penetration questions male identity, and Gothic is thus relegated to 'women's fiction'. Some of the points made by Holland and Sherman relate directly to this study. First, although neither Holland nor Sherman mentions the word 'stereotype', their analysis revolves around the type of role – both male and female – dictated by social expectations and constraints. Second, they suggest that the Gothic romance had a feminising effect on the male reader and, although the extent of a male reader's identification with the beleaguered heroine is doubtful, masculinity, allied to the idea of an active male stereotype, is often questioned and manipulated within the Gothic texts.[31]

---

[30] Holland, Norman and Leona F. Sherman, 'Gothic Possibilities', in Elizabeth A. Flynn and Patrocinio Schwieckart (eds.), *Gender and Reading: Essays on Readers, Texts and Contexts* (Baltimore and London: Johns Hopkins University Press, 1986), 215-33.

[31] It seems more likely that the male reader might have placed himself in the position of titillated observer, rather than sharer, of the spectacle of female distress. D.A. Miller, however, has convincingly argued in an analysis of the gender relations in Wilkie Collins's *The Woman in White* that the male reader is indeed 'feminised' by identifying with female sensation within the text. '*Cage aux Folles*: Sensation and Gender in Wilkie Collins's *The Woman in White*', Jeremy Hawthorn (ed.), *The Nineteenth-Century British Novel* (London: Edward Arnold, 1986), 106.

No definitions of the Female Gothic have been entirely satisfactory in relation to the earliest Gothic romances. The blanket statement of Moers's initial definition, that the Female Gothic encompasses works written by women in the Gothic mode since the eighteenth century in which fear has been joined to female experience, was not even borne out by her restricted choice of illustrative texts. The evidence does not support the suggestion that anxiety associated with the heroine is a distinctive property of Female Gothic. Actual danger surrounding the female and anxiety consequent upon it also appears in works written by men. One part of Fleenor's definition of the Female Gothic indicated the reflection of a destructive patriarchal paradigm, but the patriarchal paradigm that appears in the earliest romances is common to male and female writers and is not the one she defined. Also those critics who identified the Female Gothic as a search and a struggle for female identity have simply added an adjective of gender to what is demonstrably an integral part of the Gothic formula in the late eighteenth century.

IV. Gothic as 'Political' Anxiety

Some critics have set the Gothic in the context of literary development, i.e. in relation to the Romantic Movement or as a reaction to the 'realistic' novels of Defoe, Fielding and Smollett; others have set the Gothic in a context of specific contemporary fears. Feminist critics focused on the contemporary fears, and repressed anxieties of the woman's experience: a further group of critics have considered the Gothic as an entirely different expression of contemporary anxiety. David Punter, Ronald Paulson and Chris Baldick have all associated the fears expressed in the Gothic with contemporary political anxiety – though not necessarily the same political anxieties.[32] Writing from a Marxist stance, David Punter regarded the genre as a product of the middle class, suggesting that the aristocratic

---

[32] David Punter, *The Literature of Terror: A History of Gothic Fictions from 1765 to the Present Day* (London: Longman, 1980). Ronald Paulson, 'Gothic Fiction and the French Revolution', *ELH* xlviii (1981), 532-54. Chris Baldick, *In Frankenstein's Shadow: Myth, Monstrosity, and Nineteenth-Century Writing* (1987; repr. Oxford: Clarendon Press, 1990), and his introduction to *The Oxford Book of Gothic Tales* (Oxford: Oxford University Press, 1992).

class values within the novels represent bourgeois curiosity about a pre-bourgeois world. He further suggested that Gothic fiction served as a means by which contemporary culture might analyse itself, throwing up and exorcising troubling, dreamlike figures.[33] However, these 'aristocratic' morals and values represented and espoused in Gothic fiction are demonstrably a literary representation of middle-class ethics and can thus be interpreted as creating and upholding a middle-class moral presence in the aristocratic past. Furthermore, given the longevity and popularity of the Gothic, there must be more to the genre than the analysis of a long dead culture.[34]

Ronald Paulson did not view the Gothic in terms of class exploration. He considered the continued popularity of the Gothic, specifically the Gothic of the 1790s, in the same way that de Sade did, as an inevitable reaction to (or an expression of) the anxieties and fears aroused in Europe by the French Revolution.[35] Although Paulson concentrated his analysis only on the novels of the 1790s, his comments on Gothic as a metaphor for revolution add another dimension to the stereotype of male tyranny and the way in which a contemporary reader might have perceived it. Unlike Paulson, however, this study maintains that both Montoni and Ambrosio are manifestations of the same stereotype of villainy as the earlier Manfred (*The Castle of Otranto*, 1764) and subsequent villains.[36]

Chris Baldick, writing more recently than either Punter or Paulson, presents a concept of developing political anxiety that combines subconscious class anxieties with the specific fears generated by the French Revolution. In his introduction

---

[33] Punter, *Literature of Terror*, 425.

[34] See also Robert F. Geary's analysis of Punter's position in 'From Providence to Terror: The Supernatural in Gothic Fiction', in Donald E. Morse (ed.), *The Fantastic in World Literature: Selected Essays from the Fifth International Conference on the Fantastic in the Arts* (New York: Greenwood Press, 1987), 8.

[35] Marquis de Sade, 'Idée sur les Romans', *Les Crimes de L'Amour* (1800; repr. Paris: Gallimard, 1987), 42.

[36] Paulson considered *The Monk*, for example, to be a 'revolutionary' text while the earlier *The Castle of Otranto* reflected old mores and times past. 'Gothic Fiction and the French Revolution', 537. Horace Walpole, *The Castle of Otranto, A Gothic Story* (1764; repr. from 1798 text, Oxford: Oxford University Press, ed. and intro. W.S. Lewis, notes, J.W. Reed Jnr., 1982).

to *The Oxford Book of Gothic Tales*, his account of the Gothic tradition is similar to Punter's interpretation of the Gothic as a disturbed, middle-class reaction to history:

> It is a middle-class tradition, and its anxiety may be characterized briefly as a fear of historical reversion; that is, of the nagging possibility that the despotisms buried by the modern age may prove to be yet undead.[37]

Baldick has clearly extended Punter's interpretation: Punter's analysis pointed towards the Gothic as a vehicle through which the troubled middle class could examine its genesis and rise to power; Baldick shifts the focus of middle class anxiety from its antecedents to its present and future continuance. This quotation indicates how Baldick believes the Gothic romances demonstrate middle-class anxiety about its own stability, indicating a widespread fear of changing society, either through a reversion to a pre-bourgeois power structure and decadent, aristocratic values, or, perhaps, through working-class revolution. Taken in conjunction with other comments made by Baldick on the earlier Gothic in *In Frankenstein's Shadow*, this quotation shows the connection that Baldick makes between middle-class anxiety about the maintenance of the status quo and the contemporary revolutionary ferment in Europe.[38] Thus he seems to unite the different political anxieties explored by Punter and Paulson in one argument; the Gothic becomes an agent for the expression, whether conscious or unconscious, of societal insecurity. This, then, offers one explanation of why Gothic romances became even more popular in the 1790s; however, it does not offer a satisfactory investigation or explanation of the formula and the form through which this anxiety manifested itself.[39]

---

[37] Baldick, *Book of Gothic Tales*, xxi.

[38] Baldick, *Frankenstein's Shadow*, 16.

[39] The production (and presumably the popularity) of Gothic romances rose steeply around 1795. Dorothy Blakey's investigation of the Minerva Press shows that after this date most Minerva novels were issued in three or four volumes (prior to this two volumes was the usual

V. Definition or Division?

The critics whose ideas have been discussed under the general categories of Romantic, female and political have all attempted to define the essence of the Gothic and in so doing have imposed boundaries and divisions, discarding those works which did not conform to their Gothic blueprint.[40] Most subsequent critics of the Gothic have done the same. Indeed, most subsequent critics, whatever their ideological bias, have adopted almost identical divisions under different nomenclature.

Hume, referring to a posthumous article by Ann Radcliffe, made a distinction between 'terror-Gothic' and 'horror-Gothic'.[41] In making this distinction he was redefining (or, perhaps more accurately, refining) the Gothic, rejecting what he considered to be the over-inclusive categories of sentimental-Gothic, terror-Gothic and historical-Gothic created by Montague Summers.[42] The distinction between terror-Gothic and horror-Gothic is an important one – both thematic and chronological:

> To put the change from terror-Gothic to horror-Gothic in its simplest terms, the suspense of external circumstance is de-emphasised in favour of increasing psychological concern with moral ambiguity ... The terror novel prepared the way for a fiction which though more overtly horrible is at the same time more serious and more profound.[43]

Hume's terror-Gothic is equivalent to early Gothic, to the works of Walpole and Ann Radcliffe in which, Hume asserted, terror is dependent on the suspense of

---

format) and the prices, as well as the quantity of novels published each year, increased. See Blakey, *The Minerva Press*, 272-92.

[40] Ronald Paulson does not try to define the Gothic but, in focusing on revolution, he necessarily makes a chronological distinction between Gothic fiction written before the 1790s and that written after. Other critics have also deplored the drive towards definition, see, for example, Francis R. Hart, 'Limits of the Gothic: The Scottish Example', in Harold E. Pagliaro (ed.), *Studies in Eighteenth-Century Culture*, 3 vols. (London and Cleveland: Case Western Reserve University Press, 1973), iii. 138.

[41] Ann Radcliffe, 'On the Supernatural in Poetry,' *The New Monthly Magazine* xvi (1826), 145-52. In contrast to Radcliffe, however, Hume values horror over terror.

[42] Summers, *The Gothic Quest*, 29. Hume rather caustically observed that, 'If wearing a wool tie makes me a sheep, then *The Recess* is a Gothic novel.' 'Gothic versus Romantic', 283.

[43] Hume, 'Gothic versus Romantic', 285.

dread.[44] Horror-Gothic, which he considered more important because 'more serious and more profound,' is later Gothic in which the reader is not kept in suspense but attacked with shocking events.[45] Hume's definitions are interesting because, although one might dispute his conclusions, his chronological and thematic distinctions often appear as axes for the work of later critics.

The chronological split is particularly apparent in the work of critics who have considered early Gothic as a primitive prism through which they examine 'weightier' nineteenth-century 'Gothic' texts. Michelle Massé described this period as part two of the Gothic genre, a part which starts *after* life 'happily ever after' begins following the expulsion of the horrors at the close of 'part one' Gothic, i.e. the earlier Gothic novels, which closed with a wedding and the restoration of order.[46] Massé's own discussion of the 'early' Gothic is, like Hume's, a brief preparation for the more important work that follows. This kind of critical focus on later texts always seems to produce a reductive reading of the earlier ones: formula is relegated to the status of a primitive device for the exploration of the non-rational. As Eve Kosofsky Sedgwick observed, when commenting on Robert B. Heilman's definition of the Gothic: 'To give the description "Gothic" this full a sense, however, it is seemingly necessary to acknowledge a discontinuity between it and the Gothic novel proper.'[47] The first Gothic writers are assumed

---

[44] Obviously the crushing of Conrad and the appearance of the giant casque at the beginning of *The Castle of Otranto* is not considered shocking.

[45] Note that the authors Hume listed in connection with horror-Gothic were Lewis, Beckford, Mary Shelley and Maturin: later critics used the same group of authors in support of different definitions.

[46] Michelle Massé, 'Gothic Repetition: Husbands, Horrors, And Things That Go Bump in The Night', *Signs*, xv (1990), 690. Massé has further indicated that her interest really lies in later Gothic by developing this article into the introductory chapter of a book, *In the Name of Love: Women, Masochism and the Gothic* (New York: Cornell University Press, 1992), which deals entirely with later Gothic, specifically *The Story of O, Jane Eyre*, and *Rebecca*.

[47] Heilman's definition of the Gothic is: 'In the novel it was the function of Gothic to open horizons beyond social patterns, rational decisions, and institutionally approved emotions; in a word, to enlarge the sense of reality and its impact on the human being. It became then a great liberator of feeling. It acknowledged the non-rational–in the world of things and events, occasionally in the realm of the transcendental, ultimately and most persistently in the depths of the human being.' R.B. Heilman, 'Charlotte Brontë's "New Gothic"', in Robert C. Rathbone and Martin Steinmann Jr. (eds.), *From Jane Austen to Joseph Conrad: Essays Collected in Memory of*

to have relied on conventions; later Gothic writers – Heilman concentrated on Charlotte Brontë – indulge in an original exploration of feeling.

Hume's thematic distinction between terror-Gothic and horror-Gothic was consciously developed into a distinction between 'male' Gothic and 'female' Gothic by Juliann Fleenor in her introduction to *The Female Gothic*:

> Horror-Gothic (*Frankenstein*) would be an expression of the author's fear of ambiguity and patriarchal structures; terror-Gothic (*Castle of Otranto*) is an expression of the heroine's predicament in what proves ultimately to be a reasonable world. Horror of the self, of female physiology, is closely tied to the patriarchal paradigm.[48]

Like Hume, Fleenor privileged horror-Gothic. For her it became 'female Gothic,' an expression of the conflict surrounding female identity. Her classification of authors is not the same as Hume's, however, as her conception of 'female Gothic', the horror of the female self and the fear of the patriarchal paradigm, results in a, perhaps inevitable, division of authors by gender.

In contrast, although she did not acknowledge Hume as a starting point, Kate Ferguson Ellis used almost the same grouping of authors in order to present her division of the Gothic into either masculine or feminine Gothic.[49] Unlike Fleenor's 'female Gothic,' the authors are not grouped according to the gender of the author but, it seems, according to the gender of the protagonist. In her introduction, Ellis described the 'feminine Gothic' as the type of plot in which the woman, imprisoned inside what should be a domestic refuge, breaks out, exposing the villain's usurpation and transforming the prison into a home, thus reclaiming a domestic space: 'masculine Gothic', by contrast, shows a man exiled from the home, wanting access to the domestic space occupied by women. In a later chapter, Ellis subtly changed this definition so that the focus is shifted to the domestic space rather than the gender of the protagonist:

James T. Hillhouse (Minneapolis: University of Minnesota Press, 1958), 131, cited in Sedgwick, *The Coherence of Gothic Conventions*, 3.

[48] Fleenor (ed.), *Female Gothic*, 7.

> A castle turned into a prison and reconverted into a home (or destroyed so
> that its prisoner can establish a home elsewhere) is the underlying structure of
> the feminine Gothic. ... When the home is destroyed utterly and the destroyer
> continues to wander upon the face of the earth, we have the Lewisite or mas-
> culine Gothic.[50]

Ellis's first definition of 'feminine Gothic' began with the works of Ann Radcliffe
and, if we examine the implications of the later development, Walpole too must
be included in this category. She originally used Lewis as the type of 'masculine
Gothic' but the works of Mary Shelley and Maturin are also encompassed by this
later definition. The same works that for R.D. Hume indicated terror-Gothic and
horror-Gothic, indicate 'feminine Gothic' and 'masculine Gothic' for Ellis.[51] Her
definition, however, is less divisive than Hume's or Fleenor's. She has not privileged one type (or period) of Gothic above another and the developed definition
identifies the stability or the destruction of the home as part of the Gothic formula.

The formal problems of the Gothic outlined by Elizabeth Napier can also be
identified with Hume's definitions of the two Gothic modes. She isolated two opposed currents within the genre: there is a tendency towards moral and structural
stabilising characteristic of eighteenth-century fiction, corresponding to Hume's
terror-Gothic and Fleenor's 'female Gothic'; and there is also an inclination towards fragmentation, instability and moral ambivalence, corresponding to the
moral ambiguity which Hume found in horror-Gothic. Rather than separating
these currents into two distinct types of Gothic, however, Napier considered them
together as an intrinsic part of the Gothic formula, and, for Napier, one of the reasons for its formal failure. Napier has also identified problems in the representation of the restrained heroine and in the presence of anachronistic eighteenth-
century drawing-room rituals. However, many of these 'problems' disappear if

---

[49] Kate Ferguson Ellis, *The Contested Castle: Gothic Novels and the Subversion of
Domestic Ideology* (Urbana and Chicago: University of Illinois Press, 1989).
[50] Ellis, *Contested Castle*, 45.

one considers the Gothic formula as a synthesis of generic forms. In that case, the presence of instability and a movement towards closure are not necessarily opposing currents causing the form to fail, but may be indicators of fantasy, and the romance genre has traditionally presented idealised contemporary roles and behaviour in distant settings.

Whatever the basis of their definitions, these critics have only succeeded in polarising the Gothic. A more fruitful approach to the analysis of Gothic formula fiction, therefore, is not to look for a definition of the Gothic – thereby inevitably creating divisions – but rather to work from the perspective that the formula may be a synthesis of several modes. Napier's criticism suggests that the idealised world of romance and the unstable world of fantasy may have contributed to the Gothic formula. Castles, heroes, heroines, and supernatural manifestations are essential ingredients for the Gothic writer, and a *frisson* is the standard reader's reaction. Romance and fantasy provide the staples: horror provides the spice.

---

[51] Alison Milbank's definition of female Gothic is almost identical to that of Ellis. *Daughters of the House: Modes of the Gothic in Victorian Fiction* (London: Macmillan, 1992), 11.

2

Romance, Fantasy and Horror:
Generic Influences on Gothic Male Stereotypes

The Gothic formula consists of set pieces, of obligatory scenes played out by recognisable stereotypes against a predictable backcloth. However, not everything encompassed by the formula was an original 'Gothic' creation. Were the characters playing the major roles in these formulaic scenes created in response to the requirements of the formula? Or were the techniques that writers used to create such scenes evoking the 'Gothic' atmosphere – or indeed the scenarios and characters themselves – borrowed and adapted from other genres?

I. ROMANCE

...an Heroic fable,--a fabulous Story of such actions as are commonly ascribed to heroes, or men of extraordinary courage and abilities.[1]

This definition of Romance (Clara Reeve's own, which she offered as an amplification and summary of the other definitions she had considered) demonstrates how Romance as a genre might be defined – and defended – in the late eighteenth century. Common, contemporary assumptions about the Romance reduced it either to an absurd fiction ('une conte' or 'un mensonge' as Abel Boyer had defined it) or located it, as Johnson's primary definition did, only in the Middle Ages.[2] Reeve's definition makes an appeal to her reader, rescuing Romance by classify-

---

[1] Clara Reeve, *The Progress of Romance and the History of Charoba of Egypt*, 2 vols. (1785; repr. In facsimile, New York: The Facsimile Text Society, 1930), i. 13.
[2] I have used the definition of Romance that Reeve herself cites from Abel Boyer's, *Royal Dictionary*, 2 vols. (London: R. Clavell, 1699); the same definition appears in the augmented 1773 edition and the fourteenth edition of the abridged version (1777). Note that Reeve was not citing Boyer's primary definition, which is '(a feigned story containing an amorous adventure) *un roman*' and is, therefore, less pejorative than the secondary definitions cited by Reeve, which Boyer classed as figurative expressions. Dr. Johnson defined 'Romance' as: '1. a military fable of the middle ages;--a tale of wild adventures of love and war. ... 2. A lie; a fiction.' *A Dictionary of the English Language*, 2 vols. (1755; repr. in facsimile, New York: Times Books, 1979).

ing it as a 'fable,' thus highlighting a didactic and moral function of implicit con-temporary value.[3]

The qualifying adjective 'Heroic' is also important to an understanding not only of the eighteenth-century Romance but also of the characters moving within this Romance world. In making 'Heroic' an essential part of the definition of the Romance, Clara Reeve modified Johnson's earlier concept of a 'military fable of the middle ages,' which locates the action of the story in a specific past and sol-dierly milieu.[4] By describing the Romance as 'Heroic' rather than 'military,' Clara Reeve emphasised its ideal qualities. The description 'an Heroic fable' indi-cates that, whatever the lessons to be drawn by the contemporary reader, the Ro-mance was not a story of real life or of the ordinary, but a 'fabulous Story of such actions as are commonly ascribed to heroes.' These heroes, these 'men of extraor-dinary courage,' should, in order to fulfil the moral function of the fable, be em-bodiments of the ideal rather than mimetic characters. These idealised 'heroic' characters might also be described as champions of virtue because, following ear-lier commentators, Reeve's concept of Romance heroism was closely linked to a chivalric code.

In 1762 Richard Hurd had argued, in contradistinction to prevailing criti-cism, that the Romance had a positive value of its own:

> ...may there not be something in the Gothic Romance peculiarly suited to the views of a genius, and to the ends of poetry? And may not the philoso-

---

[3] Clara Reeve's belief in a moral, didactic function of Romance is shown again in her Preface to *The Memoirs of Sir Roger de Clarendon*, 3 vols. (London: Hookham & Carpenter, 1793), in which she seems to be reacting against the spirit of the French Revolution: 'The new philosophy of the present day avows a levelling principle, and declares that a state of anarchy is more beauti-ful than that of order and regularity. There is nothing more likely to convince mankind of the er-rors of these men, than to set before them examples of good government, and warnings of the mischievous consequences of their own principles.' xvi-xvii.

[4] I have placed considerable emphasis on the importance of the word 'fable' in Reeve's defi-nition, viewing it as an indication that the improbability of the Romance was justified because the story was intended to convey a moral. This interpretation follows Johnson's primary definition of 'fable': 'A feigned story intended to enforce a moral precept.' However, three of the five defini-tions given by Johnson associate 'fable' either with fiction in general or with perverted fiction – similar definitions to those given for romance, suggesting, perhaps, that any form of fiction in the eighteenth century was regarded with suspicion.

phic moderns have gone too far, in their perpetual ridicule and contempt of it?[5]

Hurd's *Letters on Chivalry and Romance* (Clara Reeve's source for the essentials of chivalry) were intended to vindicate Spenser and to argue on behalf of the barbarous Gothic style: '...you will find that the *manners* they paint and the *superstitions* they adopt, are the more poetical for being Gothic.'[6] Publication of these letters marks a change in attitude and taste in the eighteenth century, a public recognition by the eighteenth-century literary world that the wild, the barbarous and the fantastic had a positive value of their own. In stating that the codes of conduct belonging to this antiquated period are more suited to poetry, Hurd also implied that this code and these characters were more suited to the depiction of emotion.

A combination of Reeve and Hurd's analyses of the nature of the Romance offers three points that are applicable to the Gothic. Both Hurd and Reeve indicate that the central code of the Romance is based in chivalric heroism, suggesting a certain pattern of behaviour for the hero (explored further in the chapter on the hero figure) and connecting that figure with poetry. Heightened emotions, chivalric values and poetic sensibilities are all 'Gothic' characteristics. In addition both writers located romance values and romance action in a past, predominantly aristocratic or feudal, age and this too is characteristic of the Gothic. Reeve's definition of the romance as a moral exemplum for a contemporary reader is, interestingly, the same argument repeatedly advanced in authors' prefaces to Gothic fiction to justify their use of the supernatural or the horrific.[7] These writers acknowledged that they were producing non-realistic fiction and many of them subtitled their works 'A Romance':

> Romance (generally speaking) consists of a number of strange events with a hero in the middle of them; who, being an adventurous knight, wades through them to one grand design, namely the emancipation of some captive princess, from the oppression of a merciless giant, for the accomplishment of which he must set at nought the incantations of the caitiff

---

[5] Richard Hurd, *Letters on Chivalry and Romance*, (London: Millar, 1762), Letter I, 4.
[6] Hurd, *Letters on Chivalry*, Letter VI, 54-5.
[7] See Chapter Seven, 183-5.

magician; must scale the ramparts of the castle; and baffle the vigilance of the female dragon, to whose custody his heroine is committed.[8]

The context in which this quotation appeared indicates how closely the Romance and the Novel were connected in the eighteenth century. George Canning, who wrote this analysis whilst still a schoolboy at Eton in 1747, described the Romance at length only to demonstrate that the 'realistic' fiction of the mid-eighteenth century had a decidedly non-realist root. He followed this description by a series of parallels between romance characters and those of the contemporary novel. Although the performers have changed, he suggested that the characters remain the same: the guardian replaces the magician, but is equally ferocious, and the maiden aunt differs only from a vigilant dragon in having no claws. While the actions of the watchful guardians are the same in both romance and novel, Canning found that the figure of the hero was reduced by the transition from fabulous to realistic fiction. According to Canning, the stereotype of the hero figure in the Romance dictates certain actions, which appear ridiculous when expressed within the confines of realistic fiction:

> The hero of a novel has not indeed any opportunity of displaying his courage in the scaling of a rampart, or in his generosity in the deliverance of enthralled multitudes; but as it is necessary that a hero should signalise himself by both these qualifications, it is usual, to manifest the one by climbing the garden wall, or leaping the park-paling, in defiance of 'steel-traps' and 'spring-guns', and the other, by flinging a crown to each of the postboys, on alighting from the chaise and four.[9]

Canning's essay suggests that the formula of romance emerges in contemporary novels through the deployment of stereotypes, but the positive qualities of a romance stereotype, which are *necessary* to the representation of a hero, were adulterated when transposed to contemporary fiction. The hero figure, as Canning has described it, traditionally manifests his heroism through dramatic, effective action

---

[8] George Canning, *The Microcosm*, no. 26 (Eton, 1747), reprinted in Ioan Williams (ed.), *Novel and Romance 1700-1800: A Documentary Record* (London: Routledge and Kegan Paul, 1970), 342.
[9] *Ibid* 342.

against a malignant society and through inspiring leadership. Opposed to a private individual and leading no one, the hero of the contemporary novel is diminished.[10]

Considering that Canning found elements of the Romance formula persisting in contemporary, 'realistic' fiction, and that Gothic fiction not only contains the same stock character types, but also reintroduces the element of the marvellous which was lacking in 'realistic' fiction, is it, then, reasonable to refer to the Gothic romance rather than to the Gothic novel? As some of the dictionary definitions already quoted indicate, the term 'romance' was synonymous with 'fiction' during the greater part of the eighteenth century. In 1750, for example, Dr Johnson used 'romance' to classify fiction that dealt with ordinary or natural life (he was referring to the work of Fielding and Richardson) as well as that which dealt with the extraordinary or supernatural. He distinguished between the two by describing the former as 'the comedy of romance' and the latter as 'the heroic romance.'[11]

By the time that Clara Reeve was writing *The Progress of Romance* (1785), the term 'novel' was evidently commonly used for those works that a reader could relate directly to his or her own life – the same kind of 'realistic' fiction that Johnson had described as 'the comedy of romance':

> The Romance is an heroic fable, which treats of fabulous persons and things,--The Novel is a picture of real life and manners, and of the times in which it is written. The Romance in lofty and elevated language, describes what never happened nor is likely to happen.--The Novel gives a familiar relation of such things as pass every day before our eyes, such as may happen to our friend, or to ourselves; and the perfection of it, is to represent every scene, in so easy and natural a manner, as to deceive us into a persuasion (at least while we are reading) that all is real, until we are af-

---

[10] For a further investigation of whether the hero figure of Gothic fiction is also created after the pattern of romance, whether he, too, though in a less circumscribed environment, is as ineffectual – even ridiculous – as the hero figure Canning described, see Chapter Four, 86ff.

[11] Samuel Johnson, *The Rambler*, 4, (1750), in Elledge, Scott (ed.), *Eighteenth-Century Critical Essays*, 2 vols. (New York: Cornell University Press, 1961), ii. 571. Similarly, Walpole's second preface to *The Castle of Otranto* (1764) distinguishes between 'ancient' and 'modern' romances, corresponding to Johnson's 'heroic' and 'comedy of romance' categories respectively.

fected by the joys or distresses, of the persons in the story, as if they were our own.[12]

As Ian Duncan has observed, Gothic fiction sited itself on the border between novel and romance as defined by Clara Reeve in this quotation: it retained some aspects of contemporary real life and manners, but defamiliarised them by placing familiar mores in improbable locations and distant time periods.[13] However, in terms of nomenclature there are far more 'romance' elements than realistic ones: the use of the supernatural or the marvellous; the moral purpose frequently claimed by the authors; the idealisation of character types, and the fact that many writers chose to describe their work as 'a romance.' Therefore, it seems reasonable to term these works 'Gothic romances.'

By consciously invoking the atmosphere of the medieval romance (typically, either through the historical period in which the story was set or by isolating their characters in a building redolent with medieval associations), Gothic writers imposed limitations on their representation of character. The requirements for romance characters in a romance world have been analysed by Gillian Beer:

> The world of a romance is ample and inclusive, sustained by its own inherent, often obsessive laws. It is not an entire world; it intensifies and exaggerates certain traits in human behaviour and recreates human figures out of this exaggeration. It excludes some reaches of experience in order to concentrate intently upon certain themes until they take fire and seem to be the flame of life itself.[14]

This analysis shows the romance world to be one of exaggeration and intensity – a suitable environment for the 'men of extraordinary courage.' Romance characters, though displaying recognisably human traits, are not mimetic figures. Instead they are intensified figures, larger than life, who are deployed in order to amplify cer-

---

[12] Reeve, *Progress of Romance*, 111. Cf. John Aikin: 'Now, the writings styled *novels*, are intended to impress us like the narrations of real occurrences. They even pretend (however falsely for the most part) to instruct us in the knowledge of human life.' *Letters from a Father to a Son, on Various Topics relating to Literature and the Conduct of Life*, 2 vols. (London: J. Johnson, 1793-1796), i. 82.

[13] Ian Duncan, *Modern Romance and Transformations of the Novel: The Gothic, Scott, Dickens* (Cambridge: Cambridge University Press, 1992), 20-1.

[14] Gillian Beer, *The Romance* (1970; repr. London: Methuen, 1977), 3.

tain themes. Beer further asserts that romance can speak directly to emotional experience by simplifying character and removing the restraints of rationalism. Stereotyped characters are not only playing certain, unavoidable roles within the narrative, but specific stereotypes – those of fear or of the ideal – are fulfilling a contemporary social function, freeing 'the primal material of dreams and terrors back into fiction.'[15]

The Gothic romance is an eighteenth-century romance; it reflects eighteenth-century ideals, moral principles and, perhaps, fears. Canning's essay indicated one way in which an eighteenth-century writer might manipulate the stereotype of the romance hero. The figure of the villain also underwent an eighteenth-century transformation. One such stereotype, borrowed from the medieval romance, but significantly modified by the Gothic authors, is the feudal baron, or the lord of the castle. As exalted personages traditionally people the romance, the medieval romances are tales of the adventures of lords, ladies and knights. The lord of the castle is a familiar figure of social power, but more importantly he is a figure of social responsibility, owing allegiance to his king and protection to his dependants, over whom he has the absolute power of life and death. Much of the interest in medieval romances is generated by the lords' or knights' failure to sustain their role, the abuse of their powers, and the denial of their oaths.

The difference between the medieval and the Gothic stereotype is that tyrannical, feudal barons appear in the Gothic romance as figures of anti-social power.[16] Even when failing in their chivalric duties, medieval knights and lords are not anti-social figures. They are part of a clearly defined hierarchy with the power of life and death as a part of their status: they uphold society, they do not mock at it. By contrast, in Leland's *Longsword* (1762), Lord Raymond is presented as an anti-social, noble villain figure, who has usurped Earl William's

---

[15] *Ibid* 57.
[16] Cf. Punter: 'The figure of Manfred, laden with primal crime, is considerably larger than *Otranto* itself: his violence, his bullying, his impatience with convention and sensibility mark him out not only as the caricature of a feudal baron, but also as the irrepressible villain who merely mocks at society, who remains inassimilable.' *Literature of Terror*, 53.

lands and castle and is attempting to acquire his wife, Ela, as well.[17] Leland depicted Raymond manipulating the language of conventional knightly honour in his attempts to win Ela, maintaining the chivalric code in order to suggest that he is the moral equal of her missing husband. Leland revealed these chivalric protestations as a sham because Raymond's servants are given the power to coerce Ela physically – a power that he cannot be seen to wield himself if the stereotype of noble lord of the manor is to be upheld. Thus, Leland's villain figure is shown manipulating and perverting his supposed role as lover (for the heroine does not accept him in this role) in order to justify his tyranny and perversion of the chivalric code. Walpole's villainous feudal lord, Manfred, in *The Castle of Otranto* (1764), is similarly drawn. He too is represented as anti-social, defiant of convention, ready to commit near-incest with Isabella and to tear her from the sanctuary of the church. Forced to observe codes of traditional hospitality towards the knights who come to reclaim Isabella, Manfred manipulates his role as a responsible prince, using it to justify sending his legal wife to a convent and pursuing Isabella instead.[18]

The evidence suggests that the formula of the Romance, and the eighteenth-century understanding of it, had considerable influence over the creation of character in Gothic fiction. By adopting the title 'Romance', writers of Gothic fiction were evoking not only ideas of the marvellous but specific patterns of character type and role in the story:

> Because romance shows us the ideal it is implicitly instructive as well as escapist. By removing the restraints of rationalism it can reach straight to those levels of our experience which are also re-created in myth and fairy-tale. By simplifying character the romance removes the idiosyncrasies which set other people apart from us; this allows us to act out through stylised figures the radical impulses of human experience.[19]

---

[17] Thomas Leland, *Longsword, William; Third Earl of Salisbury: An Historical Romance*, 2 vols. (London: Johnston, 1762).

[18] As the villain chapter will show, this type of manipulation of an established male social role, and contempt for the moral code underlying social conventions, is typical of the way in which villains are represented in the Gothic romance.

[19] Beer, *The Romance*, 9.

Some stock figures of romance are idealised, and the ideals embodied must be recognisable to the reader. Thus, the hero and heroine of the Gothic romance must conform simultaneously to both the heroic pattern laid down by the romance formula and the moral ideals and patterns of behaviour that were current in the late eighteenth century. These parameters may conflict, as Canning highlighted when comparing the romance form with mid-eighteenth-century 'realistic' fiction. Later chapters in this present study will show whether writers of Gothic romances experienced similar problems in overlaying romance stereotypes with contemporary codes of behaviour.

Finally, and perhaps most importantly, both Beer's analysis and Canning's flippant essay demonstrate very clearly that the formula of the romance emerges through the interplay of stereotyped characters. Beer further stresses the potential effect that this has on the reader/text relationship. In simplifying character, in repeating certain character traits, roles and actions, writers create stereotypes whose representation and interplay act as triggers for the raising and allaying of certain emotions. The formula of the romance is thus very close to my conception of the Gothic formula.

II. FANTASY

Although Walpole asserted that his characters behaved and responded naturally within an extraordinary environment, fantasy is one of the most striking elements of the Gothic romance, which does not pretend to be a reflection of everyday reality in its representation of circumstance and happenings.[20] The fantastic, however, is not located only in the Gothic romance, nor did it first spring to life in the eighteenth century. There might prove, therefore, to be elements of the characters in the Gothic romance belonging to a wider tradition.

---

[20] 'Desirous of leaving the powers of fancy at liberty to expatiate through the boundless realms of invention, and thence of creating more interesting situations, he wished to conduct the mortal agents in his drama according to the rules of probability; in short, to make them think, speak and act, as it might be supposed mere men and women would do in extraordinary positions.' Walpole, *Castle of Otranto*, 7-8.

Gillian Beer suggested that, because it is not restrained by rationalism, the romance could reach the same levels of human experience re-created in myth and fairy tale. Once rationalism is removed, we are left with the irrational, which may perhaps be fantasy. Not only does Beer's comment suggest that the fantastic might generate a particular response in a reader, but also that romance, myth and fairy tale have fantasy as a common element.[21] Therefore, some elements of characterisation apparent in the fairy tale might be equally applicable to the creation of character in the Gothic romance.

i. Fairy Tale

Characters in the fairy tale appear to be simplified because they do not change during the course of the tale: adult characters have fixed characteristics and the story is centred on the trials and tests which beset the hero or heroine during his or her progress from child to adulthood. Fairy tale characters also typically exhibit only one strong emotion that the reader or listener interprets as the primary motive for all their actions. Because they embody a single emotion, characters from different tales with similar motives resemble each other, and are usually named after their role in the story.

These simplified characters are either completely good or completely bad: there are no moral uncertainties in the fairy tale and consequently many tales contain pairs of characters who exhibit opposite characteristics. The good, dead mother and the evil, living stepmother appear in several tales: Cinderella and Snow-White both suffer because of the vicious jealousy of their stepmothers and the weakness of their fathers; Sleeping Beauty has complementary fairies prepared to curse and to bless.[22] The prevalence and initial success of the evil character is a necessary part of the fairy tale formula because the hero, or heroine, must

---

[21] Cf. Tzvetan Todorov, *Introduction à la Littérature Fantastique* (Paris: Editions du Seuil, 1970), 98, where he categorically states that fantasy produces a particular effect on the reader that other literary modes cannot provoke.

[22] For a full discussion of the importance of fairy tales see Bruno Bettelheim, *The Uses of Enchantment: The Meaning and Importance of Fairy Tales* (London: Thames and Hudson, 1976).

suffer before winning, or being awarded, the prize of a successful and happy adult life.

The learning process is significant, not the prize. According to Bruno Bettelheim, a child is gradually taught by fairy tales that evil deeds do not bring long-term success, and that good intentions will always conquer. A child identifies with the hero, not with his virtue, but with his struggle against unfair and overwhelming odds. Considered in these terms, we can conclude that fairy tales have a perennial appeal because they work out and repeat situations and emotions, in a simplified, concretised form, which are not specific to one culture or to one generation.

When considering the fairy tale, Jung based his work on the premise that statement – by which he meant words and the way in which a subject associates or orders them – is the most important phenomenon of the psyche (Burke drew a similar conclusion in the *Philosophical Enquiry*).[23] Jung found repeated patterns, repeated characters, and repeated themes in the fairy tales he investigated. Innate ideas or the tendency to organise experience in innately predetermined patterns are the contents of the collective unconscious, or the archetypes.[24] Jung's theory argued that these autonomous, primordial images are universally present in the pre-conscious makeup of the human psyche, whose development consists of continuous movement and reorganisation of these images. As archetypes may change their form but not their substance, characters vary little from one fairy tale to another. It is the situations and the conjunctions or oppositions in which they are placed that encourage imagination, develop experience.

If it is possible to equate the archetype with an embodied emotion (as fairy tale characters seem to be both archetype and embodiment) then the simplified characters of romance, which change little from one century to another and pro-

---

[23] 'The proper manner of conveying the *affections* of the mind from one to another, is by words.' Edmund Burke, *A Philosophical Enquiry into the Origin of our Ideas of the Sublime and Beautiful* (1757), 2nd. ed. with additions (London: R. and J. Dodsley, 1759), 102.

[24] C.G. Jung, *Four Archetypes*, trans. R.F.C. Hull (198; repr. London: Ark Paperbacks, 1988), 95.

ject one emotion strongly, might also be classed as archetypes. The power of archetypal characters, and this is also true of stereotypes to a lesser degree, is that
they make an immediate appeal to the emotions of the reader. The figure that corresponds most nearly to this in the Gothic formula is the heroine, whose stereotype does not change between texts or over decades. Walpole's Matilda and
Leland's Ela are essentially the same characters (in that the same key words are
used to describe their characters, they are physically delineated in similar terms
and they respond to situations in a similar way) as Mrs. Parsons's Georgina or
Mrs. Roche's Madeleine.[25]

Superficially, writers of Gothic fiction might seem to be manipulating archetypal characters within a fairy tale framework. The Gothic formula would then
consist of goodness incarnate (heroine and, perhaps, hero), threatened by wickedness incarnate (the villain) and aided by wisdom incarnate (sound moral precepts
reinforced by the advice of the good father and the actions of providence).[26] However, as later chapters will show, education, example, and parental background
play a large part in forming character within the world of the Gothic romance and,
therefore, characters are not as simplified as those of fairy tale. In the fairy tale,
good characters are born with their moral excellence already fully fledged: in the
Gothic romance they must learn the difference between right and wrong. Although both forms dramatise a conflict between good and evil, the Gothic romance lacks the moral certainty of the fairy tale as such a conflict may take place
within one character – often the villain. Also, although the names of stock characters often echo elements of earlier Gothic fiction and thus indicate their potential
roles, simplified characters are given more individuality than those of fairy tale

---

[25] These are the heroines of Walpole's *The Castle of Otranto* (1764), Thomas Leland's
Longsword (1762), Eliza Parsons's *The Mysterious Visit* (1802), and Regina Maria Roche's *Clermont* (1798).
[26] An archetypal male figure identified by Jung, appearing in both Gothic Romance and fairy
tale, is the wise old man, who appears as a hermit, or a dying father, or occasionally as a servant.
The role is that of someone who can offer advice to the beleaguered hero or heroine, but cannot
physically oppose the villain: this is left to the actions of the hero, the purity of the heroine, an
awakening of the villain's conscience or providence.

and inhabit a more populous world.[27] The fairy tale world often consists only of the central characters, whereas the world of the Gothic romance contains a complete society from which characters are often exiled or isolated by the machinations of the villain. Both the Gothic world and the fairy tale world, however, exist at a remove from the reader's reality, 'long ago' and 'far away,' but this distance from reality is achieved through different techniques. Where the fairy tale is told in simple language and is based on the movement of timeless archetypes, the Gothic romance is told in fragmented, often archaic language and is locally based in eighteenth-century fantasy.

ii. Fantasy

In his study of the Fantastic as a genre, Tzvetan Todorov defines the fantastic moment as one of uncertainty: 'Le fantastique, c'est l'hésitation éprouvée par un être qui ne connaît que les lois naturelles, face à un événement en apparence surnaturel.'[28] According to Todorov, the hesitation experienced by a reader who is trying to interpret the text is often also present in a character, making the fantastic a part of the narrative structure and a theme. This kind of hesitation on the part of reader and character occurs again and again in the Gothic romance. Mrs. Radcliffe, for example, was notorious for introducing apparently supernatural phenomena that both terrified and perplexed her heroines and readers.[29] Similarly, Mrs. Smith, in *The Old Manor House* (1788), and Mrs. Roche, in *The Children of the Abbey* (1796), both introduce mysterious ghostly figures in half-lit

---

[27] A psychoanalytic explanation for the difference between the simplified characters of fairy tale and those of other fiction is presented by Marie-Louise Von Franz in *The Psychological Meaning of Redemption Motifs in Fairytales* (1956; repr. Toronto: Inner City Books, 1980), 10.

[28] "Fantasy is the hesitation experienced by a being who, cognizant only of the laws of nature, is faced with an apparently supernatural event." [This and subsequent translations are mine.] Todorov, *Fantastique*, 29. Not only is Todorov's definition of fantasy the one around which later theoretical works on fantasy are based, but the moment of hesitation is also directly applicable to the Gothic romance. For a survey of theoretical work done on the fantastic see Neil Cornwell, *The Literary Fantastic: From Gothic to Postmodernism* (Brighton: Harvester Wheatsheaf, 1990), 3-41.

[29] One such unearthly experience is the blue flame, observed by Emily, that plays on the soldier's spear as he patrols the ramparts of Castle Udolpho at midnight; this is later discovered to be a natural phenomenon caused by electricity in the air.

rooms or passages.[30] Both apparitions prove to be human: Mrs. Roche's ghost turns out to be the wicked, but now penitent Lady Dunreath, imprisoned in the Abbey by her unfeeling daughter; and Mrs. Smith's 'ghost' is an unromantic smuggler called Jonas Wilkins.[31]

This use of uncertainty inside the text was not a sophisticated later development in the history of the Gothic romance. It occurs also in Horace Walpole's *Castle of Otranto*, in which the interpretations of supernatural phenomena (or quasi-supernatural occurrences like Frederick's dream) by characters in the story are not only vital to the action of the tale, but enable the reader to make judgements about the character concerned. Walpole's declared intention was to put human characters into supernatural situations. Consequently, Manfred's initial reactions to the supernatural are represented as both human and natural. He is described, for example, as hesitating to accept the evidence of his own eyes when he beholds the gigantic casque which crushed his unfortunate son: 'He fixed his eyes on what he wished in vain to believe a vision.'[32] The hesitation that the villain experiences is a choice between accepting the supernatural as a 'real' event or doubting his own perception of reality. Manfred would prefer to be the victim of his own deluded senses than to be at the mercy of some vast supernatural agency interfering with his dynastic ambitions. In the moment when he doubts whether he is awake or asleep, sane or mad, he recognises the limits of his control. The facets of Manfred's character revealed by his reactions to the supernatural are a direct result of Walpole's use of the fantastic.

When Todorov mentioned the Gothic romance specifically, it was to illustrate that, although moments of fantasy occurred, the fantastic was not sustained, and such romances slid either into the 'marvellous' or the 'uncanny,' depending

---

[30] Charlotte Smith, *The Old Manor House, A Novel* (1783; repr. Oxford: Oxford University Press, ed. Anne Henry Ehrenpreis, intro. Julian Stanton, 1989). Regina Maria Roche, *The Children of the Abbey, A Tale*, 4 vols. (1796; 2nd. ed. London: Minerva Press, 1797).

[31] For a more detailed examination of the relationship between the use of the supernatural or the apparent supernatural and the male stereotyped character see Chapter Eight, 'A Miscellany of Men.'

[32] Walpole, *Castle of Otranto*, 17.

on whether or not the supernatural moment was explained.[33] Todorov regarded the explained supernatural as 'étrange' (uncanny) and the accepted, therefore unexplained, supernatural as 'merveilleux' (marvellous).

The fictional world of the marvellous is one of fairy tale and magic. Rosemary Jackson describes it as a closed world, 'whose narrator is omniscient and has absolute authority,' from which a reader is temporally distanced – a spectator rather than a participant.[34] It is a world in which supernatural operations are normal, and laws other than those of everyday reality regulate life. This is true of many Gothic novels, both major and minor: George Walker's *The Haunted Castle* (1794) and *The Three Spaniards* (1800), or Charlotte Dacre's *Zofloya* (1806) are typical examples of this type of marvellous narrative.[35] Note, however, that the long temporal perspective does not necessarily discourage reader participation. Several of the most dramatic scenes in *Zofloya*, for example, particularly the murder of Lilla, rely on the sensibilities of an engaged reader in order to raise the tensions of the story.

Nor, despite its supernatural ambience, does the marvellous preclude the inclusion of some of the realistic detail typical of a romance. For instance, when Ignatius, the hero of George Walker's *The Haunted Castle*, and his servant, La Moine, are caught in a thunderstorm, they are rescued by a hermit, who seats them by a fire and scours the rust from their armour. Touches of homely realism like this are essential to the narrative, which must retain some internal logic in order to sustain the reader's semi-belief in the coherence of the marvellous world of the tale. It is easier to accept that the portrait of Manfredi's (the murderer) wife

---

[33] "Plus exactement, l'effet fantastique se produit bien mais pendant une partie de la lecture seulement: chez Ann Radcliffe, avant que nous soyons sûrs que tout ce qui est arrivé peut recevoir une explication rationnelle; chez Lewis, avant que nous soyons persuadés que les événements surnaturels ne recevront aucune explication." ["More precisely, the fantastic effect is produced but only during one part of the reading experience: with Ann Radcliffe, it occurs before we are sure that everything that has happened can be explained away rationally; with Lewis, it occurs before we realise that the supernatural events will never be explained."] Todorov, *Fantastique*, 46-7.

[34] Rosemary Jackson, *Fantasy: the Literature of Subversion* (1984; repr. London: Routledge, 1986), 33.

pales when Ignatius stands before it, than to assume that Ignatius' armour does not get rusty when wet, which would be an unjustified supernatural event given that Ignatius possesses neither magic armour nor magic powers.

The 'uncanny,' which Todorov also described as bordering on the fantastic, is a world in which reality dominates, permitting an exploration of supernatural phenomena. Freud's essay on the 'Uncanny' defines it in broad terms as something that frightens, arousing dread and horror and exciting fear: 'The uncanny is that class of the frightening which leads back to what is known of old and long familiar.'[36] The uncanny is produced by hidden or repressed fears within the subject, which are projected onto the world around. Consequently, the subject sees the world through a veil of unconsciously repressed anxiety that changes the familiar into something disturbing. In his essay, Freud uses two levels of meaning for the German word for the uncanny, 'das Unheimlich': initially as the opposite meaning to 'das Heimlich' – familiar and agreeable – so that the antithesis means unfamiliar and alien; but 'das Heimlich' also means that which is hidden, kept secret and concealed, so that the antithesis means to reveal, to expose, to uncover that which is usually concealed. As the thing that is usually concealed is a part of the familiar, 'heimlich,' world around us, 'das Unheimlich' changes the familiar into the unfamiliar. Thus, everything uncanny is a projection of repressed, unconscious desire; the supernatural is lurking inside us, perverting our relationship with the surrounding world.

There are two ways in which the uncanny influences the creation and representation of character in the Gothic romance. First, because the uncanny is concerned with taboo – the reason for the primary repression – the actions of the villain character, who as an anti-social figure attempts to manipulate and to pervert his role within society, reveals the darker side, the taboos in the 'heimlich' society against which he acts. Second, the uncanny concentrates on the interior

---

[35] Charlotte Dacre, *Zofloya; or, The Moor: A Romance of the Fifteenth Century*, 3 vols. (London: Longman, Hurst, Rees and Orme, 1806).

life of the characters as they experience the defamiliarisation of a familiar world, and thus shapes the narrative of the Gothic romance so that it is focused on the subjectivity of the central characters.

Mrs. Radcliffe's romances are a case in point. They focus on an individual's subjective interpretation of uncanny events without using first-person narration. Her semi-omniscient narrative technique focuses attention on her heroines without making them the mouthpiece for a retrospectively told story. Thus, Mrs. Radcliffe is the teller of the tale but the reader's emotions are tuned to those of Emily or Adeline or Ellena, whose reactions and trembling sensibilities colour the narrative with fear, and make every event, every character, and every emotion larger in proportion to the heroine's weakness. It might be argued that the uncanny is an incidental effect produced in the reader by the narrative, rather than a deliberate choice modifying the form of the narrative, but Mrs. Radcliffe was acutely aware of the aesthetic differences between terror and horror, and so it is reasonable to suggest that she consciously shaped her narrative in order to produce these uncanny effects.

iii. The Effect of Fantasy on Narrative Structure

The Gothic tendencies to move both towards closure and a happy ending, and towards fragmentation, breakdown and decay are simultaneously embraced by Mikhail Bakhtin's definition which links fantasy conceptually with the idea of carnival.[37] He saw fantasy as a direct descendant of Menippean satire which violates the generally accepted, ordinary course of events. Carnival is an extraordinary experience, involving colour, excitement, and, perhaps, cruelty. Most significantly, it is a *suspension* of ordinary life. Day to day routine has stopped but, when the carnival moves on, it will start again. Fantasy can only be a tempo-

---

[36] Sigmund Freud, 'The Uncanny' (1919), trans. Alix Strachey 1955, *Art and Literature, PFL* xiv (1985; repr. London: Penguin, 1988), 340.

[37] Mikhail Bakhtin, *Problems of Dostoevsky's Poetics* (1962), trans. & ed. by Caryl Emerson (Manchester: Manchester University Press, 1984), 122-37. For an examination of 'carnival' in the

rary escape from real life. Bakhtin did not find this in Dostoevsky's work where characters exist outside the law, isolated from the community. It is, however, entirely applicable to the Gothic romance in which there is only a temporary suspension of the law, and this explains why, although the horrific and/or supernatural events were guaranteed to give an eighteenth-century reader a *frisson*, it was a very safe thrill. Normal life is restored at the end of the novels and the reader can put the volume away, reassured that the right moral values will inevitably triumph.[38] This is even the case in *Frankenstein* (1818) where the natural order is clearly disturbed and unsettling moral questions are raised.[39] For at the close of the novel, Walton the explorer gives up his quest to find a passage across the top of the world and returns home.

The influence of fantasy over the narrative structure of the Gothic romance is not confined to a happy ending; it also influences the way in which the narrative is told. Every fantastic avenue leads eventually to the relationship between the world and oneself, whether it is the hesitation experienced by a character confronted with the supernatural, or the reversal of a familiar object revealing unfamiliar desires. We see this realised in the Gothic romance where the narrative is often a tale told by fallible and sometimes bigoted human beings. There are numerous first-person narratives giving the reader a single viewpoint on the world: either the whole tale is told by the major character, usually by letter or diary, or, in cases where there is an omniscient narrator persona, there are also inset tales, anecdotes and reminiscences supplying other perspectives. Thus fantasy, concerned with individual perception and interpretation of (supra-normal) events, affects not only the narrative structure but also the representation of character.

---

eighteenth century, see Terry Castle, *Masquerade and Civilization: The Carnivalesque in Eighteenth-Century English Culture and Fiction* (Stanford: Stanford University Press, 1986).

[38] Cf. J.R.R. Tolkien on closure in the fairy tale: 'Far more important is the Consolation of the Happy Ending. Almost I would venture to assert that all complete stories must have it.' 'On Fairy-Stories', *Tree and Leaf* (1964), cited in Colin Manlove, *Modern Fantasy: Five Studies* (Cambridge: Cambridge University Press, 1975), 160.

[39] Mary Shelley, *Frankenstein, or The Modern Prometheus* (1818; repr. Chicago: University of Chicago Press, ed. James Reiger, 1982).

By using first-person narration in *Frankenstein*, Mary Shelley destabilises the reader's conceptions about heroism, monstrosity and responsibility. All three of her first-person narrators have similar, or potentially similar, spirits and vastly different experiences. Like a three-ring circus, each narrative reflects on the others and the most interesting act is saved for the core. In the outermost ring is Walton, the potentially heroic explorer; in the second ring, we find Frankenstein's narrative, a scientific 'hero' who has achieved his dream at a terrible cost; and in the centre is the monster whose narrative reveals that his monstrosity is literally and figuratively created by Frankenstein's betrayal. Even though all three narrators in *Frankenstein* speak with the same tone and the same vocabulary, the interpretative choice does not fall between three characters and three identical stereotypes, but rather between three individual characters and one complicated personality split three ways. First-person narratives like these deliberately undermine the idea that they are peopled and told by stereotyped characters.

Other writers of Gothic romances also manipulated first-person narratives, making the reader unsure of his or her interpretation of the story – though these events are not always directly connected with flagrant fantasy, i.e. super (or supra) natural events. In a romance like *The Recess* (1785), for example, Sophia Lee changed the reader's perception of the story (that chain of events which the reader retrospectively constructs) and the characters in it, by changing the discourse and shifting abruptly from one first-person narrative to another.[40] Most of this romance is told through a deathbed, memoir-letter-confession from one of the central characters, Matilda Howard. Matilda's memoir is, largely, a retrospective retelling of the love between herself and the Earl of Leicester, represented as a demi-god of mature years, perfect in character and fascinating in appearance. About two-thirds through Matilda's memoir, another first-person narrative is introduced in the form of a letter from Matilda's beautiful, but doomed, twin sister Ellinor. This narrative paints a very different picture of Leicester, as a handsome,

---

[40] Sophia Lee, *The Recess, Or, A Tale of Other Times*, 3 vols. (London: Cadell, 1785).

indulged, vain, and rather stupid man. The reader, with no reason to doubt Ellinor's narrative (until the end of the tale when she has gone mad), is left hesitating between two interpretations of character and events, both of which are presented as true insofar as the character herself sees them.

While exploring character and subjective emotion through first-person narratives, the writers of the Gothic romance were also able to extend the idea of subjective emotion into a moral discursion on the destructive effects of the passions. Charlotte Dacre does precisely this in her epistolary romance, appropriately named *The Passions* (1811), which demonstrates her interest in a theme central to most Gothic fiction: the corruption of innocence by passion.[41] From the first moment, every letter betrays something of the character that writes. Each creates his or her perception of reality, leaving the reader to try and establish the truth of the story, and to evaluate the characters, from the many versions offered.

Fantasy introduces doubts; it represents an escape from the 'real' of which it is the distorted shadow. Fantasy in literature cannot be wordless, and yet the words uttered to express something beyond what is perceived as 'real' are the language of 'real' communication. As soon as the fantastic is made concrete in language, it acquires the literalness of the everyday. As the people who utter the fantastic are grounded in their own culture, fantastic products also indicate the hidden aspirations and fears of that culture. Thus fantasy can also be horror.

III. HORROR

Of the importance of terror and horror to the writers of the Gothic romances, there can be no doubt:

---

[41] Charlotte Dacre, *The Passions*, 4 vols. (London: T. Cadell and W.H. Davies, 1811). Although I have described it as an epistolary romance, the last one hundred pages or so are written in the third person. Normal social intercourse breaks down as the relationships between the characters are destroyed. Weimar continues to write letters to his confidant, Rozendorf, but when Rozendorf befriends Julia – who has gone mad as a result of her experiences – the letters cease. The effect that this change of style has on the reader is to create the impression that, once social laws have been breached by uncontrolled passions, events rush towards a tragic conclusion – Julia's death in the snow outside her husband's house that she has been forbidden to enter.

Terror, the author's principal engine, prevents the story from ever languishing; and it is so often contrasted by pity, that the mind is kept up in a constant vicissitude of interesting passions.[42]

This comes from Walpole's first preface to *The Castle of Otranto* and indicates one of the ways in which the narrative of the Gothic romance was shaped by engaging the reader's interest through scenes of terror.[43] This terror, however, is artificial, not actual, and in creating scenes of artificial terror that would affect the reader, Walpole (and Gothic romancers writing after him) was manipulating the sublime.[44] The Aikins were among the first contemporaries to connect the Gothic romance with the aesthetics of the sublime, and their essay attempted to explain the appeal that this type of writing had for a reader:

This solution [the reader's curiosity], however, does not satisfy me with respect to the well-wrought scenes of artificial terror which are formed by a sublime and vigorous imagination. Here, though we know before-hand what to expect, we enter into them with eagerness, in quest of a pleasure already experienced. This is the pleasure constantly attached to the excitement of surprise from new and wonderful objects. ... Passion and fancy co-operating elevate the soul to its highest pitch; and the pain of terror is lost in amazement.

HENCE, the more wild, fanciful, and extraordinary are the circumstances of a scene of horror, the more pleasure we receive from it.[45]

Conversely, the Aikins argued, scenes of actual horror inflicted *real* pain on the reader or spectator and contracted rather than expanded the soul.[46] By using fantasy and terror to assault the imagination, Gothic writers were trying to elevate

---

[42] Walpole, *Castle of Otranto*, 4.

[43] Cf. John and Anna L. Aikin: 'The pain of suspense, and the irresistible desire of satisfying curiosity, when once raised, will account for our eagerness to go quite through an adventure, though we suffer actual pain during the whole course of it. ... This is the impulse which renders the poorest and most insipid narrative interesting when once we get fairly into it' from 'On the Pleasure derived from Objects of Terror; with Sir Bertram, a Fragment,' *Miscellaneous Pieces in Prose* (London: J. Johnson, 1773), 123-4.

[44] See David Morris, 'Gothic Sublimity', *New Literary History* xvi (1985), 299-319, in which he argues that the Gothic romance, beginning with *The Castle of Otranto*, significantly revised the concept of the sublime in the eighteenth century.

[45] Aikin, 'On the Pleasure derived from Objects of Terror,' 125-6.

[46] Cf. Ann Radcliffe: 'Terror and horror are so far opposite, that the first expands the soul, and awakens the faculties to a high degree of life; the other contracts, freezes, and nearly annihilates them.' *New Monthly Magazine*, xvi (1826), 149.

the emotions of their readers. In this they were following Burke's famous precept that whatever is terrible is a source of the sublime:

> Whatever is fitted in any sort to excite the ideas of pain, and danger, that is to say, whatever is in any sort terrible, or is conversant about terrible objects, or operates in a manner analogous to terror, is a source of the *sublime*; that is, it is productive of the strongest emotion which the mind is capable of feeling.[47]

Burke's investigation into the passions, his attempt to establish some rational framework that might explain man's seemingly irrational emotions and responses, led him to list and discuss certain contributory factors. Many things, Burke felt, could help to create an impression of the sublime in the reader or onlooker, and the same objects are used in the Gothic romance to elicit a similar response. Everything (and every emotion) in the romances is enlarged. Burke had already commented on the effects of vastness, obscurity and infinity – meaning the 'artificial' sensation of infinity induced by regularity and repetition – in man's emotions and understanding. He further extended his ideas about the importance of obscurity, shadow and darkness in creating the sublime effect from the contemplation of the physical (actual or represented darkness, vastness etc.) to the metaphysical. 'A clear idea is therefore another name for a little idea.'[48] He recognised the importance of shadows and the belittling effect of too strong a light. This light, which may also be interpreted as exercising the rational faculties and denying irrational impulses, has a double effect on the reader: first, reassurance, the 'safe thrill', as horrors are brought down to a human and containable dimension, and second, like Freud's second meaning of 'heimlich,' increased uneasiness. Shedding light over a scene illuminates an object; however, it also makes the shadows more obvious. The more that a human being is consciously and rationally aware, the greater and denser must be the fears lurking in the hinterland, which has fantasy as the border between consciousness and unconsciousness.

---

[47] Burke, *A Philosophical Enquiry*, 58-9.
[48] *Ibid* 108.

These theories of the sublime shaped both the narratives and the characterisation of the Gothic romances in a twofold manner. On the one hand, the focus on individual emotion and subjectivity within the texts helps to create an atmosphere of terror that the reader may experience as sublime. On the other hand, as David Morris has argued, when writers of the Gothic romance amplified Burke's concept of terror beyond a list of events, they transformed 'figurative elements of the sublime style into principles of narrative structure.'[49] Morris refers specifically to the elements of repetition and exaggeration, which, he asserts are the figures of speech shaping Walpole's narrative. Hyperbole describes the way in which characters address each other in *The Castle of Otranto*, but characters, their emotions and the supernatural manifestations causing these emotions are also exaggerated.[50] The degree of repetition within Walpole's plot is also remarkable: Manfred imprisons Theodore three times, and Isabella runs away from Manfred twice. Repetition of action, like this, is also extended to characters, who, bound by romance conventions of mistaken identity, disguise and coincidental meetings, replicate each other's emotions and double each other's roles.[51] Matilda and Isabella are interchangeable, following this principle of narrative repetition. Described as sisters throughout the text, Matilda is substituted as an accidental victim in Isabella's place. Yet, because of this doubling, had Manfred killed his intended victim, he would still have murdered a daughter. Thus a source of terror and of the sublime is found in narrative repetition. Similarly Manfred's lust for Isabella is replicated in Isabella's actual father, Frederick, who conceives an equally sudden and violent desire for Matilda. Morris further suggests that Walpole modified the Burkean sublime by forging and demonstrating a connection between terror and love, which Burke divided in his theory, through exploring the terror of potential incest – a social taboo.

---

[49] Morris, 'Gothic Sublimity,' 302.
[50] Robert Kiely also comments on writers' attempts to describe human feelings and experiences, leading to phrases like 'unspeakable horror' or 'indescribable transports of joy.' *Romantic Novel in England*, 11.
[51] Morris, 'Gothic Sublimity,' 304.

Incest, or the threat of incest, is a prime source of horror frequently utilised by the writers of Gothic fiction as a propellant for the action and a generator of anxiety. The heroines of Eliza Parsons's romances *Castle of Wolfenbach* (1793) and *The Mysterious Visit* (1802), for example, are forced into action – flight – by the amorous advances of parental figures.[52] The same device is used by George Walker in *The Three Spaniards* (1800) and *The Haunted Castle* (1794) – although the action of *The Haunted Castle* is rather different because in this case the hero is forced to abandon his bride-to-be. Such a frequent use of incest as a plot device suggests not only its efficacy, but also that the Gothic romances were liberating and simultaneously quelling contemporary fears about the stability of the family unit and the consequent stability of society as a whole. That which is socially feared can be embodied in a stereotype in horror fiction, recognised and labelled as fictitious, exploring the darker, illogical areas of human experience.[53] The Gothic romance uses social stereotypes, which, after frequent usage, can develop into widely recognised images of fear – hallmarks of the society that created them.[54]

Franco Moretti suggested, from a Marxist perspective, a very specific social need for these unrealistic symbols of fear, asserting that they – he focused on *Frankenstein* (the 1831 text) and *Dracula* (1897) – perform a reassuring function by diverting fear from the 'real' to the fantastic, transmogrified form.[55] This is an interesting theory, but difficult to accept given Moretti's definition of the 'real' fears of the society: that of the conflict between the disfigured victim and the ruthless proprietor. He suggests, for example, that Mary Shelley articulated the unconscious fears of her class by creating a monster that

---

[52] Eliza Parsons, *Castle of Wolfenbach; A German Story*, 2 vols. (London: Minerva Press, 1793).

[53] See Joseph Grixti, *Terrors of Uncertainty: The Cultural Contexts of Horror Fiction* (London: Routledge, 1989), 18.

[54] Cf. Elizabethan and Jacobean drama where Frenchmen, Spaniards and Witches stalked the stage as villains, symbolising the menace of the encroaching Catholic empire with its forked prongs of superstition and sorcery.

[55] Franco Moretti, 'The Dialectic of Fear: *Dracula* and *Frankenstein*,' *New Left Review* cxxxvi (1982), 83.

symbolises the proletariat (nameless, composed of many diverse parts, and disfigured). Moretti interprets the monster's disfigurement as the stigmata arising from the inequality of life; however, it is surely more significant to note that Frankenstein carefully chose large individual features that seemed beautiful to him, and yet, from these well-proportioned, separate elements, he created something terrible. Thus, Mary Shelley indicated Frankenstein's limitations: he has no sense of overall proportion and harmony; he is not a god.

Frankenstein's dream turned into a horrible reality – twice within the text. On an interpretative level, Mary Shelley showed the blasting of her hero's youthful hopes, as Frankenstein's narrative describes how his initial dream of being a benevolent creator is destroyed by his own repugnance at the reality he has created. The transition from dream to reality, however, is also a literal event within the text as Frankenstein awakes from a nightmare in which he was clasping the rotting corpse of his beloved Elizabeth to find the hideous face of the monster peering down at him. As Eve Kosofsky Sedgwick noted: 'To wake from a dream and *find it true*--that is the particular terror at which these episodes aim.'[56] This, comparable to David Morris's analysis of the presentation of figurative elements in narrative structure, is the horror of the Gothic romance.

The Gothic romance partakes of the same generic advantages and problems as Romance, Fantasy and Horror, and these supply the *raison d'être* for the simplified character types apparent in the Gothic formula. The elements of Romance in the Gothic formula require certain characters to be both idealised and simplified, and may speak directly to the reader's emotions through their 'poetical' effects. Fantasy affects both the content and form of the texts – the fictional world is defamiliarised through fantastic techniques before the inevitable closure, and the elements of terror/horror raise or depress the reader's emotions. Part of the special appeal of the Gothic formula, however, lies in the ways in

---

[56] Sedgwick, *Gothic Conventions*, 28.

which the writers altered existing stereotypes to suit their new mode of fiction, and the new stereotypes that it engendered.

3

The Ideal Man

The search for the ideal man, the hero of romance, begins in another form of literature: the conduct and courtesy manuals of the period. These were themselves a form of fiction insofar as they set up idealised standards, based on shared moral certitudes, that probably reflected the way eighteenth-century society desired to see itself, rather than life as it really was. Therefore, eighteenth-century conduct books contain more than a simple chart of the perfect formal manners of their age. They also indicate the moral foundations on which these manners rest, implying that perfect behaviour naturally emerges as the outward sign of a perfect soul. By contributing details of prescribed patterns of thought and behaviour the books create a composite picture of the ideal Man and Woman of the late eighteenth century. When these patterns of behaviour are examined in relation to the principal characters of contemporary fiction, it can be seen that the conduct books paralleled the concept of the Hero and the Heroine.

Conduct books thus provide one standard by which to examine the male characters in the Gothic romance, helping to set the genre within a broader context of contemporary literature dealing with social issues. They enable one to examine the degree to which these Romances reflected contemporary social mores, and to consider whether, within their fictional world, the writers of Gothic fiction shaped and created new standards, redefining accepted gender roles.

The standards of morals and behaviour promulgated by conduct literature were, on the one hand, considered to be almost universally applicable, and so the Hero and the Heroine of Romance had to embody them in order to sustain their roles credibly and recognisably. On the other hand, however, as the rest of this chapter will show, both literature and standards were being directed specifically at the middle and upper classes. The conduct writers imply that, although everyone, whatever his/her social status, should aspire to the virtues that they promote, only members of certain classes will have either the opportunity to display them or the innate sensibility required to cultivate them. This attitude is not only found in Gothic fiction but is also part of the Gothic formula: the hero and heroine must belong to a certain social status and a specific type of sensibility that not even the most worthy servant can emulate.[1]

The importance of the many conduct books written to guide the manners and morals of women cannot be ignored when considering the character and conduct of the ideal man. Unlike women, who were assumed to have the same duties and to play the same essential role across all strata of society, men might have different *duties* determined by class, but the *role* of an ideal man was delineated by his perception of, and behaviour towards women. The roles are interdependent. Conduct books written by men for women show what men expected and desired women to be, unconsciously revealing what men considered to be their own position and role. Female authors of conduct books subscribed to the same standards and proffered the same advice as their male counterparts. The concept of the desirable woman was no longer that of the aristocratic, public figure, but the woman who had become the private, domestic centre of the home.[2]

The social background of the writers of conduct books influenced their advice and the sphere for which that advice was intended. Jane West stated very specifically that she was directing her advice in *Letters Addressed to A Young*

---

[1] For the representation of servants and differences in behaviour based on class, see Chapter Eight, 'A Miscellany of Men.'

[2] For an expanded view of the development of the conduct book, see Nancy Armstrong and Leonard Tennenhouse (eds.), *The Ideology of Conduct: Essays on Literature and the History of Sexuality* (London: Methuen, 1987). The conduct writers selected here were well known. Clara Reeve included the works of Mrs. Chapone, Dr. Gregory and Dr. Fordyce in her recommended reading list for young ladies in *The Progress of Romance* (1785), and Mary Wollstonecraft cited them as familiar examples of writers who created and perpetuated popular assumptions about the role of women. Reeve, *Progress of Romance*, ii. 104-5. Mary Wollstonecraft, *Vindication of the Rights of Women* (1792; repr. from 2nd. ed. corrected, London: Penguin, 1985), 191-207.

Man (1801) to traders, merchants, shopkeepers and professional men.[3] Her letters are written to her son on his first leaving home, extolling the virtues of domesticity, family life, moderation and the middle classes. James Fordyce, son of an Aberdeen magistrate, was a Scottish Presbyterian minister preaching in London, who wrote and published sets of sermons directed at the character and conduct of young men and women. His sermons are aimed at all areas of society, particularly indicting the fashionable society and accepted habits of the time. In contrast, Chesterfield's letters are the private correspondence of a noble, accomplished statesman and man of the world, giving experienced advice to his son on how to fill a particular role in society.

Hester Chapone came from a family who had lived in a mansion at Twywell, near Northampton, for several generations, enjoying an income of £700 or £800 per year from the estate. *Her Letters on the Improvement of the Mind*, first published in 1773, were addressed to a favourite niece, the daughter of a scholarly brother living in a parsonage at York.[4] Hester Chapone came, therefore, from the same class as the Bennets in Austen's *Pride and Prejudice*: a family who owned an estate that guaranteed them an income, so they were not tradesmen, but yet were not in the highest echelons of society. The advice that Mrs. Chapone gives to her niece is, presumably, appropriate to her similar, upper-middle class station. Despite this the author of the *Memoir*, writing at a later date, states that 'her volume ought to be in the possession of all ranks in society,'[5] demonstrating that a universal concept of correct manners and morals for women exists unconfined to any one class. Women are to be the passive, cohesive centre around which revolves the family and society:

> The same degree of active courage is not to be expected in woman as in man; and not belonging to her nature, it is not agreeable in her: But, passive cour-

---

[3] Jane West, *Letters Addressed to a Young Man On His First Entrance into Life and Adapted to the Peculiar Circumstances of the Present Times*, 3 vols. (1801; 2nd. ed. London: Longman & Rees, 1802).

[4] Hester Chapone, *Letters on the Improvement of the Mind*, 2 vols. 2nd. ed. (London: J. Walter, 1773).

[5] John Cole, *Memoirs of Mrs. Chapone* (London: Simpkin, Marshall & Co., 1839), 41.

age,--patience and fortitude under suffering--presence of mind and calm res-
ignation in danger--are surely desirable in every rational creature;[6]

Mrs. Chapone introduced two keywords here – 'patience' and 'rational'. Certain
words, like these, are frequently repeated in the conduct books, endowing both the
words and the concepts they comprehend with 'gravitas.' One of the ways in
which one should judge a potential friend, according to Chapone, is to watch her
in the sickroom, observing whether her complaints are 'mild,' 'gentle' and 'restrained,' or whether she displays a 'turbulent, rebellious mind, that hardly sub-
mits to the divine hand.'[7] Submission is thus seen first as a duty owed to God,
before whose omnipotent commands and decrees the weak sinner must bend, but
the idea extends into the relationship between the sexes: man has more power and
so woman must submit. Submission is seen as her duty and also as an integral,
beautiful part of the female character, enabling her to deal with a life of suffering:

> Your whole life is often a life of suffering. You cannot plunge into business,
> or dissipate yourselves in pleasure and riot, as men too often do, when under
> the pressure of misfortunes. You must bear your sorrows in silence, unknown
> and unpitied. You must often put on a face of serenity and cheerfulness, when
> your hearts are torn with anguish, or sinking in despair.[8]

This extract from Dr. Gregory's *Legacy to his Daughters*, a posthumously published tract, reinforces the image of the woman as self-contained, unable to act
and therefore adopting a posture of saintly, martyred passive suffering. Yet this
role, artificially created by society – men work to support their family homes,
which are maintained and regulated by the women – is regarded as the essence of
femininity, however unrealistic in most individual cases. The eighteenth-century
woman is trapped by the words that define her. She must be gentle, meek, and patient, a perfect companion but also a perfect victim.[9] She must have sweetness –
like other key qualities this is associated with inner beauty:

---

[6] Chapone, *Improvement of the Mind*, i. 124-5.
[7] Chapone, *Improvement of the Mind*, i. 162.
[8] Dr. Gregory, *A Father's Legacy to his Daughters* (1774; repr. Ludlow: Nicholson, 1809), 6.
[9] The connection between the victimization of women and the stereotype imposed upon them is
explored further in Chapter Seven.

...there is, however, a certain physiognomy of beauty, a candour and sweetness of aspect, an emanation of the soul, that sometimes illuminates the countenance.[10]

Richardson actually wrote this about Mrs. Chapone herself, but the same description might apply to any fictional Gothic heroine. It is very similar, for example, to one of the earliest descriptions of Emily St. Aubert; to the description of Jacqueline, daughter of the noble knight Les Roches, in Thomas Leland's *Longsword* (1762), and to the first description of Antonia's face in *The Monk* (1796).[11] The exterior reflects the interior.

The necessity for restraint extends beyond control of one's temper to all strong emotions: A strong emotion is a passion; a passion is a destructive force and a weakness because it overrides reason:

A sweet timidity was given them to guard their innocence, by inclining them to shrink from whatever might threaten to injure it. Their passions, as they rise, are restrained from exorbitance, by a secret sentiment of shame and honour.[12]

Any quality prefixed by 'sweet,' 'gentle,' 'patient,' or 'meek' is always socially desirable according to the conduct book writers. In Fordyce's eyes, instinct rather than reason governs women: timidity and a secret sentiment of shame and honour replace the exercise of considered, rational self-regulation. Emotions are still regarded as a private experience. This sheds some light on the lengths to which Monimia goes in order to avoid a public meeting with Orlando in *The Old Manor House* (1783). She is winding linen and deliberately tangles her feet in it, falls sideways, hits her head on a metal-cornered screen and drives her scissors into her

---

[10] Chapone, *Improvement of the Mind*, xi.

[11] Ann Radcliffe described Emily in the following terms: 'But, lovely as was her person, it was the varied expression of her countenance, as conversation awakened the nicer emotions of her mind, that threw such a captivating grace around her' *Mysteries of Udolpho*, 5. Cf. Leland's description of Jacqueline: 'Yet still a greatness and elevation of soul gave dignity to her female softness.' *Longsword*, i. 112. Cf. also Lewis's first description of his heroine, Antonia: 'It was not so lovely from regularity of features, as from sweetness and sensibility of countenance.' *The Monk*, 11.

[12] James Fordyce, *Sermons to Young Women*, 2 Vols. 3rd. ed. corrected (London: Millar, Cadell, Dodsley, Payne, 1766), i. 93.

arm. This resourceful and active behaviour protects her private emotions and prevents her from betraying her guilty, clandestine meetings with Orlando.

Self-regulation extends to dress. In Sermon VI 'On Female Virtue,' Fordyce advocates Sobriety, considering it an inward habit, supporting and giving value to the whole.[13] He assures his female readers that the male population uniformly dreads marriage with an expensive woman, implying, perhaps, that one of the most compelling reasons for adopting inward and outward Sobriety is that this assists a woman to marry a discerning man:

> To divert fancy, to gratify desire, and in general to be a sort of better servants [sic], are all the purposes for which some suppose your sex designed. A most illiberal supposition! The least degree of refinement or candour will dispose us to regard them in a far higher point of light. They were manifestly intended to be mothers and formers of a rational and immortal offspring; to be a kind of softer companions, who, by nameless delightful sympathies and endearments, might improve our pleasures and soothe our pains; to lighten the load of domestic cares, and thereby leave us more at leisure for rougher labours, or severer studies; and finally, to spread a certain grace and embellishment over human life. [14]

This is the discerning man, Fordyce himself, stating precisely what he, and presumably other men of similar breeding and education, expects from a wife. He makes a significant distinction between the way that a man who has some refinement or candour perceives Woman's role, and the coarser perceptions of others. This reveals that the role of the ideal wife is defined by the way in which she complements and eases her husband, and that the difference between the illiberal suppositions of the coarse and those of the refined man rests in the language used. The wife is spiritualised, through Fordyce's language, from a physical object into a ministering angel and saint. Instead of diverting fancy and gratifying desire, the wife improves pleasures and soothes pains with her delightful sympathies and endearments; instead of being a servant, she lightens the load of domestic cares. Woman is simultaneously deified and cast down.

---

[13] *Ibid* i. 138-9.
[14] *Ibid* i. 207-8.

Gisborne and Fordyce agree that Women are best suited to the duties of the heart, as they do not have the intellectual capacity to reason or to construct a lucid argument:

> Your business chiefly is to read Men, in order to make yourselves agreeable and useful. It is not the argumentative but the sentimental talents, which give you that insight and those openings into the human heart, that lead to your principal ends as Women.[15]

All the writers deplore the essential unfemininity of argumentative women. Fordyce uses Queen Elizabeth as an example of how a woman loses her femininity when assuming a role that requires 'male' characteristics. For women should rule the home, not the world:

> The very best men are so made, as to be soothed by ready compliance, and chilled by habitual stubbornness in women ... . To female excellence they will resign the empire of the breast with pleasure. But remember, young women; *such excellence forever precludes the affectation of power, will rarely appear to exert it, and will generally prevail by submitting* [my emphasis].[16]

Men will both resign and retain power in a relationship. They will adore and worship the excellent woman, granting her power over them through their affections, but she may never consciously wield this power without diminishing her femininity. Women's power, then, lies in their ability to manipulate men without appearing to do so. There is a hint of hypocrisy, a possible difference between assumed behaviour and intention, as they are obliged to work exclusively within the passive role.

The man's role is implicit in the advice given to women, and made explicit in conduct books directed at young men. While the desirable woman is the passive, domestic centre of the home, the man is an active figure, moving between

---

[15] *Ibid* i. 273. Cf. Thomas Gisborne, *An Enquiry into the Duties of the Female Sex*, 3rd. ed. corrected (London: Cadell Jnr. & Davies, 1798), who, after listing the logical, muscular qualities of the male and comparing these with the more emotional, pliant qualities of the female, concluded that a man was possessed of 'close comprehensive reasoning, and of intense and continued application,' in a degree in which they are not requisite for the discharge of the customary offices of female duties.' 21.

the two worlds of private domesticity and active public life, which imposed a further set of duties upon him.[17] These social duties, John Aikin impressed on his son, are as important as, if not superior to, the duties of private life:

> ...are not the king, the minister, the magistrate, as much essentials of the man as the husband, the father, and the friend? are [sic] they not equally social relations, differing only from the more ordinary ones in their superior importance? and [sic] can there be any propriety in characterizing a person from his performance of the lesser duties, while he is grossly deficient in the greater?[18]

It is interesting that Aikin should advise his son that his public social duties were paramount because Jane West, when writing to her son, continually emphasised the importance of the domesticity of the male role. Perhaps here male and female writers were proffering slightly different advice based on their own experience of either the public or the domestic spheres.

Although the roles of men and women, according to the conduct books, seem polarised, both sexes are presumed to share common moral ideals and certain keywords describe desirable qualities common to either sex. 'Elegance' is a concept that recurs continuously throughout the conduct books and contemporary fiction. Defined by Dr. Johnson as 'Beauty of art, rather soothing than striking,' elegance is the essence of refinement, purity of line, and delicacy of expression.[19] Significantly, it does not denote a moral standard: 'Can anything be more elegant than the manners of Macbeth...?'[20] Every keyword explored so far has described a quality residing within, reflected on the exterior through manners, dress, and

---

[16] James Fordyce, *The Character and Conduct of the Female Sex, and the Advantages to be Gained by Young Men from the Society of Virtuous Women* (London: Cadell, 1776), 86.

[17] Thomas Gisborne produced two large volumes explaining in detail the precise duties of men in the upper and middle classes, beginning with the duties of the Sovereign and finishing with those of private Gentlemen. The duties outlined were those owed to a man's profession, to his society and to the constitution of his country. *An Enquiry into the Duties of Men in the Higher and Middle Classes of Society in Great Britain*, 2 vols. 2nd ed. corrected (London: Cadell Jnr. & Davies, 1795).

[18] Aikin, *From a Father to a Son*, ii. 42.

[19] Johnson, *Dictionary of the English Language*. 'Elegant' is defined as 'pleasing with minuter beauties.' For an examination of Johnson's own use of the term 'elegant', meaning appropriate, precise, unprolix expression, see Patricia Ingham, 'Dr. Johnson's Elegance', *Review of English Studies* xix (1968), 271-7.

[20] West, *Letters Addressed to a Young Man*, i. 115.

countenance. This use of 'elegant' is contrary to that rule: Mrs. West was not being ironic, but rather using the most appropriate adjective to describe Macbeth's polished courtly manners, which are not manifestations of an exquisite soul, for he is split between inner life and outward manners. Whilst Gothic heroes and heroines do not experience this dichotomy, the villain, who is locked within himself, does.

Both sexes should be 'mild.' It is a necessary part of Woman's passive role that she should be kind, tender, indulgent and compassionate (all qualities synonymous with 'mild' in Johnson's Dictionary). Men should cultivate mildness for another reason:

> Among the amiable qualities which contribute to the happiness of domestic life, cheerful good-humour and mildness of manner stand pre-eminent. Their influence is felt daily and hourly. And their value is best discerned by marking the glooms and constraints that pervade every part of a family, the head of which is morose, peevish or overbearing.[21]

Social considerations pervade every part of the conduct books. In the above extract men are warned that their moods and temperament affect those surrounding them. Mildness, a non-corrosive quality, enables the man to control justly and to exert a beneficent influence. His position as head of the household and the power that this gives him over the lives of his dependants is a social responsibility.

Conduct books, whether aimed at women or men, were intended to educate young people to become useful and responsible members of society: 'the same mode of thinking which forms good citizens will also form good men.'[22] Similarly Hester Chapone advised her niece:

> You must *form* and *govern* your *temper* and *manners*, according to the laws of benevolence and justice; and qualify yourself, by all means in your power, for a *useful* and *agreeable* member of society.[23]

There is a difference in emphasis. The first quotation, directed at a young man, specifically suggests membership of a public society, and furthermore considers

---

[21] Thomas Gisborne, *Enquiry into the Duties of Men*, ii. 453.
[22] West, *Letters Addressed to a Young Man*, i. 84.

this to be the formative principle – a good citizen will be a good man. Mrs. Chapone's advice, directed to a young woman, is less specific and can be interpreted as suggesting that she prepare herself for a domestic society in which her influence would be felt. The principle of self-regulation is clear in both cases: society in the mass is more important than the passions of the individual; and asserting those passions will cause either the breakdown of society or the destruction of the individual. The fates of Mrs. Lennard in *The Old Manor House* (1783) and the Abbess of St. Clare in *The Monk* demonstrate this principle. Lewis depicted the eventual result of the Abbess' vicious rage and hatred as a riot, during which she was torn to pieces by an enraged mob. Smith's unpleasant Mrs. Lennard, who had deceived Mrs. Rayland and tormented Monimia, is betrayed by her passionate nature into a violent infatuation for the repulsive Mr. Roker, gives up her dominance by marrying him and is then imprisoned by him.

An eighteenth-century reader would expect the fictional Mr. Roker to prove to be insensitive and brutal simply because he comes from the lower classes. Conduct books assert that elegance, patience, sweetness and mildness result from education and rational thought, and the lower classes had neither the leisure for nor access to such refinements. Sensibility is only for those able to afford it. In *The Mysteries of Udolpho*, for example, Ann Radcliffe comments specifically on the connection between sensibility and class through the reaction of an old servant, Theresa, to the behaviour of the heroine, Emily, who had refused to forgive Valancourt for his dissipated behaviour in Paris, although she loved him deeply: "Dear! dear! to see how gentlefolks can afford to throw away their happiness! Now, if you were poor people, there would be none of this."[24] Refined, delicate, inflexible pride is incomprehensible to Theresa, who does not have these ultra-sensitive feelings. The circumstances of birth dictate whether one has this innate delicacy: education determines whether or not one tempers it with reason. Even wickedness and villainy in the Gothic romance are more acceptable if perpe-

---

[23] Chapone, *Improvement of the Mind*, i. 78.

trated by someone with the right pedigree. The Countess, in *Longsword*, is more terrified and revolted when confronted by Grey the servile flatterer (brother to Reginhald the wicked monk) than by the nobly-born, villainous usurper Lord Raymond who wants to marry her:

> Instead of the man whose arrogance was tempered by that reverence and love with which her beauty had inspired him, Ela saw now before her an unrelenting, unfeeling vassal; in condition, such as her soul disdained to hold converse with, and in temper base and brutal.[25]

Grey's brutishness results from his base birth. Like Theresa, he is represented as incapable of experiencing elevated, chivalric feelings or of being softened by beauty. Nowhere in the conduct books do the writers suggest that the lower classes can be educated up to the moral and ethical standards they postulate. Jane West argued that ministers or favourites who come to power from the lowest ranks of society are more arrogant, extravagant, and oppressive than those who have been educated from birth towards filling some high office. She considered the class system wise because each stratum of society is educated particularly for its allotted function. She further stated that the middle ranks of society live according to the best fundamental values, those of home and the family:

> The amiable mother, who devotes her attention to the care of her rising family, and is engrossed by the interesting occupation, and happy in the conscientious discharge of her duty, had neither the wish nor the leisure to fly about the town, to condemn the conduct of Lady Rattle, who is never at home. In like manner the affectionate husband, the kind father, the good master, the laborious student, the polished cultivator of elegant acts, is contented to limit his renown to the bosom of his family.[26]

Before achieving the status of uxorious family gentleman, the young man has to explore and discover his role in an active fashion, essential to the eighteenth century concept of idealised masculinity. Fordyce, in one of his early Sermons, wrote that young men should respect themselves, as they are possessed of

---

[24] Radcliffe, *Mysteries of Udolpho*, 626.
[25] Leland, *Longsword*, i. 157.
[26] West, *Letters Addressed to a Young Man*, iii. 48-9.

many noble, innate qualities that might be improved or spoiled by subsequent experiences and education. He cited an impressive list:

> Lively fancy, ready understanding, retentive memory, resolute spirit, warm temper and tender affections, quick sense of humour and disgrace, irresistible love of action and enterprise, an ambition to be admired and praised (especially for probity, manhood, generosity, friendship, good nature &c.). Strong propensity to amusement, company and imitation, high relish of existence, sanguine hopes of happiness, exalted ideas of the world; candour and truth extending even to an easy credulity and honest bluntness, keen appetite for pleasure, restless attachment to the other sex, impatient of controul [sic], a thirst for liberty, an eagerness of information; a passion for what is wonderful, curious or new.[27]

All are active, outgoing qualities. Even the attachment to the other sex is 'restless,' implying continual motion and meaning an attachment without rest – continually renewed, rather than shifting affections from one woman to another. Proclivities repressed in women are encouraged in men. Men are admired for their impatience and eagerness, and are allowed to indulge a passion (the only occasion found where a passion is sanctioned) for exploration and discovery, stimulated and sanctioned by the approbation of society. Men were expected to have exalted ideas and sanguine hopes: women were counselled to expect a life of suffering. Mrs. West wrote that 'the configuration of his body, and the faculties of his mind, prove that he is formed for action.'[28] She continues by speaking scathingly of 'slothful drones' (again the importance of living for and contributing to society is stressed), contrasting this behaviour with the man who exercises his natural powers according to the decrees of divine law.

Although the evidence suggests that the required pattern of man's behaviour be dictated by a need to protect his family and preserve his society, the responsibility for man's heroic behaviour can also be attributed to the woman, or to the love she has inspired. Honourable love is one of the most elevating emotions that a man may experience; it is that which

---

[27] Fordyce, *Addresses to Young Men*, i. 16.
[28] West, *Letters Addressed to a Young Man*, iii. 296.

...yet fills with lofty conceptions, and animates with a fortitude that nothing can conquer – what shall I say more? – which converts the savage into a man, and lifts the man into a hero![29]

This powerful force, stimulating all that is best in human nature and depressing the vices, is capable of elevating any man to heroic status (though not, perhaps, a true elevation for those of ignoble birth). He must be worthy of his ideal woman. She becomes a symbol, a goddess to be revered and adored from afar: 'He will ascribe to the attractive object, a purity, an elevation, a supereminence of worth, that places her above the rest of her sex.'[30] Consistent with woman's passive role, she is the inspiration for man to act. Excessive love, however, is as destructive as any other passion:

> Violent love cannot subsist, at least cannot be expressed, for any time to-gether, on both sides; otherwise the certain consequence, however concealed, is satiety and disgust.[31]

Note that violent love cannot be expressed on *both* sides: moreover, in the context of the romance it is a male prerogative. A man may declare his passion but a woman must keep all her emotions locked within herself; women who do declare their passions are typically older in relatively assured social positions who are en-amoured of young heroes – like Mrs. Courtney (*Castle of Wolfenbach*, 1793) and the Baroness Lindenburg (*The Monk*). Betrayal of that type of emotion leads the woman eventually and inevitably to a state in which she is regarded with con-tempt by her lover because, by declaring her passion, the woman has destroyed the idealised, passive symbol that the man has created, and believed her to be. This is what happens in *The Monk* between Ambrosio and Matilda: he had ideal-ised her portrait as a Madonna (static, unapproachable, eternally virginal yet eter-nally exposed for his gaze and in his exclusive possession), but after the initial conflagration of passion, he grows to loathe her, blaming her for his self-betrayal. Self-betrayal here means a literal betrayal of one's self-image, the idea that one

---

[29] Fordyce, *Sermons to Young Women*, i. 24.
[30] Fordyce, *Addresses to Young Men*, i. 187.
[31] Gregory, *Legacy to his Daughters*, 47.

has of one's position in the world. The true lover destroys his own self-image willingly: he copies the temper of his mild and self-regulated lady, doubting whether he is worthy of the regard that he wishes for and dreading, above all things, a rebuff. Even with this self-effacing attitude men are ultimately responsible for the course and the conduct of a relationship. Women have less experience of the world and are supposed to have a weaker understanding than men: their innate desire (according to Fordyce at least) to please men can be manipulated by the strong and unscrupulous. He views the Fallen Woman as betrayed both by man and her own nature, rather than as innately vicious:

> ...is it not some mitigation of their guilt, and should it not obtain some compassion for their frailty, that their natural solicitude to engage the attention and tenderness of the men has been turned into a handle for their destruction?[32]

The role of the man is delineated by his responsibilities. If he fails to recognise and discharge his responsibilities and duties to society and to those dependent on him, his manliness is diminished. He is formed, as Jane West said, for action.[33]

Chesterfield's *Letters to his Son* (1774) are worth considering because they chart a system intended to educate a son to fulfil the requirements of a very specific male role, yet were never intended for publication – unlike Dr. Gregory's book, which was found among his papers after his death.[34] Chesterfield's son Philip died in 1768, aged thirty-six, leaving an unsuspected widow – Mrs. Eugenia Stanhope – and two young sons; Chesterfield himself died in 1773 and Mrs. Stanhope sold the correspondence for £1500 in the following year. Almost certainly, Chesterfield himself never wanted his private correspondence made public and the *Letters* therefore give a very frank and accurate picture of the ideas, manners and morals of an eminent eighteenth-century nobleman, as well as

---

[32] Fordyce, *Character and Conduct of the Female Sex*, 51.

[33] Cf. Aiken, writing about the evils of a secluded life: 'Men of virtuous principles have, I think, been too much afraid of contaminating them by entering into active life, and have listened too readily to the siren strains of poets and philosophers, who have praised the silent vale of retirement as the true abode of pure and exalted virtue.' *From a Father to His* Son, ii. 47.

the polish and education necessary to move in aristocratic and diplomatic circles. His advice thus differs materially from that of the other conduct writers.

By 1739, when Philip was seven, Chesterfield had already begun to write advice on a subject that would form the main theme of their thirty-year-long correspondence: the primary importance of correct and appropriate manners:

> ...a gentleman, who is used to the world, comes into company with a graceful and proper assurance, speaks even to people he does not know, without embarrassment, and in a natural and easy manner. This is called usage of the world, and good-breeding: a most necessary and important knowledge in the intercourse of life. It frequently happens that a man with a great deal of sense, but with little usage of the world, is not so well received as one of inferior parts, but with a gentleman-like behaviour.[35]

Chesterfield's letter pictures a world in which surface appearance and social graces are pre-eminent, and are the means by which people are judged. He did not suggest that morals are unnecessary, simply that the world in general does not have either the wit or will to recognise them unless they are clothed in an acceptable form, which consists of the current social modes. The adoption of good manners and polite forms of behaviour within society, therefore, is an expedient measure, serving the purposes of dissimulation better than violence and confrontation:

> Courts are, unquestionably, the seats of Politeness and Good-breeding; were they not so, they would be the seats of slaughter and desolation. Those who now smile, and embrace, would affront and stab each other, if Manners did not interpose: but Ambition and Avarice, the two prevailing passions at Courts, found Dissimulation more effectual than Violence; and Dissimulation introduced the habit of Politeness, which distinguishes the Courtier from the Country Gentleman.[36]

No heroes here! Manners are tools to deceive others and advance one's own career. Chesterfield cautioned his son that a young man required 'inward firmness and steadiness' but should have 'exterior modesty' and 'seeming diffidence'; he

---

[34] *Letters written by the Late Right Honourable Philip Dormer Stanhope, Earl of Chesterfield to his Son, Philip Stanhope Esq*, 2 vols. (London: J. Dodsley, 1774).

[35] Chesterfield, *Letters*, i. 93-5. The Letter is presented in the original French with a translation appended by Eugenia Stanhope.

should display 'apparent frankness and openness' but this should conceal 'inward' caution and closeness. The young man at court had as difficult a role to play as a passive young woman acquiring unobtrusive power through submission. This description marks, perhaps more than any other single comment, the difference between Lord Chesterfield and the other conduct writers. He was familiar with, came from, and wrote about a completely different stratum of society. The court is a separate society, heading English society in general but not mixing with it. Chesterfield's *Letters* provide a counterpoint to the other – middle-class – authors. The heroes of Gothic fiction are always well-born (even if they do not know it themselves), but the morals and attitudes they espouse are not Chesterfield's. He was less concerned with motives than with results: 'Give me but virtuous actions and I will not quibble and chicane about the motives.'[37] His *Letters* create a picture of an eighteenth-century nobleman who, if he were a character in a Gothic romance, might well be a villain, not a hero.

Like Jane West's comment on the manners of Macbeth cited earlier, there is a contrast between what is felt and what is displayed. There is not necessarily any implication of deceit, of feeling one emotion and displaying its opposite – consider the other conduct writers who all say that strong emotions must be endured with no overt display at all. Chesterfield advises discretion rather than abstinence:

> A real man of fashion and pleasure observes decency; at least, neither borrows nor affects vices; and, if he unfortunately has any, he gratifies them with choice, delicacy and secrecy.[38]

Good-breeding seems to be postulated as a substitute for self-regulation and moral choices. A courtier must know how to handle his vices and other people, and flattery is merely another useful tool to use when one is conversant with the weaknesses of others. Throughout the letters sounds an echo of Chesterfield's intellectual and social arrogance. He always represented himself as an absolute

---

[36] *Ibid* i. 443.
[37] *Ibid* i. 329-30.

authority, the man who knows, the manipulator with the power, attempting to advance his son into a similar position.

Despite the attacks made upon him by other conduct writers, like Fordyce, for example, he did share some common ground with his detractors. The following quotation reads like a piece of Chesterfield's advice but is in fact the work of Jane West:

> The world has long since decided, that a knowledge of the art of pleasing shall be a passport to its favour; and can it be wondered, that it refuses to receive a suppliant who does not come thus accredited.[39]

Mrs. West and Chesterfield share similar views on the necessity of 'pleasing,' though she asserted that it should be bound by prudence to guard the unwary young man against affectations, and Chesterfield set no discernible bounds whatsoever. His advice to Philip to 'strike through the passions' echoes the prevalent idea that passion is a dangerous and a destructive weakness. The other writers simply warned their readers against indulging in overt passion, Chesterfield advised his son to watch for and use any manifestations that betray a man's obsessions. When the passions are engaged they can override reason and the entire framework of society and the rational world is vulnerable.

The publication of Chesterfield's *Letters* provoked some extreme contemporary reactions. His frankness and cynicism shocked readers who preferred to believe that they were part of a fundamentally righteous society. Instead they were told that politeness and good manners were the socially expedient tools of a corrupt and self-seeking world. There were immediate replies.

The most provocative issue was Chesterfield's concern with manners as a means to success, apparently at the expense of morals. Fordyce condemned him:

> An universal popularity, obtained by whatever superficial accomplishments, or trivial recommendations, purchased at whatever expence [sic] of truth or virtue, the celebrated and the elegant Chesterfield is perpetually inculcating

---

[38] *Ibid* i. 213.
[39] West, *Letters Addressed to a Young Man*, iii. 27-8.

as the grand object of study, labour, ambition to a Young Man whom he loved above all others.[40]

Fordyce considered the *Letters* both indelicate and vulgar. Seeking popularity is represented as the equivalent of prostituting one's principles, and furthermore, the accomplishments enabling a young man to obtain this universal favour cannot be profound. He must hide his virtue if it conflicts with the opinions of those with whom he is talking; he cannot tell the truth if it is offensive to his companions – only the external is privileged.

In the society with which Chesterfield was familiar, dissembling is part of the normal intercourse of life; the other conduct writers prized honesty above fashionable, social success.[41] Chesterfield never advanced religious principles in his letters; all is based on common sense rather than divine law. This is one reason why the argument for self-love as the prime motive underlying virtuous behaviour was also attacked. Self-love and self-gratification will lead to the indulgence of the passions, which afford, at least, a temporary pleasure, and may lead away from the duties owed to society and the ties of friendship. Self-love has no religious foundation, which is the basis for self-regulation, and can be irrational, contrary to the ethos of an ordered society. Self-love and a lack of concern for others lead eventually to bad or offensive manners as a 'travestie' published in 1809 shows.[42] It sets forth a code of repulsive manners and advises the reader to follow them.[43] If manners are the only standard by which people are judged, with no moral basis for assumptions about acceptable social behaviour, then bad selfish manners could become as acceptable as good ones.

---

[40] Fordyce, *Addresses to Young Men*, i. 93.

[41] Cf. John Aikin's advice, which is more representative of other conduct writers: 'it is my decided advice to you, who are beginning the world, not to be intimidated from openly espousing the cause you think a right one, by apprehension of incurring any man's displeasure. I suppose this to be done within the limits of candour, modesty and real good temper. These being observed, you can have no enemies but those who are not worthy to be your friends.' *From a Father to A Son*, i. 15.

[42] *Chesterfield Travestie; or, School for Modern Manners* (London: Tegg, 1808).

[43] E.g. It recommends staring at women in the street – if they blush they are modest, if they do not, your way is clear. Talking to oneself and gesticulating wildly in public is also advocated because you will then be taken for a poet, an actor or, if well dressed, an MP.

Because Mary Wollstonecraft took the conduct books and their sphere of influence so seriously, and also because James Fordyce's *Sermons to Young Women* went through four editions in the first year of publication, it is clear that a reading public was available and eager for this type of literature. To have the time to spend reading (or writing) three volumes of sermons on conduct surely argues a considerable amount of leisure. This points to a public composed of the sort of middle-class woman whose husband's business was no longer directly connected with the home. It had probably expanded sufficiently for them to move to the suburbs and for the woman to have more servants, less involvement with the actual business and, therefore, more leisure to enjoy reading, which is also a very private pleasure.[44] Whether the conduct books provided opportunities for this type of pleasure is uncertain at best, but fiction and poetry of the period undoubtedly did.

The conduct writers were aware that they were addressing a public who regularly read fiction, including poetry and novels, and warned the reader against Romances:

> [They] have conspired to mislead unguarded minds on this subject. How? By exhibiting gaudy pictures of a passion which is originally but too alluring; by, in a manner deifying that passion, and the imperfect beings who excite it; by frequently holding up to view an excellence more consummate and more wonderful than ever existed among mortals; in fine, by placing its gratification, and the whole apparatus with which Art, not contented with the simplicity of Virtue, has embellished it, in such lights as beguile the credulous votary with expectations that can never be answered.[45]

Romances create a fantasy world, parallel to our own, in which everything is perfect. Every heroine is sweet and gentle, every hero the most magnanimous, generous, accomplished and athletic man in the entire world. Their love for each other is mutually deifying and mutually consuming. Fordyce felt that this raised expec-

---

[44] Such a family case history is discussed by Leonore Davidoff and Catherine Hall in *Family Fortunes, Men and Women of the English Middle Class* (London: Hutchinson, 1987), where the Cadbury family moved from the centre of Birmingham to the suburb of Edgbaston as the business developed and they no longer needed to live in rooms over the shop.

[45] Fordyce, *Address to Young Men*, i. 204.

tations for the reader that could not ever be fulfilled. The above exhortation was addressed to young men, who are also assumed to be undiscerning novel readers. Nevertheless, Fordyce, who hoped to change society by preaching sermons, writing conduct books and educating the young, did find a pattern of masculinity in the old romances, where he considered the men to have been real heroes:

> The men were sincere, magnanimous, and noble; the women were patterns of chastity, dignity and affection. They were only to be won by real heroes, and this title was founded in protecting, not in betraying the sex. The proper merit with them consisted in the display of disinterested goodness, undaunted fortitude and unalterable fidelity.[46]

The pattern of heroism that Fordyce admired is similar to Hurd's chivalric code: the hero protects women, and is distinguished by his unselfishness, his goodness, his courage and his loyalty. He must deserve the heroine whom he wins. By comparison, Fordyce considers English society of the late eighteenth century to be corrupt, its values bankrupt because there was a prevalent and 'growing indifference about the regards of reputable women, and a fashionable propensity to lessen the sex in general.'[47] He called the age 'luxurious and effeminate,' a mixture of 'sensuality, softness, and concealed selfishness.'[48] Manliness and heroism are absent, qualities that should be judged, Fordyce felt, as they were in the old Romances, by the ways in which men behave towards virtuous women. The spheres of influence of the male and female characters are different, yet interdependent.

Conduct books and changing social conditions established the ideal of the passive, desirable and potentially domestic woman who can attract the generous, ardent, discerning man when the beauty of her soul transfigures her still face. They also unconsciously created the dichotomy between action and inaction, between what emotions move the heart and what, if anything, can be shown in public. The ideal man is the perfect complement to the still woman; he appreciates

---

[46] Fordyce, *Sermons to Young Women*, i. 150. Note that Fordyce, in common with most other writers, disapproved of impressionable young women reading fiction because novels painted an exaggerated picture of what might be expected from life.

[47] Fordyce, *The Character and Conduct of the Female Sex*, 8.

[48] Fordyce, *Addresses to Young Men*, i. 293, 292-3.

her passive goodness. He, himself, is an intensely moral figure, an upholder of social values, often not in the forefront of high society, rather, a family man. This marks a radical departure from the conquering heroes of antiquity who were fighting to build or to protect a society from tangible dangers. An ancient hero would have no problem dealing with the various supernatural manifestations; they would be recognised enemies, not symptoms of a troubled society. A Gothic hero is faced with a greater problem: himself. The writers of the Gothic romances had absorbed these ideals of the conduct book and transplanted them into fantasy, not always without question, to delineate the Hero, the Heroine and their preconceptions about the world and about each other.

4

The Hero: Concierge or Builder?

I. THE FIGURE OF THE HERO

Who or what is a hero? The particular figure of idealised masculinity presented in the conduct books is a construct peculiar to the eighteenth century in which and for which they were written, while 'the hero' is a figure (or figurehead) recurring in many cultures. To find the hero of the Gothic romance, therefore, we must look beyond specifically eighteenth-century ideas and texts towards a wider tradition.

In the iconography of some early twentieth-century cinema – particularly action films – the hero is readily identifiable. Black and white film lends itself to a portrayal of moral polarities through basic colour-coding: the hero wears the white hat and rides the white horse. His clothing announces his heroic function, and his subsequent actions prove his hero status. The heroic function was, in these films as in other types of narrative, to combat evil and/or to act as a pioneer for his society.[1] In both scenarios, the hero's actions, which place him in personal danger, are selfless, undertaken on behalf of a community that, for various reasons, is either impotent against a menace threatening to destroy society, or unable to establish a new society without him. Therefore, the hero is an active figure, whose individual actions are necessarily of epic proportions since he is the active focus of an entire society. In defending society against an overwhelming threat, the hero fights for the good of that society against a common evil. He is thus a moral figure – although the hero can only be imbued with positive moral values

---

[1] For a brief discussion on the presentation of character and stock character roles in early cinema, see David Bordwell, Janet Staiger and Kristin Thompson (eds.), *The Classical Hollywood Cinema: Film Style & Mode of Production to 1960* (London: Routledge, 1985), 13-16.

when viewed and judged by the desired moral code of the society that he represents.[2]

As contemporary conduct literature demonstrated, the eighteenth-century ideal of masculinity was similarly manifested in activity and linked to a moral code. In Gothic romances too, 'hero' is a term that can only be applied to characters with positive moral qualities, although Johnson's definition of the hero as 'a man eminent for bravery' does not suggest a moral dimension.[3] By contrast, Johnson's definition of 'heroick' – 'noble; suitable to a hero; brave; magnanimous; intrepid; enterprising; illustrious' – not only lists all the qualities associated with the hero of the Gothic romance, but significantly includes the key word 'magnanimous' which, as this chapter will show, does have a positive moral connotation. Thus one may argue that the hero is the principal male figure within the plot, and also potentially the 'best' in a moral sense: he is the character who uses the activity associated with masculinity in a constructive rather than destructive manner. That the hero should be a moral figure is not only a requirement of the romance formula (and the Gothic formula) but is clearly also part of the structure of a hero persona.

The mythic hero may be understood as a creation of the people, an expression of the collective unconscious who is endowed with all the virtues. Both Lord Raglan and Joseph Campbell, having examined different examples of this collective hero myth, point to a tripartite spiritual and actual journey undertaken by the hero: birth, initiation and death – Raglan; and separation, initiation and return – Campbell.[4] Although the nomenclature is different, the development of the stages

---

[2] For an investigation of eighteenth-century hero figures as manifestations of social, cultural and economic development see Margaret Beaton Duncan, *Aspects of the Hero in Eighteenth Century English Literature* (doctoral dissertation submitted to the University of California, 1990).

[3] Johnson, *Dictionary of the English Language*. Cf. Ann Radcliffe, describing Emily's assessment of Montoni's courage: '... his very courage was a sort of animal ferocity ... a constitutional hardiness of nerve, that cannot feel, and that, therefore, cannot fear.' *Mysteries of Udolpho*, 358.

[4] Lord Raglan, *The Hero: A Study in Tradition, Myth and Drama* (London: Methuen, 1936). Joseph Campbell, *The Hero with a Thousand Faces* (1949; repr. London: Grafton, 1988). The quest of the hero as a central myth is common to most myth criticism; however the tripartite structure common to both Raglan and Campbell is readily applicable to the Gothic romance. For an investigation of the

is similar: both writers begin the hero quest with separation from the mother and settled society; continue with initiation into the rites of adulthood; and conclude with the accomplishment of the hero's task.[5] A new city has been founded: the old king's reign is over. The stages of this journey are not inconsequential picaresque but part of an unfolding pattern leading to the redemption of a whole people.

These heroes are builders: by the conclusion of their journey they have created something upon which a new society may rest. Even if the travels and travails are an inner, rather than an outer, journey, the hero concludes by transforming himself (a representative and leader of his entire culture) into a stronger, worthier member of his society, able to lead it towards future success and survival. Interestingly, heroes of Gothic fiction seem to follow the same tripartite pattern without achieving the same result.

The Gothic hero certainly appears to undergo 'separation,' often engineered through specific plot devices deployed by the writer in the course of the narrative. Sometimes the hero is forced into society with no adult protection, as a young hero and an orphan with no knowledge of his natural parents – these are typically revealed or vindicated at the dramatic close of the fourth volume. Theodore (*The Castle of Otranto*, 1764); Ignatius (*The Haunted Castle*, 1794); and Alfonzo (*Gondez the Monk*, 1805) all follow this pattern. Although this type of abandonment may be used as a device to 'separate' the Gothic hero and initiate his hero quest, it is more commonly used to propel the heroine into a situation in which she is an unprotected victim. Indeed, this structure is so frequently used that it may be argued that the writers of Gothic romances intensified and dramatised this archetypal process of 'separation' to create a dynamic plot.[6]

---

hero myth as a literary archetype (in which the quest cycle is viewed 'seasonally' in four parts) see Northrop Frye, 'The Archetypes of Literature', in John B. Vickery (ed.), *Myth and Literature: Contemporary Theory and Practice* (Lincoln [Neb]: University of Nebraska Press, 1966), 87-97.

[5] For an analysis of late twentieth-century masculinity that also explores the stages of separation and initiation, see Rosalind Miles, *The Rites of Man: Love, Sex and Death in the Making of the Male* (London: Grafton, 1991).

[6] Note that most fairy tales begin with the abandoned child, or a young person setting out on a quest alone.

Like the mythic hero, who is ritually initiated into the adult (male) world, the Gothic hero too is forced to prove his masculinity, either within or against established, adult, male social groups. Huberto Avinzo (*Gondez the Monk*) is literally initiated into a male society when he independently joins Robert the Bruce's fugitive gang and initially proves himself by giving sound advice during the council of war. Valancourt (*The Mysteries of Udolpho*, 1794) is tested by his experiences in the corrupt society of Paris, and proves his masculinity by eventually choosing the correct moral path despite initially succumbing to peer pressure. Initiation into the adult world is often connected as much with alienation from living parents as separation from dead ones. Unlike the type of initiation represented by *joining* adult groups, this test of masculinity is a metaphorical (and sometimes actual) battle for a recognised, autonomous male existence separate from the father. The hero's respect for the father figure is placed in proportion as the young man assumes or rejects his place in adult society, weighing the father's wishes, values and decisions against the hero's own sense of moral imperatives. Some heroes (usually and more accurately described as hero-villains) experience separation and initiation into the adult world through disillusionment with their previously godlike (or at least respected) fathers. Clermont (*Clermont*, 1798), Leonardo (*Zofloya*, 1806) and Frankenstein's creation are all examples of this type. Although one might suppose that these heroes experience a different type of initiation from the orphaned hero, this is not generally the case. Heroes in the Gothic romances (whether orphaned or with living parents) are frequently alienated from the public society into which they are first initiated because their idealised moral values are not those of a self-seeking world.

Only in the third stage, the accomplishment of the hero's quest, is there a difference between the mythic and the Gothic hero. For, unlike the mythic hero, the hero of the Gothic romance is rarely represented as the active builder of a new or renewed society because society itself is corrupt and cannot be changed by heroic activity. In Sophia Lee's *The Recess* (1785), for example, both her heroes, mature Leicester and young, idealistic Essex, are crushed by the machinations of Elizabeth I and her court. Gothic writers invariably represent Elizabeth the First as an absolute monarch, who, by virtue of her sex, is a threat to women and an enigma to men.[7] Paradoxically, both Leicester and Essex are represented as heroes who simultaneously protect and threaten their social order. As soldiers they are sworn to maintain the old order; but as the lovers of Matilda and Ellinor (the legitimate twin daughters of Mary Queen of Scots) they present a new dynastic challenge. As leaders of their society by virtue of their aristocratic birth, their primary responsibility is loyalty to the crown; however, their loyalties are further complicated by the devious and demanding personality of the monarch. The plot thus centres on the conflict between the private, emotional life and the demands made on the public persona.

The actions or the quest of the hero in Gothic fiction are frequently focused on conflicts between established social custom and private morality. A Gothic hero's role is less public and more domestic than that of the mythic hero because the primary function of the hero in Gothic fiction is to maintain the ideal moral values of his society.[8] A Gothic hero can be represented as engaging in an intense, inner moral struggle, displaying his heroism only through minimal physical action. Thus the Gothic hero figure is both more individual and more static than the mythic hero.

This type of 'individual' hero, Hans Schlaffer has argued, is always intimately connected with a bourgeois environment – interesting, when one considers that Gothic fiction not only features a rather static hero on an individual inner quest, but was also promoting middle-class values.[9] Schlaffer argued that in a bourgeois world social and political institutions are already established, capable of existence independent of human efforts, and that the classical goals of action

---

[7] See also Francis Lathom, *The Mysterious Freebooter, Or, The Days of Queen Bess: A Romance*, 4 vols. (London: Minerva Press, 1806).

[8] This is true even for a hero like Theodore in *The Castle of Otranto* who is used to establish a fresh regime after Manfred's downfall.

have already been accomplished, reducing heroic ideals and producing a focus on the inner man. Thus the only truly heroic action possible within the Bourgeois Novel is revolution, and the *limits* of individual heroism are recognised in the person of the hero. Schlaffer denied, however, that the Gothic romance could or did offer a realistic bourgeois critique. Referring to the Gothic novel as 'light fiction,' he dismissed the hero of popular fiction as trivial.[10] Schlaffer failed to recognise that the Gothic hero frequently, and the heroine almost inevitably, is shown as experiencing an inner struggle in his or her attempts to achieve eighteenth-century ideals and virtues founded upon essentially middle-class ethics. Rather than being a vehicle of trivial illusion, the hero becomes the concierge of the edifice of middle-class values. Values espoused and dictated by wise father-figures (St. Aubert in *The Mysteries of Udolpho* is a typical example) have to be absorbed and realised by the young hero before he can take over the patriarchal mantle and sustain his society.

Schlaffer did, however, outline the main problem faced by writers of Gothic fiction attempting to delineate the hero figure. The bourgeois hero cannot appropriate the actions or the aims of an antique hero because these have already been realised in the bourgeois hero's own society. Consequently, the hero of the Gothic romance is neither as compelling nor overtly active a figure within the formula as the primary villain. Because the principal male character is often also the villain of the tale rather than the hero, the hero category is further subdivided into hero-villains and villain-heroes. Hero-villains are principal male characters with an enormous potential for good, whose potential is perverted or corrupted during the course of the plot and who finally become destroyers: villain-heroes are principal male characters who are socially destructive throughout the plot with only one redeeming, heroic feature – usually courage.[11] The plot that features a hero-villain always has an accompanying villain, or agent of perversion, and the

---

[9] Heinz Schlaffer, *The Bourgeois as Hero*, trans. James Lynn (1973; Cambridge: Polity Press, 1989).

[10] Schlaffer, *Bourgeois as Hero*, 36-7.

plot containing a villain-hero has a complementary young moral hero.[12] These hero-villains and villain-heroes are characters of the same proportions as the Shakespearean tragic hero; they live in a magnified landscape of guilt.[13] The Gothic hero is more passive.

Rather than being constrained by 'realism' in depicting action, as Canning had suggested in 1747, writers of Gothic fiction were constrained by the stereotype of masculinity which they had to present as ideal. William Hazlitt investigated this very problem in an essay entitled 'Why the Heroes of Romance are Insipid,' in which he argued that the reader's expectations about the hero figure undermined any possibility of action:

> They are, or are supposed to be, so amicable, so handsome, so accomplished, so captivating, that all hearts bow before them, and all the women are in love with them without knowing why or wherefore, except that it is understood that they are to be so. ... When there is this imaginary charm at work, everything they could do or say must weaken the impression, like arguments brought forth in favour of a self-evident truth.[14]

The first point Hazlitt made is that the hero figure cannot act because he is a hero. He is so idealised that his presence alone effects the love story, which is the primary purpose of the romance, and thus, though he may be described in glowing terms, nothing that the hero figure can actually perform will live up to the heroic aura with which he is introduced. Hazlitt also suggested that the very fact that the hero embodies the ideals of his eighteenth-century readership further contributes to his passivity. Making a comparison between 'old' and 'modern' romances, Hazlitt praised the hero who had to perform some rude physical task 'instead of depending, as in more effeminate times, on taste, sympathy, and refinement of

---

[11] Villain-heroes are discussed at length in Chapter Six.

[12] Raymond (*Longsword*, 1762), Ambrosio (*The Monk*, 1796), and Leonardo (*Zofloya*, 1806) are examples of the first type: Manfred (*The Castle of Otranto*, 1764), Montoni (*The Mysteries of Udolpho*, 1794), Gondez (*Gondez the Monk*, 1805) and Schedoni (*The Italian*, 1797) are examples of the second.

[13] For the relationship between the Shakespearean tragic hero and the Gothic Hero-Villain see Mario Praz, *The Romantic Agony* (1933; repr. London: Fontana, 1960), 79-80.

sentiment and manners, of the delicacy of which it is impossible to convey any idea by words or actions.'[15] The terms Hazlitt used are those conduct book writers employed to depict the ideal woman. The hero's exceptional masculinity is no longer assessed by action but by the depth and quality of his feeling – the same standards that are applied to the heroine. Hazlitt evidently considered the modern romance hero to be cast in a predominantly feminised role, suitable to these 'effeminate times.' The expectations and assumptions of a contemporary reader about heroism, and the ideal gentleman had reduced the active scope of the hero figure to that of an attractive statue.

Nevertheless, the place of the hero figure within the formula – as an upholder of social values and protector of the heroine – is not changed despite the tension between the action expected of a hero and the representation of an eighteenth-century ideal. One might argue that such a tension is less likely in those romances set in more remote time periods, in which the hero could be more active. Hazlitt, however, found the same defects in the heroes of Scott's historical works: 'In fact, the hero of the work is not so properly the chief object in it, as a sort of blank left open to the imagination, or a lay-figure on which the reader disposes whatever drapery he pleases!'[16] By describing the heroes of romance in these terms, Hazlitt has acknowledged both the importance of the reader's expectations as he or she engaged with the text, and that the hero of romance had become so stereotyped that very little specific description was required to evoke the hero persona.

A similar consciousness of reader expectations and character stereotyping can be found in the prefaces or dedications of some Gothic romances. The dedica-

---

[14] William Hazlitt, 'Why the Heroes of Romance are Insipid,' in *Sketches and Essays* (London: Templeman, 1839), 257-8.

[15] *Ibid* 261.

[16] *Ibid* 271. Cf. Hazlitt's comments on Ann Radcliffe's heroes: 'Mrs Radcliffe's heroes and lovers are perfect in their kind; nobody can find any fault with them, for nobody knows anything about them. They are described as very handsome, and quite unmeaning and inoffensive. ... Perhaps, however, this indefiniteness is an advantage. We add expression to the inanimate outline, and fill up the blank with all that is amiable, interesting, and romantic.' *Ibid* 267.

tion of W.H. Ireland's romance *Gondez The Monk*, for example, demonstrates the writer's consciousness of the Gothic formula:

> Never before were heroes half so fine;
> Never did virtue half so sweetly shine;
> Never did Cupid aim so well his dart;
> Never did each so well enact his part;
> Monks, heroes, witches, lovers, nobles, all--
> The good, the bad, the fat, the short and tall,
> Must fill ye with delight.[17]

Part of the promised delight is based on the way in which Ireland's characters and his plot will meet and surpass the expectations of the reader. He obviously felt that fine heroes were an essential part of his story, and juxtaposed the role of the hero with his relationship to the heroine. In terms of the reader's expectations about the way in which idealised masculinity and heroism are manifested, this hero/heroine relationship is of prime importance. The hero's treatment of the heroine becomes the means by which man's relationship with, and responsibility towards, society might be tested. As the following quotation from another preface demonstrates, depictions of the ideal man in romances are not always intended to delight only, but serve as a pattern for contemporary society:

> Romance, from its earliest periods, has, in the persons of its heroines, taught the female world, that it is virtue which can alone give lustre to their rank and beauty; and, in those of its male characters, it has instructed the stronger sex, that they are to regard themselves as the natural protectors of the weaker, to treat the objects of their passion with the most profound delicacy and respect, and to expect the hand of her whom they love, as the reward of their virtues: and if this conduct be shown to produce happiness to those who move in a high station, it will naturally produce the same desirable consequence, if pursued by those in an inferior rank of life.[18]

The role model for the behaviour of the hero that this ideal invokes is a knight bound by a chivalric code. Lathom has suggested that the romance is educative for the male reader because it lays down an idealised behaviour pattern that should be observed in relationships with women. Like a knight, a hero is distin-

---

[17] W.H. Ireland, *Gondez The Monk*, i. v.
[18] Lathom, *The Mysterious Freebooter*, i. vi-vii.

guished by the favour accorded to him by the queen of her sex: he wins and then protects her. The end of the hero's quest, as described by Lathom, is marriage and a contented, domestic, social existence.

Like all heroes, the Gothic hero was, figuratively, wearing a white hat. The values of the society that he was attempting to protect and preserve, however, could no longer be won in single combat. Thus, although the Gothic hero figure embodied the best values of his society, the evils that he had to conquer were largely found within himself. He is a passive, meditative hero, locked, like the heroine, in battle with the passions liberated by the villain. In creating the hero figure in Gothic fiction, however, writers were not content with the mannequin outline suggested by Hazlitt. Instead writers referred to the pattern laid down in the first romances and triggered the reader's expectations before frequently manipulating that heroic stereotype, thereby raising questions about the hero, the nature of heroism, and even the nature of masculinity.

II. THE GOTHIC HERO

i. The typical Gothic Hero

Hazlitt's essay suggested that the hero of romance was a passive, stereotypical figure, whose heroic stature was supplied by the reader's imagination. As the preferred image of the hero in this period, supported both by the medieval or aristocratic settings of Gothic romances and promoted by conduct literature, was that of the chivalric knight, a reader's expectations and imagination might be triggered by certain keywords with 'knightly' and heroic connotations.

The words that James Fordyce actually used to describe the characters of the knights of old were 'sincere,' 'magnanimous' and 'noble': these, particularly 'magnanimous,' become keywords in the description of the young Gothic hero.[19] These words not only define the role of the hero from the inception of the Gothic romance and thus enter the formula, but, as is apparent after reading a large num-

---

[19] Fordyce, *Sermons to Young Women*, i. 150.

ber of these works, they also became interchangeable and interdependent. A character described as having one of these qualities may be expected to have them all. Interestingly, all of these qualities are innate, and so an inexperienced hero might have them all without displaying any wisdom, which he acquires during the narrative. The reader, however, is conditioned to expect certain responses from a hero figure because these keywords have been used to describe him.

For the writer of Gothic fiction, and for the reader, sincerity is regarded as synonymous with personal integrity. The Gothic hero is incapable of deception and is the embodiment of truth, just as the villain is the embodiment of betrayal. Magnanimity is, however, is the most important heroic quality. Based on his behaviour towards conquered opponents or to the weak, it reflects his position as leader and his sense of social responsibility. When the Gothic hero is in a position of power, able to offer protection to the weak and to defeat his enemies, he demonstrates his heroism by the responsible way in which he uses that power. Reason and justice temper his raw emotions or passions:

> "To be a hero, is to be a man! --To be a man is to act in unison with the feelings of nature! --If therefore we would be heroes, we must respect the feelings of others; and while we conquer, be merciful!"[20]

This declaration, made by a Gothic hero, offers two possible interpretations of masculinity and heroism in the Gothic romance. First, masculinity is equated with heroism and then with sensibility, which is referred back to the heroic character, suggesting that being a man cannot be equated simply with biological maleness. The essence of masculinity, as described in this passage, is successful activity tempered by sensibility. Second, one might interpret this passage to mean that *any* male might be a hero. This, however, is clearly impossible within the fictional world of the Gothic Romance. For the hero who is magnanimous and sincere must also be noble – of aristocratic lineage in addition to possessing the abstract, positive moral qualities also associated with 'noble' – although noble birth does not guarantee possession of the other essential qualities.

This is evident when one scrutinises the pattern of the hero figure established in the earliest Gothic texts, *The Castle of Otranto* (1764), and *The Old English Baron* (1778).[21] Walpole and Reeve demonstrated the necessity and inevitability of noble birth for the hero by placing their young heroes in lowly social positions where their heroic natures will not be acknowledged, although other characters in the tale are aware of the difference between their bearing and their social standing. The heroic nature of these pattern heroes is announced to the reader in various ways. Walpole chose to reveal Theodore's heroic character through his actions and the direct reflections of other characters. Matilda's first view of Theodore, for example, occurs while he is presented as a peasant: 'His person was noble, handsome and commanding, even in that situation.'[22] Given the association between masculinity and heroism, Matilda's thought may be interpreted by the reader (although the character herself does not make this specific association) as an indicator of Theodore's potential heroic status. The nobility of Theodore's bearing, despite his seeming peasant class and vulnerable situation, is an anomaly that awakens the heroine's interest, but also acts as a trigger for the reader's expectations about the role he will play.[23] Walpole's Theodore proves to be the perfect young hero: he is brave – the only character who asserts his personal integrity against the orders of the tyrannical Manfred; athletic – he is able to free himself from Manfred's grasp; and considerate – he endeavours not to alarm Isabella in the vaults and later tries to soften the news that he has wounded her father. His actions manifest and confirm the heroic character, which was apparent to the reader through the heroine's first perception.

---

[20] Spoken by Ignatius in Walker, *Haunted Castle*, i. 27.

[21] Clara Reeve, *The Old English Baron* (1778; repr. Oxford: Oxford University Press, ed. and intro. James Trainer, 1967). Although both writers created pseudo-medieval setting in which their heroes could be cast as chivalric knights, the qualities these early heroes demonstrate are those promoted by contemporary conduct literature and that appear in successive heroes of Gothic romances – including those works which were not set in the far distant past.

[22] Walpole, *Castle of Otranto*, 52.

[23] Cf. the first description of Earl William disguised as a poor pilgrim in Leland, *Longsword*: 'his look was pale and squallid [sic]; but his port erect; and a secret greatness and manly dignity seemed to break thro' all the gloom of adversity which surrounded him.' i. 3.

Clara Reeve used a different technique, inserting an authorial description of her hero's superb moral character into the text. Again the reader has privileged foreknowledge about the hero figure, who is virtually identical to Walpole's Theodore and to the pattern of the chivalric knight:

> He was modest, yet intrepid; gentle and courteous to all; frank and unreserved to those that loved him, discreet and complaisant to those who hated him; generous and compassionate to the distresses of his fellow-creatures in general; humble, but not servile, to his patron and superiors.[24]

Although sincerity and magnanimity are not actually used as keywords in this quotation, the qualities for which they stand are implied. Frankness and unreservedness (or candour) are the outward signs of Edmund's sincerity and his generosity and compassion are indicators of a magnanimous nature. Clara Reeve thus left the reader in no doubt about Edmund's essentially heroic character but revealed that certain other characters in her fictional world refused to recognise it:

> If he behaved with manly spirit, it was misconstrued into pride and arrogance; his generosity was imprudence; his humility was hypocrisy, the better to cover his ambition.[25]

Without the recognised status of nobility, the hero is in no position to exercise magnanimity: his inferior status makes him into a potential victim rather than a potential protector. In both these romances, and in others where the same device of a hero lacking heroic social status is used, the heroine always recognises the hero in the dependent. Consequently much of the story revolves around the heroine's suffering and the hero's struggle to gain recognition and status in a social hierarchy that refuses to acknowledge heroism or 'real' masculinity in any class but the highest. Of course, in both *The Castle of Otranto* and *The Old English Baron*, the hero is eventually proved to have genuine aristocratic origins, which effectively validate and reinforce the social hierarchy set up within the texts. When using this device of a hero figure placed in a lowly social position, the writer was also able to exploit the hero's struggle with his own emotions, as the

---

[24] Reeve, *Old English Baron*, 25.
[25] *Ibid* 32.

chivalric character does not permit a beloved object to be degraded by reducing her status to his own. Heroism in Gothic fiction thus also involves self-restraint and self-sacrifice to a larger ideal, something that the self-indulgent villain is represented as incapable of performing.

Both Theodore and Edmund are model young Gothic heroes and there is no discernible character difference between them that could be ascribed to the gender of the author save, perhaps, the amount of personal danger that each young hero faces. Theodore, a 'man's hero,' is nearly executed by Manfred and fights a duel against an experienced knight in which, as a peasant supposedly unskilled at arms, he was at a disadvantage. In contrast, Edmund, a 'woman's hero,' is brought up as a companion to the young FitzOwens, and the worst thing he has to fear is the loss of his Lord's favour and banishment from the castle. He is not even required to fight a duel against the usurping lord because Sir Philip Harclay assumes that honour. Nevertheless both heroes are continually challenged to prove themselves. Except when the figure of the young hero is deliberately subverted by the author, the role and essential heroic characteristics of the hero figure do not alter during the period chosen for this study.

Although the pattern for the hero figure *per se* does not alter during this period, each individual develops within the course of the narrative in which he appears. Thus the hero realises his heroic potential in a form of *Bildungsroman*, in which his morals are tested by worldly experience. Occasionally these moral tests and trials are represented literally within the plot; for example, when Vivaldi (*The Italian*, 1797) or Monçada (*Melmoth the Wanderer*, 1820) are imprisoned and tried by the Inquisition.[26] Heroic self-restraint and self-sacrifice are often appreciated by the reader and only publicly acknowledged within the text at the conclusion of the story. Thus the heroic struggle is internalised, re-emphasising that the

---

[26] Ann Radcliffe, *The Italian, Or The Confessional of the Black Penitents*, ed. and intro. Frederick Garber (1797; repr. Oxford: Oxford University Press, 1981). Charles Maturin, *Melmoth the Wanderer: A Tale*, ed. Douglas Grant & intro. Chris Baldick, (1820; repr. Oxford: Oxford University Press, 1989).

hero's quest is often an inner quest and valorising the exercise of self-restraint. One side-effect of such a struggle is that it reduces the hero's external activity; however, external passivity does not necessarily work against the idea of heroism, as Canning and Hazlitt both assumed, but may be interpreted positively as a contrast to the active self-seeking of the villain. The most heroic gesture made by Ignatius (*The Haunted Castle*), for example, is his private decision to leave his beloved Adelais when he believes that she is his sister. Alternatively, the young hero's capacity for heroic self-sacrifice may be recognised and manipulated by the villain. In such a case, the reader recognises both the restraints imposed by the heroic stereotype and that the hero must learn to judge the motives of other characters accurately.

Regina Maria Roche's Oscar Fitzalan (*The Children of the Abbey*, 1796) is one such hero whose innate nobility and sense of honour are manipulated and tested within the story as part of his maturation. Oscar is tricked into actively giving up the woman he loves, on a point of honour, believing that her father does not approve of the connection even though Oscar knows how Adela herself feels about him. The reader is privy to the reasons for the mental torture and real physical suffering which Oscar is forced to conceal from his associates, and can simultaneously appreciate and deplore Oscar's heroism, knowing that his promise to the villain Belgrave binds him to passivity while his beloved Adela is exposed to a miserable and loveless marriage.

Oscar is one of two young Gothic heroes in *The Children of the Abbey* who radically change their perceptions about the world during the course of the narrative: Lord Mortimer, Amanda's lover, also becomes more adult as the tale progresses and his preconceptions about the appearance of virtue change. Mrs. Roche tested the heroic stereotype by contrasting her two heroes' characters, behaviour, education, environment and parental example. Although these hero figures begin from different starting points, they undergo a similar learning process, giving them more experience of the differences between appearance and reality, and are brought to the same heroic conclusion – happy marriage to the women they love. Thus, not only can heroic status be achieved in a passive and private manner but the end of the heroic quest is also personal and domestic, entry into the private, domestic sphere, which is the heroine's rightful domain. By the conclusion of the story, Oscar and Mortimer (who share the same essential heroic qualities from the beginning) have duplicated each other's experience and reinforced the heroic stereotype.

Initially, however, they are presented as very different. Oscar, for example, is represented as approaching the artless Adela, who behaves in a forward and sprightly manner, with far more respect than Mortimer initially showed the extremely reserved and circumspect Amanda:

> the sacred impression of virtue, which nature and education had stamped upon the heart of Oscar, was indelibly fixed, and he neither suspected, nor, for worlds, would have attempted injuring the innocence of Adela.[27]

Oscar's delicate, heroic treatment of Adela is rooted in the same lack of worldly experience that eventually led to the misguided promise. Mortimer's contrasting treatment of Amanda is based on an excess of worldly knowledge that caused him to doubt the appearance of virtue.[28] Oscar has no experience of hypocrisy and Mortimer marks it everywhere.

Neither Oscar's innocence nor Mortimer's superficial knowledge of the world helps them to realise their heroic potential: they both have lessons to learn. By the close of the story Mortimer is forced to revise his concept of personal honour – at the start of the tale he was suspicious of Amanda because to be taken in by assumed virtue would have been a stain on his family honour. Four volumes later, he is conscious of the relationship of honour to self-sacrifice, rather than to self-aggrandisement. He is a sadder and wiser man: Lady Euphrasia (Amanda's

---

[27] Roche, *Children of the Abbey*, i. 187.
[28] Although Oscar is initially represented as more sensitive, Mortimer too is as magnanimous, though not as delicate, as the chivalric knight in his actions: even when Amanda seems most guilty (after Belgrave has been surprised in her bedchamber), he tries to assist her with money. He wants to assuage her suffering and protect her.

cousin) has jilted him on their wedding day; his revered father has been revealed as a secret gambler; and his home has been sold to retrieve his father's honour. Regina Roche has transformed Mortimer into a hero whose social world has been shaken but who has made an enormous spiritual gain. He has learnt, from his suffering and by example, to appreciate the strength of Amanda's virtue and he has learnt the importance of controlling his passions. The message promoted by the conduct books is realised in Mortimer's character: the fiery spirit, allowed and encouraged in a young man, must be trained and restrained, else it blazes into a consuming conflagration. Further, elevated natural pride and family honour must not become abstract tyrants supplanting moral ethics. In representing a hero who learns this lesson, Regina Maria Roche reinforced the stereotype of personal, inner heroism, while in the character of Oscar she demonstrated that this type of heroism must be tempered by experience and knowledge.

An essential part of the young Gothic hero's learning process, already seen in Mortimer's case, is the control or the restraint of 'the passions.' Although they are rarely explicitly defined, the passions that Gothic heroes have to learn to control are usually sexual in origin – mingling with Society is equated with a loss of innocence, even when the vices adopted are gambling rather than whoring. When these passions are awakened, a terrible internal conflict begins in the hero between self-indulgence and self-sacrifice. *The Passions* (1811) by Charlotte Dacre, written under the pseudonym of Rosa Matilda, shows such an awakening, such a conflict, and the resultant chaos. She had already explored the theme of awakening sexuality in young men and women in the Gothic romance, *Zofloya* (1806), and *The Passions*, written almost entirely in the first person as an epistolary novel, initially seems very different because it has no overtly supernatural (or even explained supernatural) manifestations. The passions of the characters, however, particularly the hate and desire for vengeance of the villainous Countess Appollonia Zulmer, acquire a supernatural potency of their own. Despite the absence of overt supernatural manifestations, the basic character types remain those of the Gothic romance and it has several Gothic trappings. The plot is simple: the perfect marriage of Darlowitz and the angelic Amelia is disrupted when he falls in love with Weimar's beautiful and engaging wife, Julia. Julia's response has been engineered and orchestrated through the advice given to her by the villain, Countess Appollonia Zulmer. The whole affair is entirely cerebral, taking place in letters addressed to their respective confidants, not in any physical act between them apart from a letter from Julia asking Darlowitz to *live* when he has gone into a decline, owing to the distress of his mind. Furthermore, Darlowitz has not undergone any testing experience before embarking on happiness ever after at the beginning of the novel.

In *The Passions*, therefore, the importance of a learning process is stressed as the reader experiences what happens when a hero marries a heroine without growing up first:

> But what is the wild enthusiasm, the ideal perfection of the choice of youth, compared with the refined judgement and sublimer conceptions of the man?[29]

Ironically Charlotte Dacre has depicted Darlowitz viewing himself as a mature adult, whereas later in the same letter his adult language fragments into incoherent ravings. This kind of self-deception is typical of Darlowitz, who has never seen clearly. Throughout the romance he is represented as an idealist, idolising those people whom he loves, extravagantly asserting that his friend, Weimar, has been an inspiration to him, and that his wife, Amelia, is an angel. These statements are true insofar as they are confirmed by letters from the one character whose impartiality the reader is encouraged to trust, Rozendorf, and by the opinions expressed by the villainous Countess Zulmer. Yet people consist of more than one idealised dimension, and this Darlowitz fails utterly to appreciate. As a result his wife dies and his best friend's family is torn apart when Julia flies from her home. Darlowitz is a type of young hero who has never undergone a learning process, and

---

[29] Darlowitz to Rozendorf, in Dacre, *Passions*, ii. 104. Cf. Rozendorf's description of Weimar in love: 'Weimar's goddess is an incarnation of a boyish desire and fancy. He thinks he has found her in Julia but surely his judgment should have matured since then?' *Ibid* i. 88.

who consequently, despite the noble qualities with which Charlotte Dacre endowed him, is unable to restrain his passions.

The story of Raymond de las Cisternas (*The Monk*, 1796) also involves the flight of a young woman from her home and indicates how important it is to control sexual passion. Lewis suggested throughout this romance that liberating passion, particularly sexual passion, crosses temporal as well as social boundaries, acquiring and awakening supernatural forces. The love between Agnes and Raymond, for example, causes them to try to exploit the superstition that, in another form, has destined Agnes for the Church, and Agnes's attempted elopement dressed as the Bleeding Nun literally brings the supernatural world into the natural. Like other Gothic heroes, Raymond has an important lesson to learn about the control of the passions and social responsibility.[30]

Mrs. Radcliffe's heroes also undergo educative trials, although these are only pale reflections of the mental anguish endured by her heroines. From his first appearance Valancourt is set up as a hero who will be undergoing the test of exposure to Society – St. Aubert remarks mournfully that Valancourt has never been to Paris – and rumour accuses him of loose-living in that city. Parisian society is frequently used as a type for fashionable decadence, in which innocence is at risk, although London society too proves to be extremely dangerous for Amanda in *The Children of the Abbey*. Although he examined Gothic heroes as protagonists in novels of education, Howard Anderson did not see the learning process as an essential part of the hero role, and stated that Valancourt's character does not develop any more than Montoni's.[31] However, Anderson based this assertion on an erroneous interpretation of the text, believing that Valancourt's behaviour in the wicked city was only rumour with no substance in fact. This is not the case:

---

[30] Howard Anderson also states that the hero's task is self-control and social awareness. See 'Gothic Heroes,' in Robert Folkenflik (ed.), *The English Hero, 1660-1800* (London and Toronto: Associated University Presses, 1982), 215. His study of Gothic heroes suggests that aspects of masculinity are divided among different male characters.

[31] Anderson, 'Gothic Heroes', 205-6.

Valancourt, some time after his arrival at Paris, had been drawn into the snares, which determined vice had spread for him, and ... his hours had been chiefly divided between the parties of the captivating Marchioness and those gaming assemblies, to which the envy, or the avarice, of his brother officers had spared no art to seduce him.[32]

The passage continues with the information that Valancourt's brother had refused to pay his debts and he had been sent to prison, where he had had time to reflect on his conduct and to repent. Although this occupies only one page of the text and is not given the same prominence or importance as Emily's forays into real life, Ann Radcliffe definitely showed that Valancourt had to reappreciate his moral values in order to be worthy of Emily's perfection. Vivaldi (*The Italian*), the most developed of Radcliffe's heroes, has to loose himself from the ties binding him to his worldly, materialist parents and redeem his society by appreciating and marrying Ellena to found a new and worthier dynasty of the Vivaldi family.

The reward for the successful completion of these trials is always the same: the hero has, at last, become worthy of the patient, suffering, passive heroine, and can retire into marriage and family life. Failure guarantees the destruction of the family, the destruction of love, the destruction of hope, and the destruction of the self. The general pattern of the learning process is something that is common to the majority of *young* Gothic heroes, no matter what the sex of the author, or what stylistic form the romance takes, or at what point in this period (1762-1820) they appear.

ii. Motifs associated with the Hero

Throughout this period certain repeated motifs play a significant role in the hero's development. One such motif is that of the hero's entanglement in the affections of an older woman, highlighting both the attractiveness and the youth of the hero figure, who is still learning how to control his passions and cannot respond in a sophisticated manner. Advances from older women are also part of the

---

[32] Radcliffe, *Mysteries*, 652.

learning process that the hero must undergo. As Howard Anderson has noted, the troubles besetting Raymond de las Cisternas come from his attempts to extricate himself from the love of one vengeful older woman, the Baroness Lindenburgh, bringing down on himself the unwelcome and unceasing attentions of one still older.[33] The passions of the past reawaken with the guilt and the sin still adhering to them, and Raymond must resolve and quieten these old passions before his own life and love can proceed. The Bleeding Nun haunts Raymond only, but the way in which he deals with the advances of the Baroness contains the seeds of Agnes's near-martyrdom. When his youth causes him to reject the Baroness' advances awkwardly – a more experienced man would surely have recognised the symptoms earlier – the focus as well as the nature of her passion changes. Consequently, Agnes becomes the victim of the Baroness' need for vengeance and is sent to the Convent, where her later indiscretion makes her the focus of yet another older woman's frustrated fury.[34] Raymond's attempts at sexual satisfaction cause nothing but devastation.

When an older woman finds the young hero sexually attractive, it signals both his nearing adulthood and his own burgeoning sexuality. In *Zofloya* Charlotte Dacre uses this device to drive her young hero-villain, Leonardo, from potential sanctuaries and towards his eventual downfall. After running away from his father's house, he is involved in an Hippolytus/Phaedra situation when Signora Zappi fakes an assault on herself after he rejects her advances. Thus, Leonardo is again driven from a home/sanctuary as a result of an older woman's sexuality – the first occasion was his voluntary flight after his mother disappeared with Count Ardolph – and this propels him towards the fateful meeting with Megalena Strozzi, which marks the awakening of his own sexuality.

---

[33] Anderson, 'Gothic Heroes,' 215.

[34] Lewis introduced this motif early in *The Monk* during the first encounter between the gallants and Leonella. What is comedy between cavaliers and the middle-aged, ugly daughter of a shoemaker in Cordova, however, turns into tragedy when both parties are of equal status and in deadly earnest.

Young Gothic heroes are usually about to discover the true nature of their feelings for the heroine at the same time that the heroine's older female friend, relation or benefactress begins to entertain warm feelings for them. Both the Count de Bouville and Lord Lymington undergo this experience when Eliza Parsons used this motif in *Castle of Wolfenbach* (1793) and *The Mysterious Visit* (1802); however, the change in focus between the earlier and the later texts marks a radical shift in authorial intention. In contrast to Lewis's frustrated elderly stereotypes, both the older women in these novels are initially presented as attractive, worthy matrons who benevolently befriend the helpless heroine. Thus, the destructive power of passion is more clearly shown as it undermines all their previous actions. Mrs. Courtney, the English lady in *Castle of Wolfenbach*, is a type for Austen's indolent Lady Bertram, were she to be deprived of Sir Thomas's moral guidance:

> Mrs. Courtney was good-natured, not from principle but constitution; she hated trouble of any sort, therefore bore anything, rather than have the fatigue of being out of humour; she was polite and friendly, where she had no temptation to be otherwise; in short, she had many negative virtues, without any active ones.[35]

Given this character, it is not altogether surprising that Mrs. Courtney should give way to her feelings for the Count de Bouville, rather than fatigue herself in attempting to restrain them. Mrs. Parsons made the conflict between passion and restraint more poignant when she created Madame Villeneuve, in the later *The Mysterious Visit*, who is first described as having 'true nobility of soul ... an upright, humane, and generous heart, which scarcely ever waited to be asked, before she flew to relieve'.[36] Unfortunately Madame Villeneuve is also a dormant volcano; the reader is informed that she had never been touched by passion before and, as soon as she conceived her love for Lord Lymington, it overcame her completely. Unlike Lewis, Eliza Parsons created a sophisticated hero, very aware of Madame Villeneuve's feelings towards him, who treats her with great circum-

---

[35] Parsons, *Castle of Wolfenbach*, ii. 68.

spection in order to avoid prejudicing her against the helpless heroine, Georgina. This lack of candour is no more successful than Raymond's awkwardness as it reassures Madame about the direction of his feelings, and her resentment towards Georgina (when her suspicions are confirmed) is consequently greater. None of these older women have had children, perhaps suggesting that their thwarted passion is both sexual and a perverted maternal drive. Although, unstated in the text, their childlessness is underlined by the fact that these women almost always adopt the heroine as a surrogate daughter while considering the hero as a possible lover. In rejecting their advances, the young hero breaks away from proffered emotional and sexual dependence on a mother figure, in addition to remaining true to his love for the heroine.

Another recurring motif, already mentioned briefly, is the imprisonment of the hero. When heroes are imprisoned – usually by the Inquisition – the painful trials of growth are present as an actual trial in a space in which ordinary social laws can be superseded or ignored as the Inquisition, acting as a *deus ex machina*, determines the truth. Removed from society and at its mercy, the hero is forced toward inner reflection like, for example, Valancourt's reappraisal of his behaviour in *The Mysteries of Udolpho*. The heroine goes through the same process, but because she is required to be passive and cannot control her own fate any space may become a potential prison for her, whereas actual bars contain the hero.

These motifs of sexuality and imprisonment reflect stages in the development of the hero character. Both place the hero in a *passive* role, either as the object of a woman's declared desire, or physically imprisoned – as often happens to the heroine. In neither case is the hero allowed to remain passive and feminised. He must demonstrate his activity by refusing the older woman's advances, or by breaking with bad habits, or by literally breaking out of jail. Although the Gothic hero can achieve his heroic potential by interiorising his activity, thus appearing externally more passive than active, this is not the same as being cast (and treated

---

[36] Parsons, *Mysterious Visit*, iii. 44.

within the text) in a passive role. His heroism is always allied to a potential activity, which he must learn to control. Heroism and uncontrolled passions are clearly incompatible.

iii. The Subverted Hero

We have already seen that the Gothic hero of Gothic fiction can be represented as both a good, moral character and one whose behaviour is less than perfect. Some authors, however, although including a learning process, have further subverted the heroic stereotype, showing a conflict between the reader's expectations about idealised masculinity and the practicalities of life depicted in the romance, thereby questioning the applicability of the masculine ideal and the nature of heroism itself.

One may see the difference between an imperfect hero, who has to undergo a learning process, and one whose representation is subtly subverted by the author in a brief comparison of Ann Radcliffe's handling of her heroes and Charlotte Smith's Orlando Somerive (*The Old Manor House*, 1783). The difference is further demonstrated in a comparison between Eliza Parsons's *Castle of Wolfenbach* (1793) and *The Mysterious Visit* (1802). In these novels the heroes are placed in identical positions regarding the heroine, yet one undergoes a learning process and the other is a subverted hero. From these comparisons, one may see that there are two types of subverted hero created by writers of Gothic fiction: one is ultimately rewarded by the heroine's hand and the other is not.

To indicate that her heroes would undergo a learning process, Ann Radcliffe implanted warnings about their shortcomings within the texts – like St. Aubert's comments about Valancourt, or the narrator's comments about Vivaldi's hot temper and impetuosity. However, Charlotte Smith included no such warning comments about her hero. Instead, she exploited the reader's expectations about the hero's behaviour, so that Orlando becomes a more realistic figure, who does not behave perfectly, arranging clandestine meetings with Monimia, and making a bargain with the smuggler, Jonas Wilkins. Orlando may be considered a subverted hero because, although he engages in what the reader can identify as questionable behaviour, no criticism is directly offered in the text and the reader is thus drawn into a conspiracy with the lovers. Monimia's tremblings, the terrors that the clandestine meetings cause her, almost become a moral barometer, a device forcing the reader to recognise that this hero is not behaving precisely according to the prescribed pattern.

All of Orlando's questionable actions – and they are few – are directly related to his love affair with Monimia. His pact to keep silent about the operations of the smuggler, of which Mrs. Rayland surely should have been informed, is undertaken in order to facilitate his clandestine meetings with Monimia and remove some of the terrors which plagued her.[37] Consequently, Orlando's essentially heroic character is never in doubt because Charlotte Smith allows us to see that Orlando's intentions and desires are all directed towards continuing to see and to protect Monimia. Although this urge leads him into disingenuous behaviour in the early parts of the text, it is shown to be part of the heroic character nevertheless, when the same principle later strengthens his sense of duty:

> He might die in the field, and leave her exposed to hazards infinitely greater than those which could befall her in England. This last consideration determined him--It decided his wavering virtue,[38]

The magnanimous protection of the weak is one of the trademarks of the hero, or the knight-errant, and it is the mainspring of Orlando's character. Charlotte Smith represented him as consistently compassionate and forbearing, even to the petty whims of Mrs. Rayland. Orlando, however, is more of a realist than a romantic hero. On hearing that his father died secure in the belief that his youngest son, at least, was a pattern of integrity and candour and the only 'hope and reliance of us all,' Orlando is prompted to sigh.[39] The reader knows that his father's confidence

---

[37] Smith, *Old Manor House*, 132.
[38] *Ibid* 337.
[39] *Ibid* 429.

was not fully deserved as Orlando had known and concealed the plans for the elopement of Isabella and Warwick:

> ...yet he rejoiced that, believing him ignorant of his sister's flight, this opinion of his integrity had not been impaired where it could have done no good to have known the truth, and would only have inflicted another wound on his father's heart.[40]

This is not sophistry. Here Charlotte Smith has forced the reader to question yet again the absolute integrity demanded of a hero figure. Does idealised masculinity or heroism consist in a perfect balance of sincerity (truth), magnanimity (mercy) and nobility? Or is one quality more important than the others in the delineation of the hero figure? Charlotte Smith's representation of heroism in the person of Orlando suggests that one cannot always assume the presence of all three virtues in an equal degree. She has sacrificed some of the potential romantic sensibility of her hero and substituted for it a more practical concern for the feelings of others. Orlando, equipped with all the correct contemporary moral ethics, must find a means of living that will allow him to survive with his morals and his love affair intact.

Orlando's behaviour creates an impression of an eighteenth-century man trying, pragmatically, to resolve the dilemma between the ideals of romantic love and the demands of real life. Mrs. Parsons's heroes, the Count de Bouville and Lord Lymington, both undergoing experiences with older women, are forced to try and resolve the same dilemma. In these heroes too, readers' expectations are subtly confounded and the hero figure is subverted. Worldly pride, which can be a virtue when it is called 'proper' pride and reflects a sense of the worth of the self, is carried to excess in both characters. Eliza Parsons did place them in a convincing social impasse by reversing the usual romance pattern, making her heroine rather than her hero the object of the birth question: both heroes are surprised by their feelings for a beautiful young girl with a dubious history and unknown parentage. When the heroine is of undisputed noble birth, she is still a passive figure

---

[40] *Ibid* 429.

under the physical control of father or guardian and can neither make a free decision to commit herself to the hero of lowly birth, nor protect him if such a commitment is made.[41] By reversing this pattern, the hero, possessed of greater activity, could choose to marry beneath his station, raise a virtuous wife to his own status and then protect her. Recognising her virtue and then braving the strictures of society by marrying her would constitute an active, heroic act. Both of Eliza Parsons's heroes are offered this chance to prove their heroic worth, but only one succeeds.

In the earlier text, Count de Bouville, who is not a subverted hero but one undergoing an education in overcoming class prejudices, has already been struck by Matilda's beauty when she flies to England. All that he knows of Matilda's background is that she is the ward of a Mr. Weimar and that rumours have been spread amongst the Parisian society hinting that Matilda's flight from him was caused by an unsuitable love affair. After journeying to England and overcoming his scruples, the Count honourably declares his passion. He has had more than pride to overcome in making this declaration. Parsons demonstrated to the reader that de Bouville makes a mature and deliberate choice, against advice, which he knows to be sound, from the Marquis de Melfort, who appreciates Matilda's virtue but believes nevertheless that her obscure birth will bring misery upon them both:

> A man of quality in France to marry an obscure young woman, without even knowing the authors of her being, would, he knew, incur everlasting contempt.[42]

The Marquis is described throughout the tale as a man of excellent *French* principles; the English notions admired by the young Count permit greater social freedoms:

---

[41] Such a situation forms the plot of Francis Lathom's *The Mysterious Freebooter* (1806). The heroine, Rosalind, is imprisoned by her father while her lowly hero-husband is forced into exile and has to survive several assassination attempts.

[42] Parsons, *Castle of Wolfenbach*, i. 183-4.

> How happy are Englishmen! free from all those false prejudices, they can confer honor [sic] on whom they please, and the want of noble birth is no degradation where merit and character deserve esteem.[43]

It seems that Eliza Parsons intended to use her hero's choice to make an attack on class prejudice, which is relocated to France; thus her attack is discreetly camouflaged, appealing to the reader's sense of English superiority whilst evoking a reader's possible francophobia. It might also serve as a reassuring displacement of anxiety – after all, Mary Wollstonecraft had viewed the aristocracy as both parent and source of revolutionary violence in France.[44] Another possible interpretation of the choice that faces this hero is that Eliza Parsons is directly promoting middle-class values by suggesting that the best choice for her aristocrat is a virtuous girl of unknown (though certainly not peasant) background. Of course, following the Gothic formula, the reader is confident that anyone as lovely and virtuous as Matilda will prove to be of legitimate aristocratic birth. So the hero is expected to make the right choice, prompted initially by love and recognition of the heroine's excellent qualities, to be rewarded by the resolution of the birth question and the money and estates that often accompany it.

Mrs. Parsons' other proud hero, Lord Lymington (*The Mysterious Visit*), is an English, not a French, aristocrat and, though faced with same dilemma as de Bouville, turns out to be a subverted hero. He is described in more detail than de Bouville, and Parsons hinted at his subverted hero status by allowing the reader to witness his acute self-regard and belief that he can control his own emotions:

> No, he could admire without being in love! If, indeed, her heart and mind should prove estimable and good from principle,--should her birth turn out to be respectable, and her connexions not absolutely disgraceful,--why, then, if all these ifs were hereafter realised in her favour, he thought it very possible *he might prefer her* to any young woman he had ever yet seen.[45]

---

[43] *Ibid* ii. 12.

[44] Mary Wollstonecraft, *An Historical and Moral View of the Origin and Progress of the French Revolution* (London: J. Johnson, 1794).

[45] Parsons, *Mysterious Visit*, iii. 200.

Although Mortimer (*The Children of the Abbey*) was also filled with family pride, he was represented as acknowledging a powerful love for Amanda, Lymington is more cold-blooded, thinking he can control his emotions and very conscious of condescending towards a being of inferior status. Significantly, and unlike many other heroes, he does not value the heroine's virtues as the romance genre demands that he should, and his behaviour *is* questioned within the world of the romance by the sensible Lady Fortescue:

> --she saw, also, the unqualified affection his Lordship had for Georgina, but she was not so well pleased with the reserve in his conduct towards her, when if he really loved why should he hesitate to avow it;--or, by an equivocal manner towards Madame, in some degree justify the idea she had adopted of his admiration of her?[46]

Lymington's rival, Sir Charles Boyle (grandson of a Cork wine merchant), accuses him of sacrificing Georgina to the demands of fashion. Not surprisingly, it is Sir Charles and not the nobler Lord who wins the heroine in the end. Although Lymington is presented as a hero figure, the potential saviour of the hapless Georgina, he does not make the heroic choice that the reader expects. In fact the aristocratic birth, one of the requirements for a hero in the Gothic romance, actively prevents the hero from following the dictates of his affections. True heroism in this romance can only be expressed by making the right choice with respect to the heroine.

Although the progress and resolution of this story seem to indicate that Eliza Parsons was actively and consciously promoting the values of the middle classes in her tales, there are other indications suggesting she was not just mounting an attack on aristocratic class prejudices. The heroine, Georgina, certainly comes from an adoptive middle-class background, and the man who adores her and eventually marries her is a scion of mercantile rather than aristocratic lineage – although his family has been recently ennobled. Note, however, that Eliza Parsons upsets the Gothic conventions in the person of her heroine as well as that of

---

[46] *Ibid* iv. 67-8.

her hero. For, contrary to the reader's expectations, Georgina's natural parents are never discovered and the first assumption made in the story – that she is the illegitimate child of an aristocrat – is never upset by other facts emerging from the past. The decision that Lymington has to make, therefore, about the perils of social mismarriage, is one that, unlike de Bouville, he would actually have to face. Georgina's eventual husband, Sir Charles, is also represented as acutely aware of the social problems which Lymington would face and that he will encounter only in a more limited degree: "'here she will be unobtrusive in the circles of fashion,--she has friends, and, as my wife, *will be respected.*'"[47]

Eliza Parsons's concept of heroism is made clear when one considers the shift in the depiction of her heroes. Her subverted hero, Lord Lymington, is finally unable to make the heroic choice because his noble birth is the source of his prejudices as well as his virtues:

> "Happy Boyle!" exclaimed he, " … --Happily removed from all those claims upon rank and connexions, you are accountable to no one;--indifferent alike to the censurers of your conduct, or the sneers of worthless beings, who form what is called polished society.--Why have not I courage to relinquish a world I despise, and live to my own heart?"[48]

Clearly, heroism consists in maintaining one's own integrity, living 'to my own heart,' and the test facing the hero may be an act of active renunciation. Lymington does not lack physical courage, but the courage of his own convictions and thus does not fulfil the heroic stereotype, although he is initially presented as a hero figure. By depicting Lymington's failure to reconcile the conflict between romantic ideals and real life, Eliza Parsons created a subverted hero.

These subverted heroes are female creations. Male authors do not develop or extend the role of the hero by subtly upsetting the expectations of the reader as these female writers have done. Both male and female authors make their heroes go through a learning process and in both cases this learning process or experience is connected with the mastery of passions. Thus, the young Gothic hero,

---

[47] *Ibid* iv. 111.

whatever the gender of his creator, is not perfected until the end of the romance when he knows more about himself and is able to appreciate and to implement in full those values that he has had from the beginning. A hero is, above all, a figure who treasures and then protects the woman whom he loves. So, although the reader's expectations about the hero figure may not always be fulfilled by an individual character's behaviour, as long as he adores the heroine and struggles to win her, he can be a hero still.

III. THE HERO-VILLAIN

If a hero figure is subverted in only one aspect, like Lord Lymington, he ceases to be a hero but does not necessarily threaten society: if, however, a hero figure is completely subverted, yet still remains the focus of the plot, he is transformed into a hero-villain.

Three young hero-villains illustrate how the nature of masculine heroism is questioned through their decline. Ambrosio, *The Monk* (1796), Leonardo, *Zofloya* (1806), and Frankenstein (1818) are first presented as potential heroes, whose heroic potential is the catalyst in their transformation from saviours to destroyers.

> It was not vainly, then, that she sought to seduce the imagination, and lure the senses of the youth. No; he had in his own high-wrought feelings, in his susceptible soul, powerful and treacherous advocates in her cause.[49]

This quotation refers to Leonardo's seduction by the evil Megalena Strozzi, but could as easily be used to describe some of the reasons for Ambrosio's moral decline.[50] Evidently, young Leonardo is betrayed by his untutored potential for greatness and does not become a hero because he lacks sufficient education in self-restraint, coupled, as his mother runs away with an Austrian adventurer at the

---

[48] *Ibid* iv. 214.

[49] Dacre, *Zofloya*, ii. 19.

[50] Cf. Lorenzo's comments on Ambrosio: "'He is just at that period of life when the passions are most vigorous, unbridled and despotic; His established reputation will mark him out to Seduction as an illustrious Victim; Novelty will give additional charms to the allurements of pleasure; and even the Talents with which Nature has endowed him will contribute to his ruin, by facilitating the means of obtaining his object.'" *Monk*, 21.

beginning of the story, with a bad parental example. Furthermore, his acute sensibility, the touchstone of the Gothic hero, can be manipulated by the unscrupulous as Leonardo's imagination is the first point of attack for the villain. Several times in Gothic romances what occurs in the imagination either prefigures the action or substitutes for it.[51] Lewis used similar scenarios in *The Monk*; once the hero-villain's imagination is seized, his unbounded masculine activity impels him to transform imagination into reality. Ambrosio is having a cerebral love affair with Matilda, entranced by her portrait, long before he sees her in the flesh, and the *vision* of Antonia bathing is what propels him further into murder and eventual rape. Ambrosio, a typical hero-villain of the 1790s, displaying many of the same character traits that can be seen in later hero-villains, is, like Leonardo, represented as hero potential destroyed by a bad education.

Lewis blamed society, specifically its substitution of superstition for religion, for Ambrosio's corruption and downfall. The following description emphasises Ambrosio's heroic potential. Just, however, as the trials of Raymond and Agnes are due to the superstitious vow made by Agnes's mother, reinforced by the cruelty of a inflexible religious order, so has Ambrosio's innately noble, daring and courageous character been reduced to pettiness, secrecy and fear by his education in the monastery:

> He was naturally enterprizing, firm and fearless: He had a Warrior's heart, and He might have shone with splendour at the head of an Army. There was no want of generosity in his nature: The Wretched never failed to find in him a compassionate Auditor: His abilities were quick and shining, and his judgement vast, solid, and decisive. ... His Instructors carefully repressed those virtues, whose grandeur and disinterestedness were ill-suited to the Cloister. Instead of universal benevolence He adopted a selfish partiality for his own particular establishment: He was taught to consider compassion for the errors of Others as a crime of the blackest dye: The noble frankness of his temper was exchanged for servile humility; and in order to break his natural spirit, the Monks terrified his young mind, by placing before him all the horrors with which Superstition could furnish them.[52]

---

[51] Consider the many dream-vision sequences, and the cerebral love affair in *The Passions*.
[52] Lewis, *Monk*, 236-7.

Ambrosio is a hero figure with too large a spirit for the confines of the monastic system, and no scope for exercising the intensified activity with which, as a potential hero, he is endowed. Thus, Lewis depicts the heroism of which Ambrosio is capable as a negative rather than a positive force, implying that there is only one possible role for the hero – action hero. In locating heroic action only within the scope of the active, masculine figure of the noble warrior, Lewis advanced a very limited image of heroism. However, as we have seen, a Gothic hero may demonstrate heroism through an inner struggle. Ambrosio is denied this opportunity for heroism also because he has not been taught to control his passions, but, in the absence of physical temptation, has simply been taught to repress them. Liberating his monastically forbidden sexual drive impels him towards breaking every barrier and social taboo. Ambrosio first undergoes spiritual decay, then implodes.

The potentially destructive nature of heroism is also exemplified in Mary Shelley's *Frankenstein* (1818), which initially appears to have little in common with the formulaic Gothic romance. Mary Shelley too, however, was using type figures, but developing the themes and preoccupations of Gothic fiction in an extreme manner: she created two hero-villains who destroy each other. Chris Baldick has made a very interesting comment on the way in which heroism is questioned in *Frankenstein*:

> Victor's victory, the triumph of his ascetic masculine heroism, is a conquest over his own social and sexual being, fulfilled in a creature to whom social and sexual ties are denied.[53]

Baldick suggests that the heroism of which Frankenstein is capable (and which is ironically highlighted in his name) is both essentially masculine and barren. Thus, Victor's quest to fabricate a super-race of which he will be the sole parent, can be perceived as the epitome of male-centred heroism: 'male-centred' (and unnatural) since Victor desires to supplant female reproduction; and 'heroic' because of the scale of Victor's vision. Mary Shelley's book can, therefore, be interpreted as a critique of conscious masculine drives towards heroism, since all such drives depicted terminate in either actual or potential disaster.

Like all hero-villains, the three narrators in *Frankenstein* are supermen. Walton (the potential hero-villain who could doom his crew to a lingering frozen death if he pursues his dream) and Frankenstein want to extend the field of human knowledge and to be heroes with power over life and death. The monster is created on a superhuman scale and kills, almost accidentally. Even if other characters have similar power, the choices of the hero-villains carry more weight because their greater powers of imagination are inevitably allied to a greater capacity for suffering.

Frankenstein, Walton and the monster are all represented as isolated characters. Both Frankenstein and Walton have initially chosen their isolation in order to pursue their respective dreams. By representing these characters as consciously separating themselves from society, and by using first-person narratives, Mary Shelley emphasised that the characters' concept of heroism is focused on their sense of self and their individual selfish dreams. Consequently, these are not real heroes.

> Anguish and despair had penetrated into the core of my heart; I bore a hell within me, which nothing could extinguish.[54]

Having been responsible for creating life, Frankenstein has now realised his responsibility for its destruction: he speaks these words as he remembers confronting the death of the innocent Justine. His creation uses the same language:

> All, save I, were at rest or in enjoyment: I, like the arch fiend, bore a hell within me; and, finding myself unsympathised with, wished to tear up the trees, spread havoc and destruction around me, and then to have sat down and enjoyed the ruin.[55]

Frankenstein's hell is created from his guilty knowledge: the monster's hell, shown by his narrative, is created from thwarted love and rejection. By refusing

---

[53] Baldick, *Frankenstein's Shadow*, 51.

[54] Shelley, *Frankenstein*, 84.

[55] *Ibid* 132.

his responsibilities as a creator and a parent, Frankenstein perverts his ability to love and care for those around him. His internal world decays and the people that he loves most in the world are systematically killed – simply because he loves them. The monster's rage turns outwards against his creator and kills to assert his self, to make Frankenstein aware of his existence. The monster cannot claim any place in the world, and resolves his existential crisis by destruction.[56]

This type of behaviour reveals the hero-villain to be an archetypal character who rebels, who asserts his individuality, who turns away from the Father. Lewis and Mary Shelley were consciously drawing on the potent figure of the first rebel, who, like Ambrosio, Frankenstein, and his creation, also carried his hell within him.[57] In the context of the Gothic romances, the rebel who rejects the old order, asserts his leadership qualities and establishes a new regime, usually finishes as the leader of a band of outlaws preying on the society – the parent – that he has rejected.

Such a description seems to align the hero-villain with the Romantic hero who is often described as beyond either good and evil or a social norm.[58] However, no species of Gothic hero ever feels free to reject social norms, but tends rather to try to preserve the *appearance* of social decency. Manfred tries to justify his abandonment of Hippolyta and his pursuit of Isabella to Father Jerome and to the visiting knights; Ambrosio wants to continue enjoying the benefits of his position as Abbot. Even those hero types who overtly reject all social norms and be-

---

[56] The destructive possibilities inherent in the parent/child (particularly father/child) relationship were recognised and exploited by almost all the writers of Gothic fiction. See Chapter Six, 'The Absent Father.'

[57] Interestingly, the language used to describe the young hero before he is transformed into a hero-villain is often associated with light or brightness. He too is a fallen angel. The description of Ambrosio, for example, that I have already quoted speaks of his 'shining' qualities, of the way that he might have 'shone' as a soldier. Cf. Jung's claim that the sun is a symbol for the archetypal figure of the hero, which symbolizes the libido. Man rises to consciousness and sinks back into unconsciousness in the same way that the sun travels across the sky. See, C.G. Jung, 'The Origin of the Hero,' in John Beebe (ed.) & trans. R.F.C. Hull, *Aspects of the Masculine* (London: Ark Paperbacks, 1989), 3-4. The sun can dazzle; its light can blind the unwary. Moreover, it is alone in its passage across the sky and thus becomes a very apt metaphor for the life of the introspective, self-obsessed hero-villain.

[58] See, for example, Walter L. Reed, *Meditations on the Hero: a Study of the Romantic Hero in Nineteenth-Century Fiction* (Connecticut: Yale University Press, 1974), 5.

come bandits, placing themselves outside society, are really rejectees rather than rejectors. Leonardo de Loredani, (*Zofloya*), for example, who finally becomes a bandit chief, living outside the law in Alpine caves, has been forced to live in danger and in hiding outside the laws that he has broken rather than choosing to free himself of societal shackles, as might be expected of a Romantic hero.

After briefly comparing the representations of these three hero-villains, it is apparent that, although the characters are still described with the same heroic qualities any hero figure will automatically possess, they become selfish individualists. Their aims and feelings are privileged over their society and this, for an eighteenth or early nineteenth-century writer, will constitute their eventual, inevitable downfall. Marked by an aura of perverted nobility, these hero-villains have an enormous capacity for imagination and for passion, dominating the other characters like a human equivalent of the magnificent, ruined abbey or castle. By portraying the perversion of an heroic nature through a conscious desire for heroism, writers of Gothic fiction were able to question the nature of a type of heroism that they themselves had helped to establish.

In fine, the hero figure in the Gothic formula is delineated through the evocation of moral qualities that are the mainspring for his masculine activity. He is a passive, self-reflective hero, a fit mate for the heroine with whom he is destined to create the micro-society of a family. Throughout the period, the depiction of the hero never undergoes any chronological, linear development: Gothic writers began with an idealised figure already present in the cultural and social expectations of the reader. As more works were written, the reader's expectations about the character of the hero were reinforced through recurring devices and thematic motifs. Once the type figure was established, some writers could then manipulate the stereotype, upsetting the expectations of the reader and questioning some of the established assumptions about heroism and the figure of the hero.

5

The Absent Father

The potency of the father as a figure outweighs that of the hero: the father is both the hero's progenitor and his destiny. When looking for the father, however, one begins with an absence, for no book of rules exists to determine his role. If the Gothic Romance is essentially formula fiction in which stereotypical characters are manipulated, then the role of the father too might be expected to be a recognisable type answering the expectations of the reader. Although contemporary reader expectations can be determined by a study of the father figures that appear and disappear within the romances, there are few alternative literary sources in which a similar father figure appears and is explained.

Yet the figure of the 'good' father is as clearly defined as that of the hero. In fairytales, and frequently in myth, the adventures of the hero culminate in his coronation: the young man has undergone trials, through those trials he has become an adult, with adult knowledge he has won a bride and will be capable of ruling a kingdom. He has equipped himself for living 'happily ever after' as a king, as a husband, and probably as a father. At the conclusion of the fairytale the young hero has transformed himself into another, and usually stronger, version of the old king.

Similarly, the conclusion of a Gothic romance is always a family environment. Unlike the myth or the fairytale ending, however, the Gothic hero does not found a new society based on his ability to defeat supernatural entities and other powerful rivals, which would require the emergence of a new hero as soon as the old 'king' had lost his mental agility or the power of his sword arm. Instead, the Gothic hero retires to a private domestic realm, having proved himself capable of upholding, cherishing, and protecting the best moral values of his society. These moral values are, of course, those embodied in the heroine whose destiny – like that of the hero – is to be a parent.

As fatherhood is both the end to which the hero aspires and often the source of his own moral values, it is hardly surprising that writers sharing a clear vision of the hero seem also to share a common ideal of the father, although this ideal is undefined and generally unremarked. Twentieth-century expectations about the role of the father are satisfied by the father persona pervading the Gothic romance, suggesting that both eighteenth-century writer and twentieth-century reader share the same vision of the father as an authority figure, as a wise guide, counsellor and protector of the young.

The first question that must then be considered is why should one still accept the same ideas about the role of the father that were already current in the eighteenth century? Either we are imposing our own ideas or, perhaps, have inherited others. Thus, it is possible that the twentieth century has inherited and absorbed certain ideas about the role of the father that may have been created in the eighteenth century. Alternatively, our twentieth-century response may show influences from some exterior, historical source or common tradition prior to the eighteenth century of which both cultures have been inheritors. Finally, twentieth-century preconceptions may rest upon twentieth-century acceptance of a construct articulated through psychoanalysis explaining the role of the father as part of a symbolic order existing within the collective unconscious of the human psyche, a construct that is, perhaps, read back into and forced upon our view of history.

The most striking aspect about any portrayal of the father is that he is set in the context of an ideal casting him as a figure of authority and power. Psychoanalytic theory describes the role of the father as archetype and symbol, and Jung, the primary example, located the source of paternal power in the pre-existent archetype of the father.[1] A father is necessarily defined through his relationship to the child, and in this child/parent relationship the father is seen/judged from two directions. From outside the family, observers will judge the father by the child, and, from inside the family, the child sees the father as a gigantic figure of strength and authority to be feared and loved simultaneously. The mother too is a figure of gigantic stature, but Jung found a significant difference here in that the mother archetype is split by the child into two mothers, one good and one bad, whereas the father archetype combines its opposites into one image of paralysing power.

Before Jung, Freud too saw the father as a figure to be idolised, feared and ultimately killed or replaced. Using the Oedipus myth he postulated that children longed for a total relationship with their mothers, wanting to supplant the father and assume his role.[2] Freud also identified the 'Family Romance' in which every growing child creates a fantasy replacing the real parents with fictional 'other' parents who are superior to the everyday father and mother.[3] Both literary and psychoanalytic theories argue that the father is defined in relation to and by the child, i.e. he will always be a construct, and that the father is never seen simply as a personal father but is always given overtones of archetype or symbol. In any case, he is not 'real' but something 'other,' belonging to the imagination and the unconscious. In the 'Family Romance' he is banished completely and a vacuum created in the most basic fantasy, which we construct as children: 'he is a phan-

---

[1] C.G. Jung, 'The Significance of the Father in the Destiny of the Individual' (1909 rev. 1949), *Aspects of the Masculine*, trans. R.F.C. Hull (1984; repr. London: Ark Paperbacks, 1989), 69.

[2] The word 'children' is used deliberately, for Freud believed that the mother was the primary choice for girls as well as for boys, but that the complex dissolved very rapidly. For his discussion on the dissolution of the complex see 'Some Psychical Consequences of the Anatomical Distinction between the Sexes' (1925), trans. James Strachey 1959, *PFL*, vii. 323-344. Also 'The Dissolution of the Oedipus Complex' (1924), *Ibid* 345-58.

[3] Freud, 'Family Romances' (1909) *Ibid* 221-25. See also Marthe Robert, who connects Freud's family romance to a basic novel structure. *The Origins of the Novel* (1972), trans. Sacha Rabinovitch (Brighton: Harvester Press, 1980), 21.

tom, a corpse, who may be the object of a cult, but whose vacant place cries out nonetheless to be filled.'⁴ In the Gothic romance, which partakes of the genre of fantasy, the father is significantly absent on all levels. Consequently, some of our search for the father within the fictional Gothic world must be conducted apophatically.

If the father's role is based in part on a historical tradition existing prior to the eighteenth century of which we too are inheritors, then, perhaps, we shall find the paradigm in the concept of God as Father. Biblical representations of God as father reveal both a stern father/King ruling through fear, pain and death, and a loving, personal father who still requires a sacrifice. His power is always absolute. One is immediately reminded of the archetype: a figure of fear and vengeance as well as of paternal love.

This dual concept of God as Father is present in certain eighteenth-century religious thought and teaching, and extends as a model into the relationship between earthly father and child. Methodism, which emerged as a major religious movement in the eighteenth century, held, in common with other Reformation churches, a very personal relationship between man and God as one of its major tenets.⁵ Just as the ideal woman was established as the centre of a private, domestic environment, a similar movement can be seen in religious thought where moral communities were set up based on individual, personal experiences of God that marked the recipient as one of God's children. The relationship of God as Father with Man was considered to reflect that of a parent and child. 'The will of a parent is to a little child in the place of the will of God.'⁶ The relationship between

---

⁴ Robert, *Origins of the Novel*, 26.
⁵ For a discussion on the rise and beliefs of Methodism see, Rupert E. Davies, *Methodism* (1963; repr. London: Epworth Press, 1985). Although I have cited Wesley's writings as evidence of eighteenth-century conceptions of God as Father and of fatherhood, the majority of readers of Gothic fiction were unlikely to have been Methodists. Wesley's sermons on parents and children, however, are often more specifically related to everyday living and contain more practical advice than William Paley's platitudinous sermons, for example, and the sentiments quoted are present in more orthodox, widely known theological texts of the period.
⁶ John Wesley, 'On the Education of Children', *Sermons on Several Occasions*, 2 vols. (London: Caxton Press, c.1825), i. 375. Cf. William Paley, 'The Duty of Children Towards Their Parents':

God and Man and, by extension, the relationship between parent and child is based on power, authority and respect; the benign use of this power indicated the measure of God's love. In one of John Wesley's sermons, 'On Family Religion,' he gave a picture of a father educating his child in this very relationship:

"Think what he [God] can do! He can do whatever he pleases. He can strike me or you dead in a moment. But he loves you; he loves to do you good. He loves to make you happy. Should you not then love *him*?"[7]

The child has already been made aware of the power of God through the opening gambit, which emphasises God's power by drawing the child's attention to nature. Wesley suggested a simple, logical progression along the following lines, 'This is the sun. God made it. These are the trees. God made them also.' As well as giving a picture of the power and authority of God in relation to Man, Wesley is also indicating one of the primary functions of fatherhood – education and the father's responsibility for that education.[8]

Without Wesley's overt religious intentions and bias, William Cobbett provided the reader with another vision of ideal, early nineteenth-century fatherhood. He too sees fatherhood as a responsibility whence, 'the honourable title and the boundless power of *father*' can only be deserved by those who have faithfully performed all the requisite duties.[9] Here Cobbett has clearly marked the importance of the name of 'father,' implying that the title is powerful, existing like an

---

'Upon the whole, parents, in respect to their children, do bear the signal stamp and image of God himself, not only as he is their Maker, but as he is their Preserver and Benefactor.' *Sermons on Several Subjects*, 2 vols., 3rd. ed. (London: Hurst, Rees & Orme, 1808), i. 296.

[7] Wesley, 'On Family Religion,' *Sermons*, i. 366.

[8] Cf. Paley, who divided the duty of parents towards their children into three parts: 'First; the maintenance of children, and a reasonable provision for their happiness, in point of circumstances and situation in the world. Secondly; education. And thirdly; the proper care of their virtue." 'The Duty of Parents Towards Their Children,' *Sermons*, i. 269. Paley continually referred to 'parents' but the examples that he gave of bad parentage – failing to provide financially for the child because of self-indulgent drunkenness or slothfulness, or abandoning the child after ruining the mother – indicate that he was actually referring to fathers.

[9] William Cobbett, 'To A Father', *Advice to Young Men, and (incidentally) to Young Women, in the Middle and Higher Ranks of Life* (London: published by the author, 1829), para. 250.

intangible garment that may be assumed by the man who deserves it. Despite the power associated with the name, Cobbett took great pains to stress that the father must be *liked* (my emphasis) by his children: 'they must like *your* company better than any other person's; they must not wish you away, nor fear your coming back.'[10] They must, in other words, be led and not driven. The requisite duties of fatherhood, according to Cobbett, are the protection of health and sanity, the inculcation of principles and the actual presence of the father:

> It is in the power of *every father* to live *at home with his family*, when not *compelled* by business, or by public duty, to be absent: it is in his power to set an example of industry and sobriety and frugality, and to prevent a taste for gaming, dissipation, extravagance, from getting root in the minds of his children: it is in his power to make his children *hearers*, when he is reproving servants for idleness, or commending them for industry and care: it is in his power to keep all dissolute and idle companions from his house: it is in his power to teach them, by his uniform example, justice and mercy towards the inferior animals: it is in his power to do many other things, and something in the way of booklearning too, however busy his life may be.[11]

Cobbett clearly suggested here that the ideal father is the present (as opposed to absent) family leader, protector and guide because all the power associated with the role is directed towards active involvement with the day to day life and education of the child. Like Wesley, Cobbett suggested that the extent of a father's love can be measured by the beneficent exercise of his 'boundless power' towards the child. Also like Wesley, there is, in Cobbett's letter, the idea that the role and name of father, unlike that of the hero, exists prior to the man who fulfils it. The importance of the presence of the natural father is stressed, yet the power of his role already exists in the title.

All the observations made so far apply to the relationship between fathers and their children. There is a difference, however, in the relationship between fathers and sons, and that of fathers and daughters: daughters had a longer relationship with their fathers based on authority, and submission to that authority, which

---

[10] *Ibid* para. 293.
[11] *Ibid* para. 307.

was a consequence of the difference in their destined sphere. Where sons were educated and encouraged towards an 'active' sphere, first in society, and then as the head of a family, daughters were designed from the very beginning to fulfil a passive and supportive role. When a daughter left the protection of her father and family environment to be married and begin her own family, she moved directly from one type of masculine protection to another.

Wesley's comments on 'Family Religion' demonstrate the weight of responsibility borne by the head of the household. The father was not only responsible for the moral education and conduct of his wife, his children, his servants, and in some cases his visitors, he was also responsible to a higher father figure. The father exists on two levels: that of the actual (or present) father and the (absent) paradigm from which he gains his power.

Within the world of the Gothic romance the 'good' father figure is almost invariably physically absent, leaving only the paradigm in his place.[12] He exists only as a vacuum, unable to exercise his role of guidance, protection and counsel over his child, whose situation excites feelings of apprehension and sympathy in the reader. Nevertheless, the presence of the father may still be inferred from the way in which the young hero or heroine comports himself or herself in a hostile and unfamiliar environment. Only through education and example can the hero or heroine acquire the moral principles (overlaying their basic, untutored goodness) which enable them to survive the vicissitudes of society.

Often, the father is dead (or assumed to be dead) before the story begins, like the progenitors of Edmund (*The Old English Baron*, 1778), Ignatius (*The Haunted Castle*, 1794), and Huberto Avinzo (*Gondez the Monk*, 1805). Each of

---

[12] In her analysis of Victoria Holt's twentieth-century Gothic romances, Barbara Bowman also draws attention to the absence of the father, indicating that this absence is an integral part of the formula. She suggests two images for the ideal father – the absent, indulgent provider or the present but emotionally distant and uncaring parent. 'Victoria Holt's Gothic Romances: A Structuralist Enquiry,' in Fleenor (ed.), *The Female Gothic*, 71.

these heroes is removed from the family environment whilst a baby and has no actual contact with his biological father. The writers then orphan their hapless heroes twice over: first as babies, and then by removing them from the protection of the surrogate 'good' father figures who have educated them. Huberto Avinzo is orphaned three times: brought to Scotland as a baby by Alzarro, an Italian who is not his father and who is recalled to Italy, he is confided to the care of Sir Alan Macdonald, a Scots noble loyal to Robert Bruce. Finally he is deprived of the paternal care of Sir Alan when he falls in battle, and the maternal care of Lady Macdonald when she dies in captivity in the Tower of London. Thus, by the age of sixteen, Huberto Avinzo has been thoroughly deprived of protection and support. This is one of the most extreme cases of deprivation of fatherly care as a plot device. Neither Ignatius nor Edmund is forced from the surrogate father at such a young age. Ignatius, befriended and adopted by a worthy knight, Du Pin, leaves his adoptive father to pursue his vocation as a soldier: Edmund is forced to leave the castle of his protector Lord Lovell, but this is after he too has distinguished himself as a soldier.

In using a device to separate the hero from the father, and then from the surrogate father (or series of fathers), the author not only focuses the reader's sympathy and attention on the hero's personal development but also creates a vacuum that the hero is compelled to fill. He has to redefine himself in another type of male relationship stronger than friendship – usually one of loyalty. Huberto pledges allegiance to the Bruce, creating a male bond of loyalty between subject and king in the place of a bond between father and son. Ignatius and Edmund become knights bound by a chivalric code that is another type of male allegiance, and Edmund accepts Sir Philip Harclay as yet another surrogate father within this knightly code. All heroes also fill this vacuum with a loving relationship with the heroine, in which they are beginning to establish themselves as father.

Even if the natural father is a 'good' father who is present within the text, he is quickly rendered impotent by the author. There are some tales in which the relationship between impotent 'good' father and hero son is used as a major plot device, but it is more common to find a helpless heroine whom the reader has already seen in a relationship with a 'good' but now powerless father. These fathers are usually living a secluded life surrounded by natural beauty. Having once been heroes, tasted the fruits of society and found them insubstantial, they have retired to a private realm, often associated with their childhood, in which their opinions and morals are the guiding force for their children and their dependants. The relationship between Emily St. Aubert and her father (*The Mysteries of Udolpho*, 1794) is a classic, indeed influential, example of this type. A family pastoral idyll is created and then destroyed in the opening chapter. St. Aubert is presented as an eighteenth-century man of sensibility profoundly moved by the beauties of the natural world (significantly, he is an accomplished botanist). He refuses to consider cutting down certain old trees, revealing both his fondness for the landscape of his childhood and a sense of history and tradition lacking in ultra-fashionable characters like Madame Cheron and Monsieur Quesnel. The first step in the orphaning of the heroine is taken in this first chapter with the death of Madame St. Aubert, throwing the reactions and relationship of St. Aubert and his daughter into relief. The lesson that St. Aubert teaches is one of restraint: undisciplined emotion is destructive and harmful. Discipline, however, does not deny the reality of love or depth of feeling. Mrs. Radcliffe shows the reader that St. Aubert had already learned this lesson when facing the deaths of his two sons in infancy some years before the death of his wife:

in consideration of Madame St. Aubert's distress, he restrained the expression of his own, and endeavoured to bear it, as he meant, with philosophy, he had, in truth, no philosophy that could render him calm to such losses.[13]

St. Aubert restrains his own emotions and as a corrective, protective father restrains those of his daughter:

> He endeavoured, therefore, to strengthen her mind; to enure her to habits of self-command; to teach her to reject the first impulse of her feelings, and to look, with cool examination, upon the disappointments he sometimes threw in her way. While he instructed her to resist first impressions, and to acquire that steady dignity of mind, that can alone counterbalance the passions, and bear us, as far as is compatible with our nature, above the reach of circumstances, he taught himself a lesson of fortitude; for he was often obliged to witness, with seeming indifference, the tears and struggles which his caution occasioned her.[14]

The child teaches the parent about restraint at the same time that the parent is educating the child. As well as teaching internal strength by encouraging the restraint of the passions, St. Aubert teaches self-reliance by encouraging independent, internal amusement: he is the source from which Emily derives her interests in poetry, reading, music and the contemplation of nature so beloved of all Gothic heroines. Thus far St. Aubert is represented as a perfect father, who concentrates on the formation of interior beauty of mind and heart in his child. Having created the perfect father, Ann Radcliffe then stripped him by degrees of the power to continue protecting his daughter; his power is first weakened by ill health, then undermined by financial ruin and finally removed with his death. Absent by chapter eight of the first book, he is a decaying figure who nevertheless remains present as a paradigm against which the actions of the worldly Madame Charon and Montoni appear even more callous.

This pattern of the good father who is set up as a paradigm and then made absent within the tale quickly became an essential part of the Gothic formula.

---

[13] *Ibid* 5.
[14] *Ibid* 5.

Four years after the publication of *The Mysteries of Udolpho*, Regina Roche's novel *Clermont* (1798), used similar techniques in order to establish Clermont as a 'good' father at the beginning of the tale.[15] Like St. Aubert, he is a father of mysterious origins living in rural simplicity with his beautiful daughter, Madeleine. He too educates his child and shares St. Aubert's appreciation and investigation of the natural world: he is a farmer and a skilled herbalist, able to minister to the young stranger wounded on the hillside. Unlike the plot of *The Mysteries of Udolpho*, which is centred on the fate and character of an orphaned heroine abandoned to the care or careless protection of relative strangers, the plot of *Clermont* revolves around the father as much as the heroine. Clermont is certainly absent from the story when his daughter requires paternal protection – having allowed an old friend, the Countess de Merville, to take Madeleine away from the valley and into her household. Removed from her father, the formula requires that Madeleine should also be removed from the care of her surrogate mother, who satisfies the formula by being stabbed by an assassin. Havens are continually being offered in this way to Gothic heroines and then abruptly removed; there is no real security outside the true family environment. Clermont's absence and seclusion in the valley, however, is caused by the unresolved relationship between himself and his own 'absent' father, and it is the working out of this relationship that ends in revelation, repentance and restoration of the original family structure.

The relationship between Clermont and Madeleine, like that between St. Aubert and Emily, is represented as one of love and respect. The bond between father and daughter, used in *The Mysteries of Udolpho* to correct Emily's oversensitive nature, is used again in *Clermont* to restrain self-indulgent emotion. This relationship is tested when a suitor for Madeleine appears in the valley and Cler-

---

[15] For an analysis of Maria Roche's literary indebtedness to Ann Radcliffe, together with a comparison and evaluation of *The Mysteries of Udolpho* and *Clermont*, see Natalie Schroeder, '*The Mys-*

mont cannot honourably encourage their mutual attraction. He combats Madeleine's romantic sorrow after the young man's departure by manipulating her filial love for him and her consciousness of the extent of his paternal love for her: 'he also frequently hinted, that she should be particularly watchful of her peace, as his entirely depended on it.'[16] Clermont protects his daughter by asking that she protect him. Later in the plot Madeleine again feels the need to protect her father at the expense of her own feelings and agrees to marry the repulsive Monsieur d'Alembert in order to prevent Clermont being declared a fratricide. Clermont is rendered impotent within the world of the text by the repercussions of the relationship with his own father and the guilty weight of the crime, which he thought he had committed. Having been the victim of an 'absent' father who deserted his mother and then denied a name to the child, Clermont tried to replace the vacuum of the father/son relationship with a fraternal bond. When this too seemed to have been betrayed by his brother and then destroyed by himself, he retired from the world with his baby daughter. Even when first introduced at the beginning of the tale, he was frequently absent, roaming the mountainside when fits of melancholy overtook him. Consciousness of guilt and an ambiguous social position enforce Clermont's absence and make him unable to protect his child.

Similarly, in *The Mysterious Visit* (1802) a 'good' adoptive father without a powerful social position is forced into absence while his daughter is at the mercy of an unscrupulous, socially powerful villain. Dr. Clifford, like Clermont, lives to be finally reunited to his daughter, forming part of a larger family unit. For the greater part of the tale, however, he is absent, supposed dead but actually imprisoned in the Bastille. His absence creates a vacuum around the heroine who, having been orphaned twice, is vulnerable to the approaches of a man who seems to be treating her kindly and acting the part of a father.

---

teries of Udolpho and *Clermont*: The Radcliffean encroachment on the art of Regina Maria Roche,' *Studies in the Novel* xii (1980), 131-43.

[16] *Ibid* i. 63.

Lack of money and enforced dependence on the bounty of others is clearly another device by which the 'good' father is undermined and forced into absence. Whereas Clermont, although suffering from guilt, was able to retire to the countryside and support himself and his daughter in independence, Fitzalan, in *The Children of the Abbey* (1796), also by Mrs. Roche, depended on patronage to support both his family and his fatherhood. Fitzalan's lack of status means that he is unable to protect his daughter from the advances of Colonel Belgrave within the family home, and thus is forced into absence, as his only method of protection is to send her away alone into Wales. Fitzalan's dependence is caused by another lack of fatherhood within the text: he had married the neglected elder daughter of an Earl without her father's consent. The 'good' father of the heroine in this text is only described through retrospective views and memories as the story begins with Amanda's lone arrival in Wales and follows her unprotected struggles for happiness. Father and daughter are eventually reunited in Ireland, but only briefly, and it is the daughter who offers consolation to her father as he dies, poor, neglected and unjustly accused:

> Ill, weak, and dispirited, she had flattered herself, on returning to her father, she should receive relief, support and consolation; instead of which, heartbroken as she was, she now found she must give, or at least attempt giving them, herself.[17]

Fitzalan is absent throughout the romance, although he does not die until the end of the second volume. Nevertheless, he is present in the fatherly paradigm which promises 'relief, support and consolation' to his daughter.

This serves to show the paradoxical nature of the representation of the father figure; although these 'good' fathers in the Gothic romance are absent for most of the action, there is still a fatherly presence operating throughout. Even when dead, fathers are present: either in the behaviour and moral character of

---

[17] Roche, *Children of the Abbey*, ii. 317.

their offspring, or as a memory forever attaching the affections of the child to one particular location, or, most obviously, as a ghost. Paternal love and power do not end in the grave, and a ghostly appearance always signals guilt, murder and the imminent discovery of the secret of the hero's birth. The father appears as a ghost to acknowledge his son, and then, having forced the son to recognise him, the father's ghost mutely demands filial respect, justice and, usually, Christian burial. Blood calls to blood. A meeting with a ghost is often the only contact that a hero has with either of his natural parents, and is frequently the prelude to an emotional disturbance equivalent to the social advancement gained through true knowledge of his birth. What Freud described as the 'Family Romance' – a child's fantasy of an absent, aristocratic father – is literally true in the Gothic romance. Alienation, the sense of being unloved, which helps to produce this childish fantasy is also reflected as reality in the Gothic romance through the child's orphaned state and through the emotional distress that the hero experiences on discovering his true parentage.

The experiences of Ignatius (*The Haunted Castle*, 1794) demonstrate both actual and emotional alienation. The groaning spirit of a man in bloody clothes and chains leads him towards the picture of a beautiful woman. Ignatius encounters his parents, therefore, only as reflections of reality, as a portrait and a spectre. Thus, although the 'Family Romance' is realised and Ignatius' social status is raised, there is no comfort in the contact with his spectral parents. Instead the meeting causes Ignatius great emotional distress and forces him to distance himself from everything he loves – not because he now realises that his parents were murdered but because he instantly assumes that Adelais, whom he loves and believes to be Manfredi's daughter, is his sister. His birth is confirmed only to doom his romantic love.

Edmund (*The Old English Baron*, 1778) is similarly identified as the rightful heir by supernatural means. Groans from beneath the floorboards and a cupboard that only Edmund can open, which contains a bloodstained suit of armour, are the sequel to a dream in which his parents approach him. Like Ignatius, the discovery of his parentage has an immediate effect on his romantic hopes. Although Edmund has now been raised to equal status with the Lady Emma, he has to claim his lands and his castle from her father in order to assume his birthright. He is, in one sense, usurping the place of his own father in that Lord Fitz-Owen had stood in the place of surrogate father and benevolent overlord to him. He is also, like Ignatius, going to marry his foster-sister.[18]

In *The Three Spaniards* (1800), a tale concentrating on the way in which the bonds of kinship between the major characters are unravelled by supernatural means and re-tied through marriage, Fernando, one of the three Spaniards of the title, is visited at key moments by a spectral wounded soldier – who is not *his* father, but the ghost of his father-in-law. Lacking a son to reveal the whereabouts of his imprisoned wife and enslaved daughter as well as the treachery of Don Padilla to the world, the spectre pursues the young Fernando, upsetting his romantic hopes. Fernando is actually married to Selima but unable to sleep with her, because the ghost sits on the bed every night and prevents him from doing so. Before enjoying the daughter, he has to placate the father, and this fulfilment of responsibilities towards the absent but still powerful father figure is the same basic requirement facing other Gothic heroes.

Just as the appearance of a ghost is the present manifestation of an otherwise absent father that helps to create a sensation of potent, active paternity for the reader, the paradigm of the father is also revealed through the action of Providence, or divine justice. The epitaph on Nicolo's tomb in *Gondez the Monk* (1805) connects Providence with divine justice, and explicitly states its twin aims of vindicating the innocent and punishing the guilty:

---

[18] Neither his bride, nor that of Ignatius are actually the heroes' sisters, nor have ever been called so, yet Adelais has been brought up with the title of Manfredi's daughter, and Lady Emma

Death cannot chill the ardour of the just;
The soul must live although the frame be dust.
In Mercy's cause, no ills appall [sic] the good,
For God, retributive, yields blood for blood.[19]

The workings of a vengeful Providence are similarly evident in *The Castle of Otranto* (1764) where not only do gigantic supernatural manifestations literally and figuratively crush Manfred's dynastic ambitions, but Manfred himself is brought to end his family when he mistakenly kills his daughter Matilda. The significant dream is also a plot device revealing the inevitable workings of Providence. Frederic's dream leads him to the wood where he has a meeting with a mysterious hermit – a spiritual father and therefore directly connected with the workings of God and of Providence – that causes his return to Otranto. The dreams and the ghostly appearances tend to show the presence of an absent but nonetheless vigilant father.

The absent 'good' father is often re-established at the conclusion of the Gothic romance. He is made present once more when his child is made aware of his or her paternity and assumes the family name. This device is used as the conclusion for most of the tales that involve the direct working of Providence through supernatural manifestations, like *The Castle of Otranto* (1764), *The Old English Baron* (1778), *The Haunted Castle* (1794), *The Three Spaniards* (1800) and *Gondez the Monk* (1805). There are, of course, variations on this device. Although *The Children of the Abbey* concludes with Oscar assuming his grandfather's title and wealth, he was always aware of his relationship to the dead Earl of Dunreath, and the action of Providence in this story is not worked through ghosts and groans, but through coincidental meetings. Historical romances, like *Longsword* (1762) and *The Recess* (1785), also have the resumption of title and birthright as a central theme. Earl William has to reassert his rights to his castle, his title and his

---

is the sister of Edmund's best friend and the daughter of a man who has adopted a paternal attitude towards him.
[19] Ireland, *Gondez the Monk*, iv. 140.

wife in *Longsword*, and the twin daughters of Mary Queen of Scots are hidden, unacknowledged and then persecuted to prevent them asserting their lineage.

There is a great deal in a name. The name of the family carries its own power, standing for wealth, estates, legal rights and a clearly defined position within a social hierarchy. The father, as head of the household, embodies the family name. Here too, the father is both an actual parent and a symbolic inheritor of previous generations of fathers. Name, family and by extension the father figure acquire a totemic force. An existent family name signifies more than kinship: absence is made present once more. Thus the father provides an identity as well as a role model for a child. Without recognisable parentage, a child has neither status nor identity. An absent father forces a hero to define himself in other male relationships and this marks the first step in the construction of an identity within a male-dominated world.

In *Frankenstein* (1818) Mary Shelley took the basic formula of the absent father with the hero's consequent search for identity and used it in an extreme fashion that locates *Frankenstein* on the edge of the Gothic tradition. Mary Shelley removed the reader's trust in the power of the paradigm. There is no beneficent action of Providence in the plot, apart from the coincidental meeting of like minds enabling the narrators to relate their stories, nor do the 'good' father figures within the text exert any positive influence. In this tale the innocent are not protected but systematically sacrificed and the crime committed is that of creation *by* the father rather than the murder *of* the father.[20] Although the impetus of the plot is provided by Frankenstein's act of creation and the monster's subsequent search for identity, it is as much a tale of an absent son as of an absent father. The mon-

---

[20] Although one might argue that Walpole also sacrificed the innocent Conrad and Matilda in *The Castle of Otranto*, those deaths could eventually be interpreted by the reader as part of a divine retributive plan resulting in the reinstatement of Alfonso's bloodline. There is no equivalent sense of divine agency at work in *Frankenstein*. Rather the plot is full of malign coincidences, placing victims in front of the vengeful monster.

ster is never given any status except that of creature or creation: he is not identified as 'son,' nor given a name. A name would fix the monster within a social relationship to someone else who would have called him by that name. Without a name the monster is an outcast and an outlaw; unrecognised, unnamed by society, he is not bound by its laws and its codes.

The power of the paradigm, the all-powerful and eternally absent father, is also diminished because Mary Shelley has shown it in a perverse form within the text in the figure of Frankenstein. When Frankenstein determines form and creates life from inanimate matter, he redefines and transcends the role of the earthly father:

> A new species would bless me as its creator and source; many happy and excellent natures would owe their being to me. No father could claim the gratitude of his child so completely as I should deserve theirs.[21]

Frankenstein's ideals express his conception of his role: creator and creation as creditor and debtor. The single act of creation is seen as sufficient in itself, deserving of gratitude. Although Mary Shelley presented the reader with a 'good' father figure in the elder M. Frankenstein, he is rendered absent and impotent, existing only as an element in Victor's retrospective account of his happy childhood. By failing to communicate with his father whilst engaging in his experiments, Frankenstein himself forces his father into absence and renders the paternal paradigm impotent. Nevertheless, the paternal paradigm is eventually reasserted and strengthened through the monster's quest for identity, which begins when he observes a 'good' father. For, during the course of the creature's narrative, Frankenstein is forced to recognise that the role of creator does not end with creation, but has duties and responsibilities like that of the father.

Thus, it is through the narrative of the monster that Mary Shelley reinstalled the paradigm of the father. It is the monster who recognises and values the fatherhood that he is denied. Continually outcast, he learns the lessons of language and social relationships through a crack in the wall of a cottage. He spies on family relations learning the significance of names: 'The youth and his companion had each of them several names, but the old man had only one, which was *father*.'[22] Once language has been learned, once names have been recognised as significant of role, family and social status: 'the strange system of human society was explained to me. I heard of the division of property, of immense wealth and squalid poverty; of rank, descent and noble blood,' the monster is inevitably forced to question, and then to attempt to construct, his own identity.[23] He does this in absence; first by invisibly acting as a son/provider to the family when he leaves them bundles of wood and then by terming them his 'protectors,' thus establishing a fictional relationship. This identity must be created in absence because there is no possibility of response or recognition – another type of 'Family Romance.' His attempt to realise the relationship and acquire a surrogate father is the next stage in establishing his identity. Rejected by the real son of the surrogate father that he had chosen, the monster is forced to realise that his identity depends on his 'real' parent also acknowledging the paradigm and accepting his responsibilities:

> But I will not be tempted to set myself in opposition to thee. I am thy creature, and I will be even mild and docile to my natural lord and king, if thou wilt also perform thy part, the which thou owest me.[24]

The monster's plea is couched in the terms of a close personal relationship. 'I' and 'thou' delineate the monster's sense of that relationship, using the intimate language of parent and child to express filial obedience and love. Like the fictional relationship between the monster and the De Lacey family, it is a one-sided construction of identity to which Frankenstein does not respond. By the close of their conversation, however, Frankenstein realises 'what the duties of a creator

---

[21] Shelley, *Frankenstein*, 49.
[22] *Ibid* 107-8.
[23] *Ibid* 115.
[24] *Ibid* 95.

towards his creature were, and that I ought to render him happy before I complained of his wickedness.'[25] The paradigm of the father reappears.

In creating Frankenstein as a present father within the text, who is shown to be abdicating from his responsibilities and perverting his role, Mary Shelley was following an established pattern. Fathers, or those assuming the role of father, whom the author allows to remain present and potent within the Gothic romance are figures of negative power. They are everything that the 'good' father is not and the paradigm of the father is made present in absent values. Heroines are particularly vulnerable to present father figures who direct the power and authority inherent in the title of 'father' inwards to enhance their own role, rather than outwards to care for the person under their protection. The defenceless heroine without natural father or legal status is seen in objective terms by the selfish present father, who easily acquires the status of guardian and protector simply by claiming that name. Just as the vacuum created by the absence of the father impels the hero forwards into new male relationships, the same situation makes the heroine even more vulnerable as, unable to assume an active role in seeking, finding and choosing the father, she is compelled to accept proffered male protection. Also, as the heroine is not educated to be independent of male protection, she would naturally expect the role of the father to be assumed by someone else – perhaps by another member of her family. In either case the heroine bereft of her father offers an easy target for an unscrupulous man.[26]

She becomes an object. The power and authority exerted by the present father/guardian is power stripped of care, concerned only with manipulating the object. The heroine is frequently considered only as a marriageable pawn, representing the acquisition of wealth or allegiance. Montoni, in *The Mysteries of Udolpho*, is only an uncle-by-marriage, yet while his party is still in Venice and

---

[25] *Ibid* 97.
[26] Cf. Bowman: 'The indulgent father, in dying, thrusts upon the heroine an unappeasable thirst for some new dependence on a protector.' 'Victoria Holt's Gothic Romances,' 72.

Emily's aunt is still alive, he has the power to attempt to coerce her into marriage with Count Morano:

> She afterwards enquired by what right he exerted this unlimited authority over her? ... .
> 'By what right!' cried Montoni, with a malicious smile, 'by the right of my will; if you can elude that, I will not enquire by what right you do so.'[27]

Ann Radcliffe intensified the reader's sympathies and anxieties about the plight of her heroine by showing us Emily's awareness of her helplessness, that 'neither Morano's solicitations, nor Montoni's commands had lawful power to enforce her obedience' yet she cannot actively fight against them, nor physically fly from them.[28] Montoni, accustomed to rule, having the power of life and death within his own domain, transfers this type of power into the relationship between himself and Emily, wrongly associating physical dominance with mental dominance, strength of arm with strength of will. Later, when Emily is completely at his mercy in the castle, Montoni again manipulates the power of the father figure by extending and removing (or threatening to remove) his protection from Emily. He continues to see Emily only as a symbol of possible material gain, therefore he transmutes a relationship that ought to be based on authority and respect into one of power and subjection. The representation of Montoni reinforces the paradigm of the 'good' father at the same time that it is perverted into that of the tyrannical guardian.

The present guardian may be characterised by selfishness: the absent father by selflessness. In absenting the self of the 'good' father from the text and from the scene of the action, the writer removes him from a physical to a spiritual sphere in which his concerns are those of non-material, generalised concepts like justice, vengeance, innocence and guilt. The concerns of the present guardian are focused in the material present. Montoni, for example, desires power that is

---

[27] Radcliffe, *Mysteries*, 216-17.

measured by wealth (Emily's Languedoc estates) and by the number of men he is able to dominate and lead. Although he perceives Emily as an object of desire, he is attracted by the material power he can acquire by manipulating her to his best advantage. Unlike other present guardians of helpless heroines in the Gothic romance, Montoni only wants Emily's possessions – she is not a sexual object for him. Despite Montoni's lack of interest, the desire to change the role of the father into that of lover or husband is another, key part of the Gothic formula. Walpole began it in *The Castle of Otranto* when he represented Manfred, a surrogate father to Isabella at the beginning of the tale, wanting to discard his wife in order to marry his ward. Walpole never overtly suggested that Manfred was either in love or sexually attracted to Isabella. She represents the potential success of his dynastic ambitions: a union between the house of Alfonso and his own, and sons to continue his family and confound the curse. Nevertheless, although Walpole gave Manfred very specific, non-sexual motives for wanting to espouse Isabella, he is attempting to change his role: 'You, my lord! You! My father in law! the father of Conrad! the husband of the virtuous and tender Hippolita!'[29] The repetition of the name of the father has the force of an invocation as each of Isabella's apostrophes is addressed to the paradigm of the father and husband, trying to reunite the character of Manfred with that paradigm. Isabella's fragmented language further indicates the shattering of stable relationships. Manfred makes himself into an absent father by attempting to change his role into that of husband. His role as father to Isabella is only present briefly in her language. A vacuum has been created in their relationship that impels Isabella, like Gothic heroes, into flight.

The threat of sexual attention from a father figure is a device commonly used by 'Gothic' authors to propel a heroine into legitimate, active flight and to intensify the anxiety of the reader. Eliza Parsons' *Castle of Wolfenbach* and *The Mysterious Visit* both feature a young and extremely innocent heroine, who is the

---

[28] *Ibid* 209.
[29] Walpole, *Castle of Otranto*, 23.

object of her guardian's sexual desire. Mr Weimar's designs on his supposed niece in *Castle of Wolfenbach* are revealed retrospectively as Matilda has already fled from his house before the plot begins. The reader is party neither to the development of his passion nor to the trusting relationship that previously existed between Matilda and himself. The threat to her chastity is simply a device to account for her unprotected state, her voluntary and justifiable flight and to introduce anxiety through the threat of pursuit. When Eliza Parsons used this device again in *The Mysterious Visit* the focus was changed to highlight further the perversion of the father role through the character of the villainous Sir William Symons, who, although outwardly adopting the role of present guardian or protector, desires to possess and corrupt Georgina's innocence:

> The possession of her person alone would not satisfy the passion he felt, without obtaining her heart; and to this purpose, to inspire her with an equal tenderness, he had controuled [sic] his impetuous desires, and employed every seductive art to soften her heart, and obtain a triumph over a pure and uncorrupted mind.[30]

Sir William, like M. Weimar and Manfred, is also represented as trying to move the heroine from one role to another. If the heroine possessed a power of passive sexual attraction which these guardian/father surrogates were unable to resist, they would, in submitting to sexual desire, be unwittingly granting or acknowledging some form of female power. The heroine, however, does not draw these surrogate fathers from one role to another. Instead, the vacuum of the absent father impels her to trust and then fly from the present father/guardian/wicked uncle, who never fulfils the role of the father even though he usurps the power of the archetype.

While there is a sharp perceptible division between the present guardian and the absent father of the heroine, present fathers of heroes in the Gothic ro-

---

[30] Parsons, *Mysterious Visit*, ii. 219-20.

mance are less easy to quantify and are used differently within the formula. As the present, natural father of a hero they must represent the father paradigm. The formula, however, requires that the son be impelled away from the father and initiated into society without paternal protection or guidance. These present 'good' fathers of heroes cannot, therefore, completely sustain their role: the formula dictates a flaw in their representation. Conscious of his position in society, the present father of the hero is usually depicted as too conscious of social pressure and this constitutes a flaw in the role, making an otherwise 'good' and responsible father indifferent to the ultimate happiness of his hero son. A similar situation may occur when a present natural father of a heroine tries to force her into an unwanted marriage because it will reflect social glory on the family (*The Mysterious Freebooter*, 1806) or prevents a heroine from marrying the man she loves (*Gondez the Monk*). The objective situation for hero and heroine are similar, yet there is a difference in the presentation of the father figure. The fathers in *The Mysterious Freebooter* and in *Gondez the Monk* are also lords of castles engaged in creating and maintaining their society in an active, violent manner.[31] Present fathers of heroes are not involved in such outward, active movement because their society is already in existence and upheld by law. Their failure or their impotence in one area of fatherhood reinforces the father paradigm. Readers and hero sons are simultaneously disappointed when their expectations about the role of the 'good' father are not consistently fulfilled by these figures. The subversion of a figure initially presented as a 'good' father – particularly when the values of such a figure are shown to conflict with those of the heroine or hero – raises questions about the necessity and extent of filial obedience. The reader's sympathies are more fully engaged because the hero is caught between his filial obligations and what both reader and hero know to be the correct, heroic choice. What these subversions of the 'good' father further reveal is that an absent father is vital to the

---

[31] As Lord William, Baron de Mowbray, in the opening pages of *The Mysterious Freebooter* is literally creating his own society, overseeing the building and fortifying of his castle.

Gothic formula. A 'good' father can only remain truly 'good' in absence, hallowed in memory as a compound of abstract virtues, because once he is a presence in the tale, he exerts more authority than the hero/heroine. Consequently, he must either be shown to be ineffectual against the power of the villain, or display some flaw in his character – otherwise there would be no conflict and no story.

Lord Cherbury (*The Children of the Abbey*) is a case in point. From the outset he is presented to the reader as a benevolent and fatherly presence. He is first introduced as an absent patron of Fitzalan, the good and absent father of Amanda and Oscar. Thus as the protector of the 'good' father, Lord Cherbury reinforces the father paradigm, buttressing Fitzalan's fatherhood, and the reader expects he will maintain this role. Only one early authorial reference hints at any flaw in Cherbury's character: 'he yet retained and was willing to obey, the dictates of humanity, particularly when they did not interfere with his own interests.'[32] Cherbury's opposition to the marriage and Lord Mortimer's reaction to it call the power and the limits of the relationship between father and son into question:

> "In chusing [sic] you as the partner of my future days, I do not infringe the moral obligation which exists between father and son; for as, on the one hand, it does not require weak indulgence; so, on the other, it does not demand implicit obedience, if reason and happiness must be sacrificed by it."[33]

The authority of the father is represented here as an exercise of reasoned strength and, if necessary, correction. Strength, however, Mortimer implies, exists on both sides of the relationship. Herein lies the difference between the relationships of present fathers and heroines, and present fathers and heroes: the relationship between father and hero-son changes as the son matures, becoming a relationship between adult males of equal strength and reasoning capacity, in which the

---

[32] Roche, *Children of the Abbey*, i. 51.
[33] *Ibid* ii. 175.

younger defers to the elder through respect. The relationship between daughter and father does not change in this way. Amanda promises her dying father never to see Lord Mortimer again, simply to protect his honour from the suggestion that he deliberately encouraged their relationship. However much the hero may be permitted to evade it, sacrifice is a keyword in the relationships of heroines. In fact Cherbury's relationship with his son has undergone a role reversal of which his son is unaware. Amanda, who consistently protects the fatherly paradigm in *The Children of the Abbey*, has acceded to Cherbury's wishes in order to preserve the father/son relationship. Cherbury reveals, in a letter, that he has embezzled his ward's money and can only retrieve the situation if Lord Mortimer marries Amanda's cousin, Lady Euphrasia:

> Great as was the injury he would sustain by mortgaging it [the family estate], I was confident he never would hesitate doing so if acquainted with my distress; but to let him know it was worse than a death of torture could be to me, his early excellence, the nobleness of his principles, mingled in the love I felt for him a degree of awe.[34]

Reader expectations about the present 'good' father role are upset again. Lord Cherbury asks Amanda to sacrifice her hopes of happiness so that he may preserve his image as father in his relationship with his son. In this text, the paradigm of the father is both potent and vulnerable. It is threatened by the perfection of the son and protected by the dutiful obedience of the heroine. Lord Cherbury is represented as a father who is conscious of the paradigm but who fails to sustain the role. Rather than admit his failure, suffering embarrassment, a loss of social reputation and a sense of diminishment in his role, he would condemn his son to potential lifelong, domestic unhappiness. As in other Gothic romances, the father's hidden guilt would be visited on his child.

The point at which the interests of the hero conflict with those of the otherwise present 'good' father is always that of the hero's intended marriage. The impulse towards marriage marks an independent choice indicating the hero's de-

---

[34] *Ibid* iii. 137.

sire to establish himself in the father's role. The motive for the father's opposition, his determination to exercise his judgement in preference to that of his son, is not always as dramatic as the one that haunts Lord Cherbury. Mr Somerive (*The Old Manor House*, 1783) is a 'good' present father whom Charlotte Smith portrayed as rendering himself absent. Through his dealings with his sons, Charlotte Smith demonstrated that, although a paternal paradigm exists, the actual father has only as much power as his sons are willing to accord him: 'his father, when he was present, and had resolution to be peremptory, still retained some power over him.'[35] Both of Mr Somerive's sons disobey their father. Philip, described above, only responds to his father's presence and authority when it is exerted. Orlando, the younger son and hero, has more respect for his father's paternal role, yet he too ignores his father's wishes when he pursues his relationship with Monimia. Mr. Somerive is portrayed as a man of taste and good breeding, a discerning man. Yet his concern for social propriety and his desire not to give offence cause him to register his disapproval through absence. He leaves when insulted at Mr. Stockton's dinner party and propitiates Mrs. Rayland by keeping out of her way. In this text, Charlotte Smith intensifies the need for the hero to assert himself in an active manner by creating a present father figure who voluntarily absents himself, whose social position and wealth are undermined by his son, whose health is consequently impaired, and who finally dies. This is a similar, although more protracted, use of the absent 'good' father device apparent in other Gothic romances. Whereas, in other Gothic romances, the absent 'good' father is rendered impotent very rapidly in the course of the story, forcing the hero into society, Charlotte Smith's portrayal of the father/son relationship shows that as the father declines in his role, the son gains in power. At the close of the tale, Orlando Somerive has replaced his father as the head of the family.

---

[35] Smith, *Old Manor House*, 209.

Spiritual fathers within the Gothic romance also represent (and are seen as re-presenting) the absent father paradigm. Writers of Gothic fiction make a sharp division between spiritual fathers living alone and those living in community. The spiritual father is incorporated into the formula of the Gothic romance, which requires good figures to prefer a more solitary communion with nature – like the good and present natural fathers within the tales. Thus, hermits (like those in *The Castle of Otranto* and *The Haunted Castle*) are instruments of Providence: direct reflections of divine will, they aid and direct the hero or the heroine during their journey. Other lone spiritual fathers who live within society without dwelling within the confines of a religious order are also benevolent figures. These spiritual fathers, representing God as Father, are dignified with that title, like Father Jerome (*The Castle of Otranto*), Father Anthony (*The Recess*), and Father Oswald (*The Old English Baron*) but are not associated with a particular religious order. The title of 'Father' is not given to spiritual fathers, particularly those in positions of authority, who are living in a religious community. These are almost invariably malevolent figures constructed around an absence. The 'good' spiritual father is transfused with the invisible power of God: the 'bad' spiritual father has a vacuum instead of faith at the core of his being.

In this part of the formula, one sees a manifestation of the eighteenth-century distrust of the social power wielded by Catholicism, which writers of Gothic fiction typically depicted as based on superstition rather than rational thought. Both Agnes (*The Monk*, 1796) and Monçada (*Melmoth the Wanderer*, 1820) are sacrificed as the result of a superstitious oath. The power of Catholicism, translated as superstition, was a tool in the hands of the Gothic writer who used it as a device separating the hero or the heroine from society. It also intensified the anxiety present within the tale, for the closed world of the monastery or the convent in a Catholic country is not subservient to the laws of society, but, as Marilyn Butler suggests, joins with the State to oppress the individual.[36]

'Good', present, spiritual fathers are as impotent in the romance world as the 'good' father who is forced into absence because neither can wield sufficient social power to protect the young hero or heroine. The power of the absent 'good' father is the power of the paradigm and is not exerted in a material manner; the power of the present, 'good' spiritual father is similarly intangible. Manfred, for example, tries to limit the sphere of Father Jerome's influence to the 'absent' or spiritual, by claiming the material kingdom as his own domain:

> Father, interrupted Manfred, I pay due reverence to your holy profession; but I am sovereign here, and will allow no meddling priest to interfere in the affairs of my domestic. ... My lord, said the holy man, I am no intruder into the secrets of families. My office is to promote peace, to heal divisions, to preach repentance, and teach mankind to curb their headstrong passions. I forgive your highness's uncharitable apostrophe: I know my duty, and am the minister of a mightier prince than Manfred.[37]

Jerome's response shows the power contained within his role which forces him to confront Manfred, as well the pervasiveness of the father paradigm which cannot be expelled completely into absence, even though it is concerned with calming and with healing intangible rather than physical wounds. Part of Father Jerome's impotence is a direct result of his lack of omniscience. He, as present spiritual father, is devoted to calming the problems of the present, while Providence operates on a larger scale, involving the past and the future. This, perhaps, is why Walpole represented him as having insufficient power to control Manfred's violence, or to offer realistic, continued protection to the princesses seeking sanctuary in the church. Similarly, Father Anthony (*The Recess*) is unable to do more than protect the young Matilda and Ellinor by concealing them while they are growing up.

---

[36] Marilyn Butler, *Romantics, Rebels and Reactionaries: English Literature and its Background 1760-1830* (1981; repr. Oxford: Oxford University Press, 1989), 160-1.

[37] Walpole, *Castle of Otranto*, 45-6.

Sophia Lee did not give him the power to create a place for his young charges within society. He is a 'good' surrogate and spiritual father figure whose impotence is due in part to the historical period in which the tale is set. Catholic monks, even benevolent ones, had no power or place in an Elizabethan society that was still smarting from the Catholic rule of Mary.

It is only when the Gothic romance is set in an overtly Catholic country that spiritual fathers are granted social influence and power, and spiritual fathers with political ambitions are always depicted as malevolent, destructive, and self-seeking. Material power is represented as a corrupting force and the writers of the Gothic romances frequently focused on the breakdown or perversion of social roles:

> Instead of brotherly affection, a gloomy mistrust was graven on the front of our conductor; and his manners were as cold, repulsive and comfortless as the internal appearance of this sanctified abode.[38]

Isolated and alone in a Protestant country, the Catholic monk or priest has no power and may be depicted as good and incorrupt: in community in a Catholic country he wields enormous power, because he is a smaller unit of the Church whose powerful arm is the Inquisition.

If a monastery is something to be regarded with fear, the Inquisition is a place where terror reigns. The inquisitors are also part of the Gothic formula, representing one side of the father paradigm. Like the hermit, they are instruments of Providence. Although guilty and innocent alike fear the dungeons of the Inquisition, it is always the guilty who suffer. The Inquisition's labyrinthine corridors and halls of judgement are often used as the setting for the revelation of guilt and for the punishment of the guilty, whose social position might otherwise protect them from the processes of the law. The complicated plots and trails of guilt in Ann Radcliffe's *The Italian* (1797), George Walker's *The Three Spaniards* (1800), Ireland's *Gondez the Monk* (1805) and Percy Shelley's *Zastrozzi* (1810)

---

[38] Ireland, *Gondez the Monk*, i. 26.

are unravelled by the Inquisitors.[39] Just as the power of the Inquisition is a fundamental part of the fabric of Catholic society as it is represented in the Gothic romance, so, too, is the paradigm of the father of which it is one present reflection.

It is not just fathers that are made absent in the Gothic romance – mothers do not figure in the texts either. Yet the figure and the role of the absent mother is not given the same power as the absent father. The absent mother, usually dead but occasionally imprisoned, is present only as a passive icon whose memory may be cherished. The obvious exception to this rule is *Frankenstein*, and here Mary Shelley has denied the mother completely by removing her from the creative/reproductive role. Thus, Mary Shelley ensures that the monster, in looking for his creator, is also looking for his father, and there is no overt suggestion that the monster is particularly conscious of the absence of the mother.[40] Only the absence of the father is used as a device to induce action in others.

There is always a paternal presence operating throughout the Gothic romance even when actual fathers in the tale are forced into absence. The 'good' father figure, offered to the reader as an archetype, is used by the author to establish the paradigm of the father. When the father is removed, the paradigm remains in the expectations of the reader and of characters within the tale. Driving the father into absence is an essential part of the formula of the Gothic tale, as it creates an atmosphere of vulnerability and uncertainty, impelling the hero, and sometimes the heroine, both forwards and inwards to construct their own identity.

---

[39] Percy Shelley, *Zastrozzi, A Romance, and St. Irvyne, or, The Rosicrucian: A Romance* Stephen C. Behrendt (ed. & intro.) (1810, 1811; repr. Oxford: Oxford University Press, 1986).

[40] For critics who do see *Frankenstein* in terms of the absence of the mother see Gordon Hirsch, 'The Monster was a Lady: On the Psychology of Mary Shelley's *Frankenstein*', *Hartford Studies in Literature* vii (1975), 116-53. Marc Rubenstein, '"My Accursed Origin": The Search for the Mother in *Frankenstein*', *Studies in Romanticism* xv (1976), 165-94.

6

Gothic Villains

I. HOW TO RECOGNISE A VILLAIN

"As to calling yourself my father, that is a stale trick, and will not pass; and as to personating (what I perceive you aspire to) the grand villain of my plot, your corpulency, pardon me, puts that out of the question for ever. I should be just as happy to employ you as any other man I know, but excuse me if I say, that you rather overrate your talents and qualifications. Have you the gaunt ferocity of famine in your countenance? Can you darken the midnight of a scowl? Have you the quivering lip and the Schedoniac contour? And while the lower part of your face is hidden in black drapery, can your eyes glare from under the edge of a cowl? In a word, are you a picturesque villain, full of plot, and horror, and magnificent wickedness?"[1]

By its nature, parody reveals the commonly recognisable stereotypes of any particular form. This passage from *The Heroine*, written two decades after the deluge of Gothic romances published in the 1790s and relying heavily on the readers' familiarity with the major romances of that period, highlights some of the problems associated with a consideration of the representation of the type of the villain. First, the well-read heroine Cherry (romantically self-styled Cherubina) Wilkinson can only conceive of a villain who conforms to specific physical characteristics already established as part of a formula. Second, by requiring a 'grand' villain capable of 'magnificent wickedness' for the plot, Barrett associated villainy with the language of the sublime. Cherry rejects her father as villain because he fails to arouse the requisite emotions of fear and dread in her, thus demonstrating that this villain stereotype is rooted in the consciousness and emotions of the romance reader. Not only does Cherry's speech imply that the villain is defined through a particular relationship with women, (the recognition or rejection of the

---

[1] Eaton Stannard Barrett, *The Heroine, or Adventures of a Fair Romance Reader*, 3 vols. (London: Henry Colburn, 1813) i. 155-6.

projected villain image by the female consciousness) but also that villainy can only be measured or considered of importance insofar as it affects the heroine. Finally, note that by 1813 the stereotype of the wicked monk was the pre-eminent image of villainy; the villain was, literally and metaphorically, the High Priest of the plot. Cherry's speech also suggests that there is only one recognisable or acceptable villain stereotype.

Critics too have commonly seen only one developing type of villain and one increasingly ambiguous response to villainy in the Gothic romance, based on a a conscious association between the nature of evil and the Sublime in the representation of the villain figure. A close examination, however, of the role and function of the villain within the context of the Gothic romance reveals not one, but two villainous stereotypes. Both are allied to the female rather than to the male role in eighteenth-century society, suggesting that, like the hero, the character role and function of the villain figure in the Gothic formula are delineated by his/her proximity and behaviour towards women.

Attention and anxiety are increasingly focused on the villain who is moved to the centre of the formula while the father is reciprocally marginalized. A distinction must be made between the developing hero-villain, opposed to the young hero through their contrasting education and subsequent development, and the fixed type of villain-hero who, opposed to the absent 'good' father, embodies the social and emotional problems that must be overcome if society is to survive. The characteristics of the 'good' father type are to be impotent, selfless, and absent: the characteristics of the opposing 'evil' villain type are to be powerful, selfish, and present. As soon as Cherry's father appears before her as a present father in place of the grandiose family relations sought in true 'Family Romance' tradition, she asserts that, if not the absent 'good' father of her imagination, he must be trying to be a 'grand villain.' However, Cherry is made to reject Gregory Wilkinson in both roles because he is 'only a sleek, good-humoured, chuckle-headed gentleman' who is sent away, fit only to 'return to your plough, mow, reap, fatten your pigs, and, the parson.'[2] Her father's social status is here presented as anti-thetical to the villain's role, suggesting that the *'grand* villain' [my emphasis] must belong to the same social rank as the trembling heroine or the noble hero.

Despite the pattern indicated by Barrett, Gothic villains are neither exclusively nor necessarily male; the representation of the female villain is both similar and dissimilar to that of the male, as her sphere of influence and social power is more circumscribed. It is when considering the representation of the female villain (and her *modus operandi*) against that of the male that one sees how the villain may be feminised – other than through simple association with the heroine. Writers of Gothic fiction explored the type of the villain in a way not usually recognised by critics, who see this representation of villainy only as one step in a literary development beginning with Milton's Satan and reaching its apotheosis in Byron's Romantic heroes.[3]

Eighteenth-century criticism clearly demonstrates the importance of the subjective response of the reader when considering the representation of the villain. In his short study of eighteenth-century criticism on the 'heroic' villain, Marlies Danziger considered the appeal and admiration for villainy displayed by eighteenth-century critics against the background of classical precedents, accepted literary taste, attitudes towards vice and virtue and theories of the sublime.[4] Beginning with seventeenth-century French criticism in translation, Danziger found changing attitudes towards villainy, paralleling a development in aesthetic taste,

---

[2] *Ibid* i. 156.

[3] For the development of the villain-hero from Satan to Byron, see Praz, *Romantic Agony*, 72-112. See also Peter Thorslev, *The Byronic Hero: Types and Prototypes* (Minneapolis: University of Minnesota Press, 1962), who argues that, unlike the Byronic hero-villain, the Gothic villain's rebellion does not engage the reader's sympathy, 52. Walter Reed, *Meditations on the Hero*, also uses moral categories to distinguish between the Gothic villain and the amoral Romantic Hero. He stresses, however, that this distinction marks a different type of character rather than implying, as Thorslev does, that this distinction marks an inferior type of character.

[4] Marlies Danziger, 'Heroic Villains in Eighteenth-Century Criticism,' *Comparative Literature* xi (1959), 35-46. For an expanded discussion on the sublime in the eighteenth century see S.H. Monk, *The Sublime: A Study of Critical Theories in XVIII-Century England* (1935; repr. Ann Arbor: University of Michigan Press, 1960). For changing perspective on the self see Peter de Bolla, *The Discourse of the Sublime: Readings in History, Aesthetics and the Subject* (Oxford: Blackwell, 1989).

that present the villain as a primary character, appreciated like the sublime, thus confusing moral and aesthetic standards.[5] The following quotation, from Blair's *Lectures on Rhetoric and Belles Lettres*, illustrates Danziger's argument:

> However, on some occasions, where Virtue either has no place, or is but imperfectly displayed, yet if extraordinary vigour and force of mind be discovered, we are not insensible to a degree of grandeur in the character; and from the splendid conqueror, or the daring conspirator, whom we are far from approving, we cannot with-hold our admiration.[6]

The villain figure is being viewed in heroic terms as an 'extraordinary' figure and, as such, is presented as a primary rather than, as Aristotle would have it, a secondary character, whose wickedness is exactly appropriate to the demands of the plot. Furthermore, though individual crimes may inspire repugnance, the scale of the villainy is such that the reader is compelled to feel ('cannot with-hold') admiration. Clearly, then, Blair acknowledges that, when considering the villain figure, he partially suspended his conventional and inflexible moral judgements, allowing himself to be swayed by an emotional rather than a rational response to aesthetic stimulus.[7]

Why should villainy be judged in a different manner to the rational, moral response demanded of the reader when considering the hero, the heroine or the father? Why should villainy (to return to Barrett) be 'picturesque,' 'grand,' or magnificent? Despite evidence that interest in Longinus travelled from France to

---

[5] Danziger did not comment on the fact that the examples, which she used to establish a pre-eighteenth-century critical trend connecting the villain figure with heightened emotions and grandeur of soul, betray a French rather than a British concern, although these writers were quickly translated and adapted into English. Neither did she alert the reader to the fact that the primary aim of these writers was to consider character in terms of dramatic poetry. The eighteenth-century British critics whom she examined, however, are concerned with a philosophical and psychological enquiry into emotion. She concentrated on John Baillie, *An Essay on the Sublime*, 1747, Hugh Blair, *Lectures on Rhetoric and Belles Lettres*, 1783, and R.P. Knight, *An Analytical Enquiry into the Principles of Taste*, 1805.

[6] Hugh Blair, *Lectures on Rhetoric and Belles Lettres*, 2 vols. (London: W. Strahan, T. Cadell, 1783), i. 54.

[7] Note that genuine responses to aesthetic stimuli are used as infallible indications of moral character in Gothic fiction.

England, creating an aesthetic of the sublime, Samuel Monk claimed that the aesthetic of terror was a peculiarly British development:

> For some reason the aesthetic of terror interested the eighteenth-century Englishman. In a sense it is the aesthetic of the ugly, for neither the ugly nor the terrible is agreeable. It is in this connection that the English show their independence.[8]

Edmund Burke was the first to develop an aesthetic system of terror but David Hume's essay on Tragedy (1757) shows a similar critical preoccupation. Hume did not mention character but concentrated exclusively on finding some rational explanation for the pleasure derived from experiencing disagreeable emotions:

> Objects of the greatest terror and distress ... please more than the most beautiful objects that appear calm and indifferent. The affection, rousing the mind, excites a large stock of spirit and vehemence, which is all transformed into pleasure by the force of the prevailing moment.[9]

Hume's distinction between the effects caused by terror and distress and those caused by the contemplation of beauty – the rousing or allaying of emotion in the onlooker – is the same distinction that Burke made in *A Philosophical Enquiry* between the beautiful and the sublime. We see, therefore, that the sublime and terror exacted the same response and were described in the same language.

Thus, a villain may be described as 'grand' or 'magnificent' because the emotions that his figure induces are those of the elevating sublime, the language of which describes the heights and plumbs the depths. It is in Hell that one finds the archetype of the 'grand villain': Milton's description of Satan, mingling passion with physical characteristics has the greatest bearing on the description of the later Gothic 'grand villain':

> ...but his face
> Deep scars of thunder had intrenched, and care
> Sat on his faded cheek, but under brows
> Of dauntless courage, and considerate pride

---

[8] Monk, *Sublime*, 52.
[9] David Hume, 'Of Tragedy', *Four Dissertations* (1757), repr. ed. by Scott Elledge, *Eighteenth-Century Critical Essays*, 2 vols. (New York: Cornell University Press, 1961), ii. 807.

> Waiting revenge. Cruel his eye, but cast
> Signs of remorse and passion to behold
> the fellows of his crime,[10]

Every lineament is described subjectively. Milton 'reads' the face of the Fallen Angel, particularly those features which impart expression – the eyebrows and eyes – interpreting each part as if it were a plastic entity fixed only by the passions. The passions that Milton marked in (and on) the face of Satan are the same ruling passions evident in the 'grand villain' – courage, pride, cruelty and a desire for revenge – coupled with the breaking of a social or religious taboo.[11]

Ann Radcliffe's first description of Schedoni (*The Italian*, 1796) displays the same combination of passion and suspected broken, moral sanctions that characterise Milton's Satan.[12] As Barrett's usage of the word 'Schedoniac' indicates, Schedoni was accepted as the definitive type of the 'grand villain':

> His figure was striking, but not so from grace; it was tall, and, though extremely thin, his limbs were large and uncouth, and as he stalked along, wrapt in the black garments of his order, there was something terrible in its air; something almost super-human. His cowl, too, as it threw a shade over the livid paleness of his face, encreased its severe character, and gave an effect to his large melancholy eye, which approached to horror. His was not the melancholy of a sensible and wounded heart, but apparently that of a gloomy and ferocious disposition. There was something in his physiognomy extremely singular, and that can not easily be defined. It bore the traces of many passions which seemed to have fixed the features they no longer animated.[13]

Here the reader is given a brief physical description accompanied by the author's simultaneous metaphysical interpretation. Like Milton, she has chosen to delineate character through perception and subjective reaction. Everything tends towards sublimity: Schedoni is described through obscurity, he is wrapped in

---

[10] Milton, *Paradise Lost*, I. 600-606.

[11] Marcia Pointon, *Milton & English Art* (Manchester: Manchester University Press, 1970), 96, points out that representations of Satan in the 1790s were both human and heroic – suggesting, perhaps, that Satan, like the experience of the sublime, was now located within the human heart.

[12] Mario Praz has commented on the similarity between Milton's description of Satan and Ann Radcliffe's Schedoni, *Romantic Agony*, 75-8.

[13] Radcliffe, *Italian*, 34-5.

shadows and created from darkness. Even his physiognomy is elusive, being compounded of shadows and definable only by negative 'traces' of passions. This elusive quality intensifies the sensation of menace for the reader whose expectations about the villain character have already been triggered by certain keywords in the passage. One of the hallmarks of the 'grand villain' and a keyword in his description is 'severe.' This, coupled with pride, indicates not only austerity, but also a fundamental lack of that magnanimity or benevolence which characterise the hero and the father.

II. 'GRAND' AND 'SIMPLE' VILLAINS

A feminist reading of Gothic fiction might see male character types as literary articulations of a female desire for power and a protest against powerlessness because some male types (the hero) are emasculated, bringing them closer to the feminine sphere of influence, while others (the 'grand villain') express female anger.[14] In her examination of twentieth-century 'Gothic' romances with a reflection on their eighteenth-century precursors (specifically *The Mysteries of Udolpho*, 1794), Tania Modleski found convincing evidence of a world informed by feminine paranoia.[15] Interestingly, the evidence Modleski identified – fears of and arising from separation, victimisation, and lack of identity – seems to be the same as that used by David Morris to prove that writers of Gothic fiction revised the Burkean concept of the sublime.

Morris, dealing specifically with *The Castle of Otranto* (1764), isolated the potential doubling and victimisation of the heroines, the difficulties of separation from filial dependency and the threat of acute physical and potential sexual

---

[14] Tania Modleski commented on the tendency for women 'to divide men into two classes: the omnipotent, domineering, aloof male and the gentle, but passive and fairly ineffectual male,' seeing this as a fundamental trait of Gothic fiction written by women. *Loving With A Vengeance: Mass-produced Fantasies for Women* (London: Methuen, 1984), 79. Elaine Showalter drew similar conclusions about the underlying motives for representations of male types by nineteenth century female writers in 'Feminine Heroes', *A Literature of Their Own* (1979; repr. London: Virago, 1988), 133-52.

danger to women. Morris' interpretation of these disturbing elements in Gothic fiction, considered alongside Modleski's thesis, suggests that danger and anxiety surrounding the female is (and has always been) an intrinsic part of the Gothic formula: a part that need not necessarily be perceived as marking the Gothic as peculiarly female territory. If the excitement of the Gothic arises from the victim's fears, then villainy must be construed as the greatest threat to the weak and the innocent. This is apparent in Gothic fiction in which the villainy of the villainous stereotypes, however different they may appear, is commonly defined by its effect on women.

i. The Grand Villain

Horace Walpole's representation of the first Gothic 'grand villain' typifies the close relationship between the villain figure and women. His tyrant, Manfred, is never described physically, but his tyrannical nature is established in the opening pages via one of the keywords of villainy; Manfred's family dare not question his decision, 'apprehending the *severity* of their prince's disposition [my emphasis].'[16] Walpole made the connection between tyranny, villainy and female distress explicit when Isabella reflects on her probable future:

> ...she was not sorry to be delivered from a marriage which had promised her little felicity, either from her destined bridegroom, or from the severe temper of Manfred, who, though he had distinguished her by great indulgence, had imprinted her mind with terror, from his causeless rigour to such amiable princesses as Hippolita and Matilda.[17]

Again Manfred is characterised as 'severe,' and this is made apparent and defined through female perceptions and as a threat to the happiness of the women in his family. One might argue that Manfred's tyranny is apparent in his relations with

---

[15] Modleski, *Loving with a Vengeance*, 59-84. Unfortunately, Modleski tended to ignore any male contribution to the development of the eighteenth-century Gothic romance, preferring to view it as an exclusively feminine province, shaped by female anxieties.

[16] Walpole, *Castle of Otranto*, 15.

[17] *Ibid* 18.

all his dependents, and that this definition and delineation of villainy in relation to the female is a consequence of Walpole's focus on the family situation. Manfred behaves differently, however, when faced with the defiance of a subordinate, yet courageous, male like Theodore:

> This presence of mind, joined to the frankness of the youth, staggered Manfred. He even felt a disposition towards pardoning one who had been guilty of no crime.[18]

In a situation in which two men confront each other, involving a mutual display of masculine honour, Walpole allowed Manfred to respond to courage. His villainy is not similarly tempered when he is confronted with a courageous and defiant young woman: when Isabella attempts to repulse Manfred, his reaction is physical coercion. Of course, Theodore's defiance is not immediately connected with Manfred's overwhelming passion, unlike his relations with Isabella, and furthermore, Isabella should be doubly in Manfred's power – as subject to Lord and as woman to stronger man. Her defiance and flight are, therefore, a challenge to his masculinity and a diminution of his power. When Isabella flees, Walpole again showed the reader Manfred's tyranny in a rape of female happiness:

> ...she did not doubt but Manfred would seek her there [in Hippolita's chamber], and that his violence would incite him to double the injury he meditated, without leaving room for them to avoid the impetuosity of his passions.[19]

Flight (passive opposition) is the only possible reaction to violence that Isabella is allowed. Her inability to confront Manfred forces her from the comparative familiarity and security of the palace into the insecure and gloomy labyrinth of the dungeons and secret passage.

Further evidence of the association between the villain and the woman (or women) upon whom he exercises his villainy in *The Castle of Otranto* occurs in Walpole's reference to Manfred's 'exquisite villainy' when:

---

[18] *Ibid* 30.
[19] *Ibid* 24.

Presuming on the unshaken submission of Hippolita, he flattered himself that she would not only acquiesce with patience to a divorce, but would obey, if it was his pleasure, in endeavouring to persuade Isabella to give him her hand[20]

Manfred's villainy consists in manipulating the role of the ideal wife to further his own designs and incidentally to destroy her happiness. He is conscious of the power of virtue and the feminine ideal, while wilfully perverting it, and such a deliberate perversion of good through an abuse of the female role marks Manfred's villainy as 'exquisite.' From the earliest Gothic romance, then, the treatment and perceptions of women reveal the villain fully as much as the hero.

ii. The Simple Villain

The other villainous stereotype operating within the Gothic formula differs from the 'grand villain' in several respects, despite occupying the same place in the formula. Although, both villainous stereotypes are antithetical or perverted representations of the absent 'good' father and can be identified by their relations to women within the tale, Gothic writers handled them differently. The 'grand villain' is an aristocrat, described in sublime terms, and is increasingly used as a primary character occupying his own isolated location. In contrast, the 'simple villain' is usually lower class, described in repulsive rather than elevating terms, and has no private domain.[21] Rather, the 'simple villain' is a social parasite adept at manipulating his host and, operating covertly within society, adopts a seemingly passive role.

In a dependent position, the 'simple' villain is servile. Thomas Leland created such a character in *Longsword* (1762) in which Grey the flatterer is the prime mover behind the usurping Lord Raymond:

---

[20] *Ibid* 35.

[21] 'Simple' is used here in the sense of pure villainy, uncomplicated by an ambiguous reader response.

Subtle and expert he was in the arts of fraud and circumvention; ever attentive to his own private interest; patient, persevering and sagacious in the means of advancing it.[22]

Like all villains, Grey's villainy manifests itself primarily through his behaviour towards the unhappy wife of Sir William. Yet, as a 'simple' villain, Grey is not used as a primary character: his plotting and prompting lure a weak superior into overtly villainous behaviour. The 'simple villain' of base birth is incapable of inspiring a sublime response and is often portrayed as perverting the behaviour of a potentially noble character. For example, Lord Raymond is encouraged by Grey to use 'gentle violence' – a term also used by Walpole to describe the behaviour of the princesses in removing Hippolita to her chamber – in marrying Ela without her consent.[23] The baseness of Grey's birth, according to Leland, has formed him into 'an unrelenting, unfeeling vassal,' and shapes the evil of which he is capable because of his 'temper base and brutal.'[24]

Charlotte Smith also used this villainous stereotype to create the character of Sir Richard Crofts and his relationship with Lord Montreville in *Emmeline* (1788).[25] Sir Richard Crofts might be a model for the 'simple' villain:

He had less understanding than cunning; less honesty than industry; and tho' he knew how to talk warmly and plausibly of honour, justice, and integrity, he was generally contented only to talk of them, seldom so imprudent as to practice them when he could get place or profit by their sacrifice.

He had that sort of sagacity which enabled him to enter into the characters of those with whom he conversed: he knew how to honour their prejudices, and lay in wait for their foibles to turn them to his own advantage.

To his superiors, the cringing parasite; to those whom he thought his inferiors, proud, supercilious, and insulting;[26]

All his ideas are directed towards profit or self-aggrandisement and his advisory

---

[22] Leland, *Longsword*, i. 149.
[23] *Ibid* ii. 43.
[24] *Ibid* i. 157.
[25] Charlotte Smith, *Emmeline, The Orphan of the Castle*, ed. and intro. Anne Henry Ehrenpreis (1788; repr. from 2nd. ed., Oxford: Oxford University Press, 1971).
[26] *Ibid* 87.

relationship with Lord Montreville perverts a potentially admirable character, directly affecting the heroine's destiny and happiness. Like Grey the flatterer, he is a purveyor of second-hand evil, relying on the power of his host to advance his ends, and marked as a 'simple' rather than a 'grand' villain in two significant particulars. Although both types are incapable of abstract thought, 'simple' villains are also incapable of mustering the raw, bestial courage that the 'grand villain' displays in the defence of his honour or the pursuit of his plans. Another of Charlotte Smith's 'simple' villains, Sir John Belgrave, behaves improperly (villainously) towards Monimia (*The Old Manor House*, 1783) but is too effete to repulse Orlando. 'Sir John, who was quite the modern man of fashion, did not much approve of the specimen Orlando had given him of his athletic powers.'[27] Because the 'simple villain' cringes to his superiors, he cannot be considered or described in sublime terms, and seeming subservience is his second distinguishing characteristic. Nowhere in the description of a 'simple villain' does the reader encounter the magnificent villainy or excessive pride that marks the 'grand' villain: excessive servility usually accompanied by physical cowardice delineates his counterpart.

Even if the 'simple' villain does not display cowardice, he triggers very different emotions to those evoked by the 'grand' villain. Sir William Symons (*The Mysterious Visit*, 1802), for example, fulfils all the 'grand' criteria but is not a source of sublime emotions and is, therefore, a 'simple villain' of relatively aristocratic birth:

> ...one who wore the semblance of honour, without a single particle of it in his soul; and to every vile propensity that disgraces human nature, had completely attained to the climax of wickedness, by a system of the most detestable hypocrisy, to impose upon the truly good and unsuspecting heart by an affectation of every virtue, as a covering to the most abandoned principles, and with a view only to deceive and betray.[28]

---

[27] Smith, *Old Manor House*, 87.
[28] Parsons, *Mysterious Visit*, i. 148-9.

Unlike Radcliffe, Eliza Parsons did not describe her villain in terms of barely repressed passions that might be interpreted by the reader. There is no possibility of an ambiguous reader response, no representation of fascinating evil, no suggestion of daring or feats of anti-social courage. Instead the writer took care to alert her readers to the misery of the villain's situation:

> ...involved in the most nefarious plots, and entangled in a maze of intricate schemes, he was for ever mistrustful and wretched, from the constant apprehension of some untoward chapter of accidents crossing him, to develope [sic] his dark designs, and cover him with infamy.[29]

A villain, conscious of the differences between appearance and reality in his own character and aware of the thinness of the veneer, can trust no one because suspicion and fear are the natural consequences of villainy.[30] This, together with the importance of restraining the passions, is the message that Gothic writers continually promoted. Clara Reeve had already made this moral point in *The Old English Baron* (1778) through the villainous Walter Lovel: 'From that fatal hour I have never known peace, always in fear of something impending to discover my guilt.'[31] Fear of apprehension – which is not the same thing as the consciousness of guilt or remorse – is another characteristic peculiar to the 'simple villain.' Such fear is unknown to 'grand' villains like Manfred who declares he will brave Hell itself to further his designs, or to Montoni who scorns the feelings of lesser men: '"No existence is more contemptible than that, which is embittered by fear."'[32] The 'simple' villain manipulates the rules of his society: the 'grand' villain ignores them.

---

[29] *Ibid* ii. 208.
[30] E.g. the words given to Mr. Weimar: 'tis the fate of villainy never to be secure; and the constant apprehension of detection embitters every hour of their lives who once plunge into guilt.' Parsons, *Castle of Wolfenbach*, ii. 167.
[31] Reeve, *Old English Baron*, 105.
[32] Radcliffe, *Mysteries*, 244.

iii. Society

Society, by which is meant high, or fashionable society ordered by corrupting superficial values, is the natural home of the Gothic villain, whose character, allied to the nature of the world he inhabits, provides a critique on facile social values:

> ... the middling and lower classes of people ... are more to be depended on for character, than the higher ranks in society, who view men and manners through an artificial medium, without taking the trouble of investigation.[33]

In society, as Gothic writers portray it, reputation (in the twin senses of personal reputation and rumour) is all-important. The importance of penetrating the surface manners of an insidious villain is evident in *The Mysteries of Udolpho*, in which the superficial fallibility of social judgement is demonstrated within the text. Ann Radcliffe showed her readers a fashionable and stupid woman, Madame Cheron, betraying both her ignorance and her artificial judgement as she asserts her superiority over her dead brother, St. Aubert: "'What has a man's face to do with his character?'"[34] Had Madame Cheron been as skilled as Emily in the metaphysical interpretation of countenances, she would not have been deceived by Montoni's gentlemanly veneer. Their subsequent marriage is based on deception and false repute: he believed her to be considerably wealthier than was the case and hoped in marrying her to 'delude society' and 'regain the fortunes he had lost'; she believed him to be a man of good character and settled property.[35] Ann Radcliffe used this double deception as a device whereby Montoni was forced to remove himself and his entourage from Venice, returning to Castle Udolpho.

By retreating within the walls of an enclosed world, the villain recreates his own landscape, denying Nature. Fortified castles are never regarded as homes in the Gothic romance, possibly because the home is a domestic, female sphere. Castle Udolpho (*The Mysteries of Udolpho*), Castle Ray (*The Mysterious Visit*),

---

[33] Parsons, *Mysterious Visit*, i. 18-19.
[34] Radcliffe, *Mysteries*, 112.
[35] *Ibid* 190.

the Castle of Otranto, and the Castle of Wolfenbach are decaying, labyrinthine prisons for women trapped in the villain's sphere of influence. Even in Barrett's parody, the heroine's attempt to inhabit Monkton Castle is unsuccessful – she abandons it after realising that she will have to share her bedchamber with thirty men. Instead the reader is invited to share the fantasy that rural cottages and countryside estates offer the security and haven of home denied by a fortified castle.

Montoni's retreat to Castle Udolpho marks a mid-point in the depiction of the villain with regard to society. In the earliest Gothic romances the villain figure is an usurping tyrant who, as absolute overlord, makes the laws of his society, shaping his own environment, like Manfred or the villainous Mal-Leon in Leland's *Longsword*. By 1797, when the villainous figure of Schedoni appeared, the villain figure had been incorporated into a tight social structure of which he was no longer the apex, although he was often placed at the head of a subsidiary, semi-autonomous society like a religious order, or a castle household. Montoni's retreat, however, shows the reader a 'grand villain' who, although adept at manoeuvring within a social milieu, always has the possibility of rejecting society's standards and retreating (when necessary) to a stronghold outside that society.

Ann Radcliffe's Montoni (*The Mysteries of Udolpho*, 1794) is poised as a character type between Manfred and Schedoni, and reveals all the dominant qualities of the Gothic 'grand villain' in and out of society. His villainy is manifested and registered through women, and he is introduced to the reader trying to manipulate a social situation in order to enhance his social power. Montoni also displays the potentially admirable characteristics that all 'grand villains' share. He is the leader of a band of mercenaries, exacting unquestioning obedience from his followers by virtue of his decisive nature and 'the vigour of his thought ... to which most of his companions submitted, as to a power, that they had no right to question.'[36] Grand villains typically exert a near mesmeric influence over those around them. Ambrosio (*The Monk*, 1796) is not only the youngest monk to be

Abbot of his monastery but is also a powerful, persuasive preacher. Similarly, John Melmoth (*Melmoth the Wanderer*, 1820) arrests attention whenever he appears. Passions are so concentrated in the person of the 'grand villain' that the attention of others focuses on him.

iv. Subjective reader: Objective villain

All the characteristics of the villain, whether 'grand' or 'simple,' and his place in formula depend upon the reader's subjective response to an atmosphere of menace and uncertainty, triggered by a shared understanding of the vocabulary of feeling. The sublimity ascribed to the 'grand villain' is located in the emotions of the reader. The 'simple villain' has a less powerful emotional effect, but the representation of the villain and his place in the formula of the Gothic romance demand that the actions (rather than the character) of this figure should also create sensations of fear or anxiety for the reader. In either case, the villain figure is invariably objective in his/her perception and goals, opposed to 'good' characters within the text and the reader outside it: all the emotions are evoked by the villain and felt by the reader.

An archetypal 'good' father like St. Aubert (*The Mysteries of Udolpho*) is portrayed as a man of conscious feeling and sentiment, and the hero and heroine are represented as types who, acutely aware of their own sensations and feelings, respond strongly to external stimuli. Valancourt and Emily, for example, vent their overcharged emotions through the mutual shedding of tears. The reader is invited to share their perceptions and feel their emotions, commonly expressed through poetry, which is a contained and shaped response to external stimulus, an exercise in the ordering of emotion by a rational mind. Thus a reader experiences emotion at second-hand: the correct subjective response is already present in characters in the text, rationalised and filtered through authorial narrative.

---

[36] *Ibid* 288.

The opposite effect is obtained through the representation of the villain, who does not respond to external stimulus by emitting sentimentalised emotion. Instead he is the one figure within the formula who exists both as an external stimulus on a par with natural forces and as a character in his own right. Everything, for the villain, is an object that may be manipulated or acquired to build his own powerbase.. Even the 'grand' villain's mesmeric influence over his men or associates is part of the active desire for dominance in a one-way power relationship. In the villain's egocentric world, other human beings are reduced to objects representing different aspects of the villain's power. Montoni, for example, is represented as incapable of friendship: 'associated with them [the vicious aristocrats, Bertolini, Orsino and Verezzi] only to make them the instruments of his purpose.'[37] Montoni's chosen companions are simply his tools, in the same way that he perceived Emily as an objective embodiment of the Languedoc estates. Manfred's desire for immortality is likewise perceived and expressed in objective terms as dynastic continuance.

Since everything surrounding the villain is perceived by him as an available object, he is necessarily represented as a figure of extreme outward action. This in itself is enough to create an atmosphere of threatened violent physical action that is anathema to the idealised, gentle, thoughtful and passive female. Not only is the villain represented as an active figure of potential violence within the text, however, but also as one constitutionally incapable of enduring inaction. When thwarted, the passions of the Gothic villain are either liberated in rage or turned back against himself. Wenlock's response (*The Old English Baron*, 1778) is typical of a villain at bay: he 'flew into a passion, raged, swore, threatened, and finally denied every thing.'[38] The usurper Lord Raymond (*Longsword*) is also represented as continually giving way to his passions in fits of 'distracted violence.'

---

[37] *Ibid* 182.
[38] Reeve, *Old English Baron*, 96.

Typically, the villain figure is compounded of gigantic, unrestrained passions that distort his soul and reshape his countenance:

> Georgina was drowned in tears, terrified by his [Sir William Symons] passion, which had so inflamed and altered his features that he really looked quite horrible.[39]

Even when the villain is frustrated in his desires and rendered powerless, his passions still vent themselves in some active, physical manifestation. Whilst Lord Dunlaney and Lady Symons were exclaiming over the pathetic innocence and beauty of young, fatherless Georgina, Sir William – responsible for the incarceration of Georgina's father – bites his nails and gnaws at his fingers. Unable to further his plot at that time, the villain turned that outward, destructive passion against himself. Count Wolfenbach also demonstrates that personal peace is neither attainable nor desirable for a passion-filled villain. Through his conversation with his suffering wife, Victoria, Eliza Parsons reveals the villain's dominant urge to gratify the baser passions:

> "Because, (said he, furiously) because I prefer revenge to my own quiet; because I will be feared, and make your destiny hang on my pleasure."[40]

The same restless, passionate urges and corresponding delight in violent action can be found in Montoni:

> He delighted in the energies of the passions; the difficulties and tempests of life, which wreck the happiness of others, roused and strengthened all the powers of his mind, and afforded him the highest enjoyments, of which his nature was capable.[41]

The Gothic villain is directed towards action and conflict; he is not generally concerned with abstract concepts.

Honour is the one abstract conception that the 'grand villain' commonly entertains and even this is objectified, becoming synonymous with social reputation and masculine status. Honour revolves around the idea of the self; often

---

[39] Parsons, *Mysterious Visit*, ii. 116.
[40] Parsons, *Castle of Wolfenbach*, i. 263.
[41] Radcliffe, *Mysteries*, 182.

rooted in pride or the reflection of one's self in others, it is a suitable obsession for the villain, who is self-motivated, self-propelling and self-absorbed. Clara Reeve used the villain's tendency to objectify his situation in order to create a dilemma and punishment for the materialistic Walter (*The Old English Baron*): 'He was unwilling to give up the world, and yet more so to become the object of public shame, disgrace and punishment.'[42] Here the villain abjures the world in order to prevent the deflation of his self-image or to become an object for others – sustaining this self-image is what constitutes honour. Similarly, Ann Radcliffe represented Montoni as a character obsessed with his honour, synonymous with self-will and masculinity. The villain may see others in objective terms, but may not be so seen himself. He considers his honour at stake whenever his will is thwarted or his designs challenged. Thus he invokes it as a motive for coercing Emily into a marriage with Morano: 'my honour is now engaged, and it shall not be trifled with.'[43] It is also offered as the reason for Montoni's anger at Morano's suggestion that Montoni obtained the castle by foul means: 'with respect to my honour; no man shall question it with impunity.'[44] In this case, honour is advanced as an acceptable masculine inspiration for anger where the true inspiration is guilt. As soon as 'honour' is mentioned, it is understood as a challenge or a block beyond which there is no room for appeal or negotiation: violent action can be the only result. The reaction of Leland's Mal-Leon (*Longsword*) to the public disclosure of his dishonourable conduct not only demonstrates how the loss of honour reflects a loss of power, but that an injury to a villain's pride only aggravates his operant passions:

> ...[Mal-Leon] whose imperious spirit could but ill endure the piercing wound his honour had now received; discomfited, disgraced and doubly conquered, now felt the most malignant passions rankling in his breast.[45]

---

[42] Reeve, *Old English Baron*, 123.
[43] Radcliffe, *Mysteries*, 198.
[44] *Ibid* 289.
[45] Leland, *Longsword*, i. 36.

George Walker also represented his 'grand' villain, Don Padilla (*The Three Spaniards*, 1800), as acutely and hypocritically conscious of honour in the abstract when he 'resolved, with obstinate firmness, to submit to any infliction, rather than bend to a confession which must overwhelm him with infamy.'[46] The initial description of Don Padilla as 'a gruff old Don, proud as a bashaw, and grim as a starving wolf' has already prepared the reader to expect an anti-social character capable of predatory, rapacious violence.[47] Honour, a natural consequence of pride, is produced as the excuse for having mistakenly stabbed his daughter whilst she attempted to flee from a convent with her lover:

> "you know how necessary it is that the privacy of a superior, or indeed or any individual, should be sacred: you will not wonder then that I was transported almost beyond the bounds of reason at so flagrant a breach of honour."[48]

Interestingly, this, like every occasion that causes Montoni to unfurl the flag of honour, is concerned with a woman's situation or reputation.

One of the villain's traits is to shift moral responsibility for his 'honourable' actions to the woman who has inspired them. One such shift occurs over the assassination of the Countess de Merville (*Clermont*, 1798) by her villainous son-in-law, Monsieur D'Alembert, an action commended by his father as 'a proof of real spirit, which would not quietly submit to ill-treatment.'[49] The murder is less important than an assertion of masculine activity and dominance over a female obstacle: it is treated as a matter of honour. D'Alembert himself uses the same argument to justify his desire to rid himself of his wife: 'a noble soul will ever try to break chains which are oppressive.'[50] When Mrs. Roche described d'Alembert's attempts to justify his behaviour by representing his own deeds and motives as those of the masculine ideal – a noble, chivalric knight combating injustice – she represented the classic villainous stereotype who perverts the ideal of

---

[46] Walker, *Three Spaniards*, iii. 198.
[47] *Ibid* i. 67.
[48] *Ibid* ii. 191.
[49] Roche, *Clermont*, iv. 213.
[50] *Ibid* iv. 223.

masculine activity. D'Alembert justifies himself once more by transferring the responsibility for his own villainous actions to the heroine Madeleine:

"though solely in my power, I never will make an ungenerous use of that power, by using any violence. I will not force you to return my love; but if you continue much longer to disdain it, I shall not hesitate to surrender your father to the fate he merits."[51]

D'Alembert appears to recognise both his villainy and his responsibility towards a helpless young woman, yet makes a merit of physical restraint while he applies emotional blackmail. In effect, he declares that he recognises and fulfils *his* masculine duty towards women, and uses Madeleine's strong sense of filial duty to compel her obedience. Mr Weimar (*Castle of Wolfenbach*, 1793) is represented as using exactly the same technique for apportioning guilt and responsibility: "'It was my intention to have married you, unless you rejected me--in that case you must take the consequences.'"[52] Montoni also appeals to Emily's perfect femininity, with a subtext of underlying duty, in order to persuade her to accede to his demands: "'you have none of those contemptible foibles, that frequently mark the female character.'"[53]

In each case the villain first accorded due respect to the perfect heroine and then demanded a sacrifice from her. These are further examples of the villain whose villainy is apparent through his manipulation of the female role and, although the authors quoted above were all women, it is a device commonly used by all writers of Gothic romances. Walpole used the same technique in the description of Manfred's behaviour and motives when he attempts to relinquish his wife. Thomas Leland also used it in describing how Lord Raymond accedes to the kidnap of Ela's baby son, transferring the responsibility for that action from his own desire to Ela's refusal to marry him. Every occurrence, every person, every

---

[51] Roche, *Clermont*, iv. 171.
[52] Parsons, *Castle of Wolfenbach*, ii. 171.
[53] Radcliffe, *Mysteries*, 380.

motive is measured, considered and justified in the light of the villain's overween-
ing ego.

A concern or obsession with personal honour is not confined to the villain
– every major character in a Gothic romance partakes of such a concern, although
only the villain sees it in objective terms. Honour is a particularly loaded concept
for women in the Gothic romance, as it involves not just their own reputation but
that of their family, and is often based on maintaining their sexual integrity which
extends even to thoughts. Heroines are thus the most sensitive and vulnerable to
attack:

> you must make some allowance for the natural character of man, influenced
> as it moreover is, by his unrestrained habits and education. He is not, like
> woman, accustomed to view the smallest wanderings of his ideas as crime--
> he assumes, and by compact as it were, is granted an independence of con-
> duct and opinion, which in woman would not be tolerated.[54]

Female honour is equated with integrity of role. For a woman, this often consists
of the active defence of a passive purity, involving painful restraint. When a
'grand villain' invokes the honour concept, however, he asserts his right to an active male role, re-establishing domination and confirming power over others. Villain and heroine are thus linked once more through their opposed conceptions of
honour.

---

[54] Countess Sternach to Amelia: Dacre, *Passions*, iii. 133.

III. THE FEMININE VILLAIN

... he could adapt himself to the tempers and passions of persons, whom he wished to conciliate, with astonishing facility, and generally with complete triumph.[55]

A successful villain is a chameleon, adept at recognising, disguising and adapting his own passions to suit the environment around him. Capacity for adaptation and manipulative passivity are as much a part of the ideal role of woman as a necessity for the successful villain and villains cast in this 'feminine' role are those whom writers of Gothic fiction represent as neutered by social disadvantage.

i. The Young Villain

Young villains in the tales, of whom there are few examples, rarely have enough social power to threaten the hero or the heroine significantly. Wenlock and Markham (*The Old English Baron*) join in attempting to destroy Edmund's reputation and favour with his protector, Lord FitzOwen, but their plotting is ineffectual and unsuccessful. Clara Reeve did not use them as an opposing device obstructing the hero's destiny or as figures of evil to enthrall the reader, but as foils counterpointing Edmund's excellence. As such they underline the need for moral education and restraint of the passions in the young. Alwin, the villainous young page in Francis Lathom's *The Mysterious Freebooter* (1806), serves the same purpose as a foil to the excellences of young Edward.

These young villains are not characterised in the same way as adult Gothic villains: their villainy is not defined through their behaviour towards women, nor are they perceived as a threat through female consciousness. Instead, they partake of the feminine role to some extent, being dependent like the heroine, and forced to exploit their dependency, vulnerability or childishness in order to achieve their ends: 'mixing the manners of cunning with the playful childishness natural to his

---

[55] Radcliffe, *Italian*, 35.

years, and exercising them to the best advantage.'[56] The technique used by Clara
Reeve's young villains, Wenlock and Markham, to discredit Edmund is calumny
and false report inspired by jealousy; the same technique and the same motive
used by the ladies of Irish provincial society to justify their scorn of Amanda (*The
Children of the Abbey*). There are obvious similarities existing between the position and techniques of the young villains and those of women.

ii. The Wicked Monk

The figure of the Wicked Monk became a common topos for the writers of
the Gothic romance, who recognised and exploited the dramatic potential inherent
in a character forever wearing a mask, split between an outward show of spiritual
benevolence and an inner reality of selfish passion. He is also a highly feminised
character: rumour has it (in *The Monk*) that Ambrosio, like the heroine, Antonia,
has been educated in ignorance of the sexual differences between men and
women. There is an even stronger parallel than this instance might suggest between the role of the monk and that of the woman. He is at a disadvantage in society and is denied any overt social power. Further, his monkish role requires him to
triumph over the grosser passions and to embody the moral stature of his rational
society while upholding irrational faith. The monk or priest is given some status
through the rituals of public ceremony or the intimacy of the confessional. This
power, however, is both acknowledged and emasculated: public ritual (like the
procession of the nuns in *The Monk*) serves as mass entertainment rather than a
visible reminder of spiritual authority, and the seal of the confessional confines
the priest's power to a spiritual rather than a social realm. The ideal woman is in
almost exactly the same position, having no social power except in the home. She
is expected to be the embodiment of all domestic virtues and experienced in containing all passions while commonly supposed to have a weaker and less rational
understanding than a man.

---

[56] Lathom, *Mysterious Freebooter*, i. 188.

Like other villain figures, the Wicked Monk inhabited a mysterious, closed world with its own social hierarchy and power structure; unlike other villains, however, as a perverted holy man, he was poised on the brink of eternal destruction, thereby intensifying the horror and the dramatic tension. The mystery and mystique of Catholic religious practices were also suited to the representation of an atmosphere of suspicion and vague, though elevated, emotions:

> Neither Catholic dogma nor religious life is thought to be worthy of the intellectual assent of reasonable beings. Yet, Catholic dogma in practice can provide situations highly pleasurable to the emotions, and the appurtenances of religious life have qualities extremely satisfying for the lover of the picturesque. Catholicism in Gothic fiction, therefore, presents ample materials for the exercise of both sense and sensibility. Sense rejects dogma; sensibility revels in the decorations. [57]

After a study of more than one hundred novels, Sr. Tarr concluded that the elements of Catholic practice appearing in Gothic fiction, including architectural setting, the piety and frequent devotions of major characters, and spectacular religious ceremonies, are used mainly to evoke an atmosphere of pseudo-medievalism. Accordingly, Gothic writers ignored the principal tenets of Catholicism, subordinating it to a convenient stage-setting in which emotion could be released. A secondary result of this religious miasma concentrating on the effects of irrational superstition, Sr. Tarr felt, is a vindication of eighteenth-century rationalism: 'a sense of relief that the eighteenth century has been delivered from the fanatic superstition of earlier times.'[58] In addition to appealing to aesthetics, a writer could exploit an actual fear of Catholicism in order to enhance the sensations of horror. That there was an awareness of Catholicism, coupled with a popular ground swell of strong anti-Catholic feeling, in late eighteenth-century England cannot be denied. 1762-1820 was a period of social and ecclesiastical

---

[57] Sr. Mary Muriel Tarr, *Catholicism in Gothic Fiction: A Study of the Nature and Function of Catholic Materials in Gothic Fiction in England (1762-1820)* (Washington: Catholic University of America Press, 1946), 72.

[58] *Ibid* 21.

revolution. The notorious Gordon Riots of 1780, during which Roman Catholic chapels were pillaged and burnt and London was under mob rule for several days, were a direct response to a proposed Act of Parliament according limited toleration to Roman Catholics. Sympathy shifted towards persecuted clergy and people who fled to England in order to escape the activities of the French revolutionary government, and an Act of Relief for Roman Catholics was eventually passed in 1791; complete religious freedom with full legal rights and protection was not granted until 1829. Historically, this was a period in which attitudes towards Catholicism, Dissenters and the established Church were undergoing radical shifts and changes.

Distrust, suspicion and superstition are not the only contemporary social conditions reflected by the depiction of the Wicked Monk in the Gothic romance. Daniel Watkins, for example, (concentrating on *The Monk*) has suggested that the representation of religious life also reflects an eighteenth-century preoccupation with class division.[59] Much of what Watkins has discovered in *The Monk* is also applicable to other Wicked Monk figures and may be considered as an essential part of the stereotype. Basing his criticism on the fact that, although his father is an aristocrat, Ambrosio's mother, Elvira, is the daughter of a shoemaker in Cordova, Watkins asserts that Ambrosio's fate dramatises the evil resulting from crossing social divides. 'Ambrosio is from birth doomed to exclusion from and isolation within society, as his tenure in the monastery symbolises, and thus his desires and power are the desires and power of the hopelessly alienated.'[60]

Watkins does admit that Ambrosio's villainy is not reducible to his mixed heritage. However, his central point, that the circumstances of Ambrosio's birth exclude him from any true social power and that the monastery is a shadow world outside society in which he can rise to eminence, is pertinent to representations of

---

[59] Daniel Watkins, 'Social Hierarchy in Matthew Lewis's *The Monk*,' *Studies in the Novel* xviii (1986), 115-124.
[60] *Ibid* 117.

the Wicked Monk in general. The Wicked Monk is frequently described as having chosen the religious life, either to escape social condemnation for his crimes or because the monastery offers the only environment in which he may exercise a degree of power inappropriate to his status in 'normal' society. Leland's Reginhald (*Longsword*) is the earliest Wicked Monk of the latter type: he comes from the lower classes and is even more repugnant than his villainous brother Grey.[61] In contrast, the most famous of all the wicked monks, Schedoni, is an aristocrat, but he too was initially denied the social power and status he desired because he was a younger son.[62] Similarly, Abbot Gondez (*Gondez the Monk*) is eventually revealed to be the bastard son of Cardinal Nicolo Gonzari and the Abbess of the Della Pietà convent. In each case, the stereotype of the Wicked Monk is created from social disadvantage and used as a device to first alarm and then reassure the reader as power is ultimately returned to the traditional authorities.[63]

Although Watkins's analysis is founded exclusively on *The Monk*, his remarks are applicable to any Gothic romance in which a wicked monk is a major character. For example, both Gondez and Schedoni perish in the prison of the Inquisition. Thus, their social power is terminated, innocence is vindicated, the truth made apparent and the social order is stabilised. In sum, the Wicked Monk is an eminently suitable villainous stereotype for the Gothic romancer. Masked in an outward show of spiritual benevolence and opposed, in the formula, to the father whose role he perverts, he has his own enclosed location to which he may retire. Furthermore, as a socially disadvantaged character professing a suspect religious faith, he may be used as a device to disquiet the reader. His social disadvantage fuels his passions, the abnormal strength of those passions combine with the role

---

[61] Leland, *Longsword*, ii. 2.
[62] Cf. Thomas Paine on the evils of primogeniture: 'By the aristocratical law of primogenitureship, in a family of six children, five are exposed. Aristocracy never has more than *one* child. The rest are begotten to be devoured.' *The Rights of Man*, Pt. 1. (London: J. Johnson, 1791), 69.
[63] Watkins, 'Social Hierarchy,' 118.

of outward passivity belonging to his profession as monk, creating the outline of a figure who is denied true male activity.

IV. THE FEMALE VILLAIN

Women villains in the Gothic romance are accorded no sympathy for their conduct and their villainy, though necessarily covert, is effective. Male writers, in the texts considered, have included few female villains in their plot, and those who do appear are almost invariably characterised by some religious or super-natural connection.[64] Matthew Lewis, for example, crammed *The Monk* with an exceptional number of female villains with supernatural or religious overtones. Most obviously, Matilda, who seduces Ambrosio, and assists him with her magic powers in his lust for Antonia, is finally revealed to be a demon, but the other female villains, like Baroness Lindenburg and the Abbess of the Convent of St. Clare in Madrid are also associated with the supernatural. George Walker only introduced one female villain into *The Three Spaniards* – a sorceress and a 'picture of corrupted death' – who plays a minor part in the development of the plot.[65] Beckford also created a stony-hearted sorceress, the mother of Vathek, to demonstrate the cruelty that dominates his fictional oriental world.[66] It seems that male writers of the Gothic romance have tended to reflect unquestioningly a patriarchal society in which it is inconceivable that women should wield sufficient social power to act as a villain, unless possessed of some additional superhuman powers.

In surrendering himself to vice, villainy, and Matilda's guidance, Ambrosio is feminised and, as Matilda gains in ascendancy, her character becomes more markedly masculine:

---

[64] Although Percy Shelley's Matilda di Laurentini (*Zastrozzi*, 1810) is not associated explicitly with the supernatural in the text, he based both his plot and her character on *Zofloya* (1806) – the work of a female writer.

[65] Walker, *Three Spaniards*, ii. 153.

[66] William Beckford, *Vathek* (1786; rep. from corrected 3rd. ed. 1816, Oxford: Oxford University Press, ed. and intro. Roger Lonsdale, 1983).

But a few days had past, since She appeared the mildest and softest of her sex, devoted to his will, and looking up to him as to a superior Being. Now She assumed a sort of courage and manliness in her manners and discourse but ill calculated to please him. She spoke no longer to insinuate, but command: He found himself unable to cope with her in argument, and was unwillingly obliged to confess the superiority of her judgement.[67]

Connecting the female villain with supernatural powers may reflect more than patriarchal assumptions about power. It might also suggest a degree of masculine fear about female power, particularly when associated with female sexuality.[68] Female sexuality itself acquires both a supernatural and socially disruptive force – particularly in novels like *The Monk* in which Ambrosio's spiritual decay is rooted in sexual temptation. In this context note that all of the male writers quoted (with the exception of George Walker) were in their late teens and early twenties when they wrote their romances, and were young enough to have absorbed the social assumptions of their society without questioning them through experience. Also note that at least two of the writers mentioned, Beckford and Lewis, were overtly homosexual and may have found demonstrations of female sexuality distasteful.

In striking contrast, female romancers almost invariably include a female villain (Clara Reeve is the only exception to this rule) and the *raison d'être* of these villains is never supernatural. In the majority of cases, the female villain is a secondary character assisting in the destruction of the heroine's happiness and in isolating her from society, while the major movement of villainy – an active physical assault – is undertaken by the male villain. Like the male villain, female villains in tales created by women are recognisable and defined by their treatment of other women. The Marchesa's villainy (*The Italian*) is made apparent through her plots to destroy Ellena's happiness. Megalena Strozzi (*Zofloya*) is branded as a villain when she stabs her innocent rival, Julia. Mrs. Hood (*The Mysterious*

---

[67] Lewis, *Monk*, 231-2.
[68] Cf. Nina da Vinci Nichols, 'Place and Eros in Radcliffe, Lewis and Brontë,' in Fleenor (ed.), *The Female Gothic*, 192.

Visit) lusts after Sir William Symons and aids him in his attempts to seduce Georgina's mind and body. Lady Greystoke (*The Children of the Abbey*) is initially presented as a shrewd, discerning woman in striking contrast to the pettiness of Irish provincial society. She too, however, is selfish, easily turned towards villainy through her desire to marry Lord Cherbury, and assists in the destruction of Amanda's reputation and happiness. Female villains created by female writers owe nothing to the supernatural but everything to passion.

Female authors seem to perceive female villainy as an assault on feminine integrity and the attempted destruction – whether in the heroine or within themselves – of conventionally acceptable feminine sexuality. Appollonia Zulmer (*The Passions*) is a primary character within the tale, a figure of towering and overpowering evil:

> I will not stand alone, I will pull down others to grovel with me in the abyss of misery and sin. Like a malignant fiend--the knowledge that I am myself the uttermost boundary of evil, that there is none beyond me, renders me outrageous and confirms my malice.[69]

Through the character of the wicked Countess, Mrs. Roche made an explicit connection between the woman and the role of the villain. In the letters exchanged between Appollonia Zulmer and her governess, the writer explores the underlying passion and contempt of the apparently passive woman:

> Oh! Men; ye lordly despots, what mere machines are you in the hands of those ye affect to govern; on what do ye ground your pretensions, for are ye not in reality our tools? ... So should it be--*man* must believe himself invested with sovereign power, *woman* only should possess it.[70]

A belief in the superior manipulative skill and clearer perception of women, with a corresponding contempt for the complacent blindness of men, is glaringly apparent. An overwhelming belief in his/her superior judgement is, however, characteristic of a villain, as is the ability to manipulate covertly the passions of

---

[69] Roche, *The Passions*, ii. 229. Countess Zulmer is also establishing herself in the role of archetypal rebel, cf. Milton, *Paradise Lost* IV, 73-5.
[70] *Ibid* i. 55-6.

others. As Appollonia Zulmer gradually gains an ascendancy over Julia's mind, Regina Maria Roche also showed the reader the skill with which her female villain manipulated the common bond between women. The Countess begins her campaign by making woman to woman jokes at the expense of man's understanding:

> In vain may the most brilliant genius, the most polished understanding, the most sensible and delicate soul, exist beneath an unattractive exterior; no man will *discern* it--no man will *love*.[71]

The Countess persuades through half-truths couched in negative terms, asserting that no man will discover the perfect soul if it is trapped in an ugly body and the grain of underlying truth, which makes her statement easier to accept, is that men do notice and are attracted by beautiful women. Regina Roche's skill, and the skill of her villain, is to present one idea, evoke another, and to suggest that the partial truth of one substantiates the other. Julia's reaction to this womanly banter – the Countess continues by stating that men hate women who possess superior intellects and, unlike women, are incapable of friendship – is laughter and complicity. She is allying herself with Appollonia in a woman-woman bond, which later she does not want to break by showing the letters to her husband. Woman, in this tale, is the most perfect and successful villain figure conceivable, as her position and influence over the heroine (within this female sisterhood) is much stronger than that of any potential male villain.

Female writers frequently polarised their fictional worlds into male and female spheres, according to a plan that male writers did not seem to recognise. A male writer located his heroine in a world in which friendship or support between women is assumed, but is never questioned and is rarely active. Women in distress do cling to each other, like the female inmates of *The Castle of Otranto*, but Isabella flees alone. Female writers, however, make the reader aware of a network of sympathetic relations existing between women allied against men. This is very

---

[71] *Ibid* ii. 14.

clearly represented by Charlotte Smith in *Emmeline* in which the major female characters (Emmeline, Mrs. Stafford, Augusta and Adelina) are allied in mutual protection against the male world of impetuous action, business and double-dealing represented by Delamere, Sr.Richard Crofts and Lord Montreville. Appollonia Zulmer's arguments in *The Passions* make both this female allegiance and the potential devastation of its disruption or perversion clear. Intimate knowledge of supportive female relations is apparent in most Gothic romances written by women, presupposing a similar knowledge of their betrayal. This may explain the difference in representation and frequency of occurrence of the female villain figure in romances written by men or by women.

Some female villain figures appear in both male and female-authored romances. The Abbess makes a convenient villain for both male and female writers, as the titular head of an enclosed and exclusively female world depicted as a sink of passions, 'the last retreat of disappointed women.'[72] As the head of this enclosed world, she is invariably represented as a woman of strong and disappointed passions, as 'severe and violent' as any villain whilst remaining 'a Woman of a violent and revengeful character, capable of proceeding to the greatest extremities.'[73] As the female counterpart of the Wicked Monk, the Abbess is described and treated in almost the same way by both male and female writers, although she is never socially disadvantaged – as an aristocratic woman her social disadvantage is an automatic part of her sex.

Queen Elizabeth I, in a position of supreme social power, is also used, rather surprisingly given her solid Protestant background and successful reign, as a convenient villain figure by men and women authors alike. She suffers from the clash of two different stereotypes: popular conceptions of the Elizabethan period, as a Golden Age of English expansion and trade presided over by a successful and astute monarch outwitting the predatory Catholic kings of Europe, conflict with

---

[72] Lee, *Recess*, ii. 111.
[73] Radcliffe, *Italian*, 121, and Lewis, *Monk*, 190.

popular conceptions of ideal womanhood. In the works of both eighteenth-century conduct writers and historical romancers, therefore, she is praised for her understanding and statesmanship whilst criticised for her lack of essential femininity. The Gothic romancers, whether male or female, represented this symbol of female power as both disturbing and unrestrained:

> although possessed of a solid and refined judgment, [she] had a foible ... with her it was a sin, in those whom she permitted about her person, and those with her were intimates, for confidants she had none, to arrogate to themselves the slightest degree of that authority which she considered, and was resolved to maintain, hers alone and indivisibly.[74]

Both Sophia Lee and Francis Lathom presented the same picture of Elizabeth I: a woman of masculine understanding, possessed of absolute power that corrupted her femininity, and both portray her using the role and power of Queen to ensure the continuance of her self-image as a desirable woman. The writers tended to 'feminise' all of Elizabeth's actions and motives, even when those actions might have been politically motivated. For example, despite the threat posed by her Catholicism, Mary Queen of Scots is consistently represented as a patient and beautiful victim of Elizabeth's feminine envy rather than as a political opponent or symbol of dangerous religious views.

V. THE END OF THE VILLAIN

Finally, the Gothic villain must be removed from the plot. Having been depicted as a malignant force of such potency that only his (or her) removal is sufficient to guarantee a stable society and continued happiness for the hero and heroine, the self-obsessed villain is destroyed. Not all villains are killed, however, female villains and some petty villains, with their circumscribed social spheres and limited capacity for damage, are permitted to live, punished only by the crushing disappointment of their plans. Appollonia Zulmer is an exception who is

---

[74] Lathom, *Mysterious Freebooter*, i. 44-5.

removed from the scene, unrepentant, in a fatal carriage accident. Victoria (*Zofloya*) shares the same fate as Ambrosio: both cheat the Inquisition through diabolical means and both are cast down from a great height in physical and spiritual torment. Most male villains, killed at the end of the tale, are unrepentant and still dangerous. Those hardy types who faced the terrors of the Inquisition without flinching, commit suicide or are executed. Schedoni dies unrepentant, rejoicing in having killed his accuser; Don Pedro (*The Three Spaniards*) dramatically stabs himself over his daughter's corpse; and Gondez, in W.H. Ireland's typically exuberant style, is privately burnt to death once his crimes have been revealed. Sir William Symons undergoes bouts of transitory remorse but, when his villainy is finally revealed through the ignominy of a servant's testimony, he slits his veins with a shard from an ink bottle. Few male villains who are primary characters are permitted to live, those who do are retired, crushed by guilt and the consciousness of their crimes. Manfred, for example, retires to a nearby religious house, having destroyed his family and given up his hopes of dynastic power.

Close examination of the villain figure in the Gothic romance reveals that, unlike the type characters of the absent father or the active hero, a linear development does exist and may be traced through the sublime 'grand villains' who can be found in the well-known peaks of Gothic writing. This development appears to be located in the increasing association between the villain and women who are menaced by the figure's machinations. There are also, however, unconditionally evil villains who do not undergo any psychological development, and who are neither accorded nor invite the sympathy of the reader. They are not sublime and many of them are women.

7

The Victim

Alongside every dark-visaged villain in the Gothic romance there must always be a helpless victim. The victim is an integral part of the Gothic formula as a necessary emotional and moral standard by which to judge the behaviour of other characters objectively, and a means by which the plot may be furthered and readers' emotions heightened.[1] However, unlike other stock figures, the victim is not an identifiable stereotype but a dramatic role created by the exigencies of the plot. Heroes, fathers and villains can all be cast as victims but their characters will be diminished, only the heroine's status is augmented by her position as victim.

More than one type of victimisation was created by the formula of the Gothic romance. Characters are victimised 'directly' inside the text, but there is also a perceptible form of 'indirect' victimisation operating from outside. The victim described above, a figure conjoined to the villain, is an example of 'direct' victimisation. Within the text, characters are menaced, imprisoned, threatened to the point of death and sometimes killed by the machinations of other characters. 'Direct' victimisation within the text is not only obvious but is frequently articulated by the victims themselves. 'Indirect' victimisation occurs in the very formation of the character stereotype: characters are victimised, not by the author, but by the parameters for character delineation that are imposed by the formula of the Gothic romance and the expectations of the reader.[2] The hero must embody all the characteristics of the ideal man: the heroine is required to be the pattern of ideal femininity. These patterns, the outward manifestation of the code of morality un

---

[1] Although she focuses only on the sexual charge of the relationship between villain and victim in her consideration of the demon-lover motif, Toni Reed makes the same point about the necessity of the victim figure in *Demon-Lovers and Their Victims in British Fiction* (Lexington: University of Kentucky Press, 1988), 18.

[2] In the Introduction to *The Female Gothic*, Fleenor makes a similar point about the relationship between a literary form and social convention, 15.

derpinning the fabric of the Gothic romance, not only predispose certain character types towards 'direct' victimisation within the text but also prevent others from adopting that role. As women are more frequently cast as victims, did social stereotyping, which dictated the boundaries for male and female roles, become a form of 'indirect' victimisation operating outside the plot but influencing what went on within it?

Victim and villain are morally opposed yet physically close within the Gothic romance. The figure of the victim is, therefore, as familiar a stereotype as that of the villain, and the common conception of both is determined by gender. Certain physical characteristics were popularly associated with the person of the 'grand villain' and the foremost of those was his dominant, active masculinity. The victim was equally typecast in the popular imagination as passive, suffering and female. The description of Lilla (*Zofloya* 1806), beloved by the noble Henriques, bereft of his protection, and being carried up the side of an abyss to her death, typifies such a victim:

> ... her fragile form lay nerveless, her snow-white arms, bare nearly to the shoulder (for a thin nightdress alone covered her) hung down over the back of the Moor; her feet and legs resembling sculptured alabaster, were likewise bare, her languid head drooped insensible, while the long, flaxen tresses, escaping from the net which had enveloped them, now partly shaded her ashy cheek, and now streamed in dishevelled luxuriance on the breeze.[3]

Every element in this description suggests helplessness, purity and innocence. We are assured twice that Lilla is unconscious, effectively preventing a reader from projecting any sense of complicity or guilt onto her 'nerveless,' unresisting form. By rendering Lilla unconscious, Charlotte Dacre is also able to present her as a body at the mercy of the elements – unable even to control her own hair, which has developed an active life of its own, 'escaping from the net.' Everything that would normally be restrained, tied up or concealed is laid bare or loosed: hair, arms, legs, feet and the hint of a body under a thin nightdress, yet Charlotte Dacre

---

[3] Dacre, *Zofloya*, iii. 33.

avoids an overtly erotic representation by describing Lilla in shades of white and in terms of statuary. She might, from the description, be a corpse already. The whiteness assures the reader of Lilla's purity, her unconsciousness guarantees her innocence and lack of responsibility, while her 'fragile form' and drooping head invite sympathy through a direct contrast with the athletic darkness of the Moor. Her physical weakness and her passivity (taken to the extreme of unconsciousness) make her vulnerable, create a victim persona for her and yet, at other points in the text, are also emphasised as part of the attraction of her essential femininity. For Lilla's fragility and childishness are the qualities which have made the noble Henriques love her. He is not attracted by 'the masculine spirit of a Victoria,' characterised by activity and strength.[4]

Thus, one may see the process of victimisation operating in both the ways outlined. The reader is introduced to a state of 'direct' physical and emotional victimisation within the text engineered through actions taken by other, more dominant, characters: a victim of plot. The very stereotype itself, however, is a form of 'indirect' victimisation, from which both Lilla and Victoria suffer and which helps to form the plot structure. Just as Lilla's femininity, formed after the stereotype of perfect womanhood, is paradoxically both her justification as woman and destruction as victim, so too is Victoria victimised because she fails to fulfil the criteria for perfect femininity and there is no other axis along which she can be judged. Thus, although all characters are fictional constructs designed by the author, a process of victimisation is apparent in their representation. The reader is not led to interpret dominance and activity or passivity and suffering as characteristics applicable only to the specific role of villain or victim in a certain type of fiction, but as part of the ethos around which gender roles are constructed. Those women who fail to conform to the prevailing stereotype (Laurina, Megalena and Victoria in *Zofloya*) are 'indirectly' victimised by the expectations attendant on

---

[4] *Ibid* ii. 275.

that stereotype, and may thus be seen as victims of the formula and of the reader's expectations.[5]

This type of 'indirect' victimisation is not applicable only to the female stereotype of perfection. Men, too, are 'indirectly' victimised within the text, although rarely through the action of the plot, but like the women discussed above, male characters are victimised by the standards and pattern of behaviour created for them by social expectations. This is particularly true of those cast as potential hero figures, who have the double obligation of pursuing an active masculine role that will also fulfil the lofty moral expectations expressed by the heroine. Unsatisfactory heroes, like Delamere (*Emmeline*, 1788) and Lord Lymington (*The Mysterious Visit*, 1802) who, though fascinating, are unworthy of the heroine's love and are not rewarded with her hand in marriage, are 'indirectly' victimised by the inflexible standards ruling the Gothic hero. Through the plot, the stereotype of the hero is reinforced and the reader's expectations are confirmed and affirmed. Thus, the hero stereotype has influenced both character and plot development, predestining the fate of characters like Lymington and Delamere, and is thus a form of 'indirect victimisation.'

Many characters within the texts are described as 'destined' victims, implying that, in the society depicted in the Gothic romance, providence chooses the character predetermined for the role of victim. In most cases in which a character is described as a 'destined victim' an element of mock religious sacrifice is introduced into a situation redolent with thwarted sexuality.[6] This does not only apply to women. Appollonia Zulmer, for example, makes constant references to the fate

---

[5] For a similar argument (based on psychoanalytic methodology) which specifically treats the depiction of women, in Gothic novels written by women, as a recognition of trauma with its basis in the restrictions of contemporary social life – a position very close to 'indirect' victimisation, although Massé does not apply the same principles to male characters – see Michelle A. Massé, 'Gothic Repetitions.'

[6] Lewis uses 'destined victim' with a completely different effect in *The Monk*, 356, where the Abbess is described as the 'destined victim' of the enraged mob. In this instance, the coupling of destiny and victim intensifies the reader's sense of horror by predicting the Abbess' inevitable death. Like all victims, however, her death may be interpreted as a ritual of appeasement.

she intends for Weimar after he spurned her sophisticated advances and married a naïve girl from the mountains:

> Who then shall snatch from my brow the wreath which Nemesis bestows? Who shall rob my altar of its destined victim? My revenge has fed upon his ruin, it can be satiated only by giving him--death.[7]

Such an element of mock religious sacrifice occurs when a character within the text assumes the position of an agent of providence – only blood or death can appease thwarted sexuality. Thus, when characters within the text usurp the power of providence, 'destined' becomes synonymous with 'desired.'

The emphasis shifts, however, when providence itself works in the text bringing misfortune to selected victims through coincidence: 'destined' then becomes nearly synonymous with 'necessary.' The preface to *The Haunted Castle* (1794) indicates the place of suffering in the romance:

> The reader will, no doubt, discover, that the leading traits of this romance are, to shew [sic], that however mysterious the ways of providence may appear to us, who can view only the present, yet, that in the end they are productive of good; and by unforeseen ways, and apparent afflictions, bring about ends which would not otherwise have existed.[8]

George Walker presented a justification for suffering in this preface which goes far to explain why the victim is an integral part of the formula of the Gothic romance. 'Unforeseen ways and apparent afflictions' comprise, the preface suggests, necessary stages in the workings of providence towards a state of eventual 'good.' Thus the victim's duty is to suffer in order that 'good' may be attained, and responsibility for suffering is removed from the victim as all the action is predetermined. Suffering becomes part of the essential sacrifice made to ensure those 'ends which would not otherwise have existed.'

The restoration or establishment of an eventual 'good' through the actions of providence, however frightening and inexplicable, is what George Walker promised in his preface. Other authors justified the improbabilities of romance by

---

[7] Dacre, *Passions*, iv. 72.
[8] Walker, *Haunted Castle*, i. vi-vii.

stressing another heavily-pointed moral lesson commonly contained in the action of the plot: vice is displayed only to be despised, while candour, self-control and self-regulation according to religious or humane principles are consistently shown to be admirable and eventually rewarded:

> "Years of reflection in my horrid prison have convinced me of the danger, the folly, and the guilt of gratifying our passions at the expense of our integrity, or attempting to impose upon the world, by a system of hypocrisy, which leads progressively to the commission of the most abandoned vices"[9]

So says Clifford at the end of *The Mysterious Visit*, the absent 'good' father returned home after ten years (and two and a half volumes) incarceration in the Bastille. This dictum concerning the primary need for self-control and regulation of the passions has been demonstrated throughout via the effects of licence and vice practised by villains upon a series of innocent victims – first Clifford, then his unprotected, adopted daughter, Georgina.[10] Similarly, the narrator declaims in the penultimate paragraph of *The Mysteries of Udolpho* that: 'O! useful may it be to have shewn [sic], that, though the vicious can sometimes pour affliction upon the good, their power is transient and their punishment certain; and that innocence, though oppressed by injustice, shall, supported by patience, finally triumph over misfortune!'[11]

Superficially, there is a difference between Ann Radcliffe's assessment of the forces surrounding the potential victim, 'the vicious can sometimes pour affliction upon the good,' and George Walker's preface underlining the power (and indeed necessity) of a benevolent providence performing the same actions. However, the basic message – that the good must suffer – is the same, and the apparent

---

[9] Parsons, *Mysterious Visit*, iv. 270.

[10] Similar morals are promulgated at the conclusion of the majority of Gothic romances, e.g. Dacre: 'Dreadful is the war of the passions in the heart of man, and terrible are they in their might. Bestowed on him for his happiness, and to be retained in the subjection of his reason, they become the sources of his misery, when permitted to have sovereign sway.' *Passions*, iv. 233. Or the warning given by the unhappy Laurentini di Udolpho: '"Sister! beware of the first indulgence of the passions; beware of the first! Their course, if not checked then, is rapid--their force is uncontroulable [sic]--they lead us we know not whither--they lead perhaps to the commission of crimes, for which whole years of prayer and penitence cannot atone!"' Radcliffe, *Mysteries*, 646.

[11] Radcliffe, *Mysteries*, 672.

difference is explicable if one considers the place of the supernatural in *The Haunted Castle* and *The Mysteries of Udolpho* respectively. George Walker could allow the presence of an inexplicable, yet ultimately benevolent, providence because his romance is full of supernatural phenomena, but Ann Radcliffe was notorious for the way in which she rationalised and explained every apparently supernatural occurrence. Providence manifests itself only through coincidence in her romances and so the afflictions visited on the victim are presented simply as the work of malevolent human agency. Significantly, neither makes the victim responsible for his or her affliction, and innocence thus appears to be a prerequisite for one type of victim figure used as a device to point a moral lesson in the Gothic romance.

Some types of characters are uniquely qualified for the innocent victim's position by virtue of their social vulnerability. Children are the weakest, most vulnerable members of society and thus one might assume that the Gothic romancer would employ them as the most poignant of victims. For they can have no personal responsibility for acts done to them and no redress for or means of articulating their suffering; their helplessness is so acute that no excuse could be found for the villain who oppresses them. There are, however, very few child victims in Gothic romances, apart from William Frankenstein, who dies at the hands of the monster, and Agnes's putrefying baby (*The Monk*, 1796), because child victims suffer wordlessly. The Gothic writer, demonstrating that certain moral tenets triumph over affliction, can only use the child victim as an incidental feature. In *Frankenstein* (1818) the reader is led to identify with the suffering of the monster through the first-person narrative and, therefore, perceives the death of young William Frankenstein only as an indication of the monster's increasing rage and alienation.[12] A comment made by Mr. Weimar (*Castle of Wolfenbach*,

---

[12] William's death inspires great grief in the text but is a less sorrowful experience for the reader. For an extreme view of the reader's indifference, see Stephen King, *Danse Macabre* (1981; repr. London: Futura, 1988), 69-70.

1793), during his deathbed confession, may be usefully transferred to a consideration of victimisation in *Frankenstein*:

> "It [visible partiality bestowed on one child] lays a foundation for much fu-
> ture misery in the family; creates every vice which envy and malice can give
> birth to, and the darling object is generally the victim."[13]

One might interpret every murder victim in *Frankenstein* as the result of faulty
familial structure.[14] The death of young William, motivated by sibling rivalry,
suggests that the monster himself is, in a sense, an articulate child victim refusing
responsibility for his actions. The formula requires an innocent, helpless, yet articulate victim.

Only the heroine corresponds to all three of these requirements. Obviously, all women (save Queen Elizabeth I) are physically weaker and more vulnerable than any man. Society *per se* offers no protection to a woman, particularly
a young woman, who is dependent on the good offices of men. Equally, social
status offers no automatic barrier of respect to protect women against the unwelcome attentions of men. Women, therefore, make ideal victim figures. Thus, the
concept of a 'female Gothic' becomes tenable: initially, because the majority of
victims are women; and then because the word 'victim' is frequently used by female characters in the work of women writers, indicating a way in which women
are marginalised into passive victim figures – through language.

There is a particular and sometimes disturbing language of sacrifice, with
its roots firmly embedded in the popular stereotype of femininity, associated only
with women in the Gothic romances. Women are expected to embrace sacrifice,
which has more positive connotations than 'victim' as it suggests a difficult but
ultimately beneficent action of renunciation enjoined by a god, and self-denial, as
duties. In the following quotation, Amanda (*The Children of the Abbey*, 1796),
speaking of herself in the third person, stands over her mother's tomb:

---

[13] Parsons, *Castle of Wolfenbach*, ii. 154-5.
[14] George Levine also stresses the importance of the family structure in *Frankenstein* in
'*Frankenstein* and the Tradition of Realism,' *Novel* vii (1973), 24-5.

Oh! if she is doomed to tread a path as thorny as the one you trod, may the same sweetness and patience that distinguished you, support her through it: with the same pious awe, the same meek submission, may she bow to the designations of her Creator.[15]

Here we see the same assumptions apparent in George Walker's preface, that providence afflicts the innocent – one may be 'doomed to tread a thorny path' – and that suffering is part of a divine plan. The only valuable response possible, Roche suggested, for a woman dealing with suffering or oppression, is meek submission and patience, which applies not only to afflictions imposed by providence, but to all human relations:

"Well, Sir, (said Matilda, hastily) it is fit you should prefer your own happiness to mine, I have no right to refuse nor any way of discharging the obligations I owe you for the care of my early life, but by the sacrifice of the maturer part of it."[16]

Matilda is addressing her uncle, Mr. Weimar, and it is obvious that the social position of women dictates her self-sacrifice because she has no active option through which she can 'discharge the obligations' she owes. Significantly, Matilda has borrowed from the language of business and honour in order to express her sense of the indebtedness by which she is bound. Renunciation and self-denial are the only activities that the heroine is called upon to perform voluntarily, and this type of sacrifice is always praised by the narrator or by a character within the text.

Every occasion of female renunciation of happiness is valorised. Georgina (*The Mysterious Visit*) swears she would not marry Lord Lymington, '"if such an event would *give one pang to your heart*,"' and Madame Villeneuve is 'sensibly touched by this heroism.'[17] Charlotte Smith also showed the relationship between the discourse of sacrifice and the maintenance of the feminine stereotype, when Augusta Delamere (*Emmeline*) projected this language of sacrifice and heroism onto Emmeline, using it to interpret her behaviour:

---

[15] Roche, *Children of the Abbey*, i. 63.
[16] Parsons, *Castle of Wolfenbach*, i. 196-7.

> She [Augusta Delamere] was deeply read in novels, (almost the only reading that young women of fashion are taught to engage in;) and having from them acquired many of her ideas, she imagined that Delamere and Emmeline were born for each other; ...
>   She fancied that Emmeline could not be insensible to Delamere's love; she even believed she saw many symptoms of regard for him in her manner, and that she made the most heroic sacrifice of her love to her duty, when she resigned him: a sacrifice which heightened, almost to enthusiasm, the pity and esteem felt for her by Augusta Delamere.[18]

Obviously this type of sacrifice is intimately connected with a stereotypical struggle between love and duty, but Charlotte Smith also pointed clearly to the falsity of interpretation that restricts feminine behaviour to such a stereotype, a form of 'indirect' victimisation. The expectations of an experienced novel reader are present within the text as concrete social standards of female behaviour and projected, incorrectly, upon the figure of the heroine. It is clear from the tale that Emmeline, has not, in fact, made a heroic sacrifice: Delamere is impetuously passionate and the aggression of his love frightens Emmeline more than it thrills her. In their first tête à tête, in which Delamere surprises Emmeline while she is resting on a log after a walk, the pattern is set for all their subsequent encounters:

> Delamere, who was really captivated at the first, and who now thought her more beautiful than he had done in their former interviews, hesitated not to pour forth the most extravagant professions of admiration, in a style so unequivocal, that Emmeline, believing he meant to insult her, burst into a passion of tears, and besought him, in a tremulous and broken voice, not to be so cruel as to affront her, but to suffer her to return home.[19]

Delamere is also a victim of 'indirect' stereotyping here. Of fundamentally good character, he fails to behave like a conventional, considerate hero, while Emmeline behaves like a conventional victim; his display of aggressive love reduces her to a state of trembling terror. She is similarly afflicted later the same night when Delamere bursts into her room and her terror initially robs her of any active or rational faculty: 'Emmeline was infinitely too much terrified to speak: nor

---

[17] Parsons, *Mysterious Visit*, iv. 77-8.
[18] Smith, *Emmeline*, 71.
[19] *Ibid* 23.

could her trembling limbs support her.'[20] Charlotte Smith depicted her heroine as a quivering object bereft of all kinetic energy. Faced with overt aggression, women in the Gothic romances commonly intensify their femininity: "'But I am in the grasp of the lion," she said to herself, "and I must try, by gentleness, to disengage myself from it.'"[21] The very qualities of the feminine stereotype keep the heroine in a victim's position, a position that is, to some extent, valorised through the promotion of self-sacrifice.[22] Self-sacrifice and patient submission are continuously promoted as the essence of attractive femininity, rather than an adjunct to it: 'the soft dejection of her manner, and the patient sweetness with which she bore her situation, soon gained a complete conquest over his heart.'[23]

Men are rarely placed in the position of victim. There are a few occasions in which a male character is victimised within the text. Edmund in *The Old English Baron* (1778) and Edward in *The Mysterious Freebooter* (1806) are both young, socially disadvantaged victims of the villain. Edmund is the only victim in *The Old English Baron* and, although he is forced away from his home, he is able to salve his honour and assert his position by means of active soldiership. No tensions are raised by Edmund's victimisation because he can actively prove his worth. Most of the tension or menace within Clara Reeves' story is introduced through fleeting supernatural manifestations. Edward (*The Mysterious Freebooter*) is placed in a different position; although betrayed into a foreign prison by the agency of the evil Rufus de Magincourt (alias the freebooter, Allanrod) who proves, eventually, to be Edward's father, he is not the only victim figure. His incarceration is an important part of the plot but the reader's anxieties are focused

---

[20] *Ibid* 32.

[21] Roche, *Clermont*, iv. 177. The description of Mary Queen of Scots confirms that submission is the only defence for the beleaguered woman: 'Amid all these fears and mortifications, submission was Mary's only measure. She had learnt, young as she was, to submit with dignity, and demand a degree of generosity, by not seeming to doubt of finding it.' Lee, *Recess*, i. 50.

[22] Mary Brunton's novels, *Self Control* (1810) and *Discipline* (1815) both present this type of self-sacrifice as the female response/interpretation of Christianity, showing that the social assumptions about role underpinning the Gothic formula are often shared with those found in other contemporary fiction.

[23] Roche, *Clermont*, ii. 37.

on his wife, Rosalind. Abandoned (however unwillingly) by her husband, bereft of her baby and her father's love, imprisoned for long periods twice within the tale, and threatened with an enforced bigamous marriage, she embodies vulnerability. The plight of the male victim within the Gothic romance never includes that element of total vulnerability: men can always fight to defend their honour and to reject the status of victim. When unable to fight, the active man can be temporarily as oppressed by affliction as a passive heroine. In Leland's *Longsword* (1762) for example, the following passage indicates a relationship between the consciousness of affliction and the consciousness of the victim. William reflects on his rescue: "'No longer the helpless victim of fell revenge, no longer crouching under the ruthless arm of a ruffian, I felt my afflictions no more.'"[24] The difference between William's consciousness of victimisation and that of the heroine is that Leland allows William to articulate and recognise his status as victim *after* his situation had changed and he was once more a free man.

Oscar (*The Children of the Abbey*) is one of the very few men who are represented as applying a code of sacrifice, similar to that of the 'female Gothic' to their own lives. Trapped by the stereotype of hero, Oscar is unable to retract a promise honourably given, though dishonourably extorted: 'after his fatal promise … a self-devoted victim.'[25] In the same text, however, Mrs. Roche also demonstrated that when most male characters in the Gothic romance refer to 'sacrifice' in the context of their own relationships with women, the concept of sacrifice is denigrated. Lord Cherbury, for example, is represented as taking a moral standpoint early in the tale: "'I can make no allowance for a deviation from integrity, or for a sacrifice of honour and gratitude at the shrine of interest.'"[26] Although Cherbury is a benevolent father and patron, the sacrifice he asks of Amanda is precisely that which he has already condemned. Thus, Regina Maria Roche ironically underlined the double standards applied by male characters: a pillar of society, a

---

[24] Leland, *Longsword*, i. 62.
[25] Roche, *Children of the Abbey*, i. 209.
[26] *Ibid* ii. 216.

hero and a villain figure all behave as though sacrifice is an action undertaken by others. The hero, Lord Mortimer, and the villain, Colonel Belgrave, are linked in a selfish attitude, which pays no attention to a woman's feelings when the gratification of their desires is at stake. 'A trifling sacrifice' is how Mortimer refers to a clandestine marriage and Belgrave to the action of becoming his mistress. In both instances, a woman is being asked to flout all social conventions for the sake of love.

The action of the Gothic romance and other contemporary fiction supports the idea that society is prepared to tolerate a different sort of behaviour from men by virtue of their activity. Many libertines are at large in society which condemns but partially condones their actions as the result of impetuous passion, whereas the objects of that passion are forced from society and undergo great physical and emotional suffering. Fitz-Edward (*Emmeline*) is such a man, redeemed only by the love and essential purity of his victim, Lady Adelina Trelawny, who descends into the depths of melancholy madness, fever and near-death.

Few men in Gothic fiction are permitted such a fate. They are restricted by the masculine stereotype of activity that rarely allows them to occupy the place of the victim. Responsibility for action, in that case, cannot be evaded. Thus, when a man is described, like Oscar, as a 'victim,' the author signals to the reader, indicating innocence and, in this case, impotence. Delamere is also posthumously described as a victim: 'She considered him as the victim of his mother's fatal fondness and his father's ambition.'[27] However, this does not indicate culpable passivity on Delamere's part but rather establishes his innocence and his lack of responsibility.

Most men violently repudiate the very idea of being cast as a victim. Even on his deathbed, Mr. Weimar rejected the passive role: '"I will not be the victim to procure happiness for others."'[28] This reaction is typical not only of an active

---

[27] Smith, *Emmeline*, 527.
[28] Parsons, *Castle of Wolfenbach*, ii. 152.

villain but also of an active man. A woman's reaction to adversity or threat in the Gothic romance is represented as an intensification of passive femininity; similarly, a man also reacts to adversity by intensifying the stereotype. Weimar's anguished reaction (*The Passions*, 1811) to Julia's letter shows both shame and rage at having been placed in a passive role:

> [She]--dared to tell me that I had been her tool, her puppet--the wretch on whom she had practised at pleasure, her powers of damned deception. ... I was as a wounded lion, raging and terrible in my anguish.[29]

Significantly, perhaps, Charlotte Dacre did not permit Weimar to call himself a victim, but the ideas expressed in this quotation are all passive – a 'tool,' a 'puppet,' and a dupe clearly suggest victimisation. Weimar's physical reaction is also significant: no attempt at rational self-control is described. Instead he rages like 'a wounded lion,' an intensification of thwarted activity very unlike the wasting illness exhibited by the wife of the other guilty party. The stereotype of masculinity, in which honour is mingled with activity, dictates his behaviour. Similarly, in *The Mysterious Visit* there is a description of the masculine character that links both essential activity and a lack of rational intelligence:

> "--Men, I fear, are too like restive horses, proud of their power and strength, they resist opposition and coercive treatment; but a little gentle stroking, a few coaxing manoeuvres rarely fail of producing the desired effect both on man and beast."[30]

Spoken by a benevolent doctor, this is a jocular comment on the obstinacy of men, whose intelligence, it is suggested, is on a par with that of a brute beast and can be managed as easily. However, the comment also implies that men are bound by their constitutional masculinity, their stereotype of superior 'power and strength' and that this 'pride' dominates their reactions, making them easier to control. The female stereotype is also present as a superior, manipulating intelligence whose 'gentle stroking' produces 'the desired effect.' Again the efficacy of

---

[29] Dacre, *Passions*, iv. 5-6.
[30] Parsons, *Mysterious Visit*, iv. 59-60.

the stereotype of ideal femininity is reiterated but the threat of brute violence is always present.

The stereotype of femininity lends itself to the depiction of the victim. Popular impressions are correct, the victim figure is usually a woman, who responds to aggression by intensifying her passivity and reinforcing the stereotype.[31] Note, however, that women writers represent their heroines as *aware* of their position as victim. Women within the text of the Gothic romances frequently declare themselves to be victims of male aggression: "'…is it me, the helpless child of sorrow, Lord Mortimer sought as a victim to illicit love!'"[32] The narratives do not just represent and repeat a traumatic situation but articulate a conscious experience. If a 'female Gothic' may be said to exist, it exists in the consciousness of these victim figures, these heroines who are prepared to assert their status as victims, denying responsibility, conscious of oppression and conscious, also, of innocence.

The victim figure in the formula of the Gothic romance is essential in the formation of the subject. Definitions of stereotyped self are constructed around the victim figure; women intensify their passivity, and men further demonstrate their activity. The figure or role of victim thus acts as a catalyst on all the male characters, emphasising and strengthening their masculine activity. 'Direct' victimisation forces the male to display his masculinity by escaping from the victim's role. 'Indirect' victimisation, caused by the imposition of the active male stereotype, ensures that no primary male character in the Gothic romance can evade action or responsibility: though they may be victimised, men cannot be victims.

---

[31] Cf. Massé, 'Gothic Repetitions,' 693.
[32] Roche, *Children of the Abbey*, i. 132.

8

A Miscellany of Men

Men are part of the landscape. Not only are the majority of characters represented in the Gothic romance male but male characters also perform the same function within the Gothic formula as landscape. Indifference to scenery marks the villain as surely as sensibility towards it marks the sympathetic hero: reactions towards landscape indicate character and role. Minor male characters in the Gothic romance are similarly used as devices by which major characters or plot situations may be revealed and measured.

Both landscape and the minor male characters are ancillary devices, confirming the expectations of the reader and validating the emotional perceptions of the heroine, whose judgements are not confined to the threatening or adoring figure of the primary male characters. Like the landscape, minor male characters are often filtered through the perception of the heroine to create an appropriate emotional ambience for the relationship between heroine and villain, or, occasionally, heroine and hero. Montoni's condottori (*Mysteries of Udolpho*, 1794), for example, are perceived *en masse* and at length entirely through Emily's eyes:

> a large party of horsemen, dressed in a singular, but uniform, habit, and completely, though variously, armed. They wore a kind of short jacket, composed of black and scarlet, and several of them had a cloak, of plain black, which, covering the person entirely, hung down to the stirrups. As one of these cloaks glanced aside, she saw, beneath, daggers, apparently of different sizes, tucked into the horseman's belt. She further observed, that these were carried, in the same manner, by many of the horsemen without cloaks, most of whom bore also pikes, or javelins. On their heads, were the small Italian caps, some of which were distinguished by black feathers. Whether these caps gave a fierce air to the countenance, or that the countenances they surmounted had naturally such an appearance, Emily thought she had never, till then, seen an assemblage of faces so savage and terrific. While she gazed, she almost fancied herself surrounded by banditti; and a vague thought glanced athwart her

fancy--that Montoni was the captain of the group before her, and that this castle was to be the place of rendezvous.[1]

Mrs. Radcliffe returns the reader continually to the increasing detail of Emily's observation and the emotions that the scene arouses in her heroine. The passage moves to a climax as Emily first records detail in a painterly fashion and then interprets it in an emotional response. The verbs that Mrs. Radcliffe uses to refer the reader back to Emily as the focal point also indicate a progression in the way in which Emily 'reads' the scene before her. Initially, she 'saw' parti-coloured details of clothing and black cloaks. Daggers of various sizes trigger another level of response: instead of simply recording general impressions of the mass as she has been doing, she makes a deliberate comparison between band members, 'she further observed.' These mounting observations create an atmosphere of threat from sartorial detail: the caps surmounted by black feathers cast a sinister shadow whereas the black and red jackets indicated only some kind of martial uniform. Instead of concentrating on the facts of the scene outside, Emily internalises the scene and begins to interpret it, 'an assemblage of faces so savage and terrific,' leads her to the conclusion that 'she almost fancied herself surrounded by banditti.' She is not 'observing' – with the detachment and clarity that the verb implies – any longer and this is reflected in 'she gazed.' Thus Mrs. Radcliffe moves her heroine from sight to acute observation to a fixed stare that covers considerable internal agitation. The climax of the passage coincides with internal reflection rather than the sight that occasioned it. Equally significantly, the climax of the passage is not the concept of the 'banditti' but the revelation that Montoni must be their captain and the castle their rendezvous.

The men represented are not significant in their own right as characters. All the menace built up through their description is transferred to Montoni at the climax, which coincides with Emily's awakened sensation of personal fear. He is the epitome of the threatening male although he takes no part in the following

---

[1] Radcliffe, *Mysteries*, 301-2.

raid. The representation of this armed band and Emily's reaction to it is used in several ways. First, this massed group of ferocious males creates a sensation of disquiet in the heroine through whom the reader views the scene – they form part of the emotional landscape of fear. Second, the sensation of disquiet generated by the condottori is focused and projected onto the figure of their putative leader, Montoni. Similar reflections may be applied to any group of minor male characters, who, whether banditti, monks, members of the Inquisition, servants or demons, are only important as part of the landscape, and as a suitable background for the primary figures.

I. BANDITS AND BRIGANDS

Gothic authors consistently used Bandits and Brigands as part of the landscape, yet the idea of the bandit and the outlaw gang is peculiarly suited to the Gothic romance and might have been exploited very differently.

So much of the Gothic formula revolves around a suspension of 'normal' life and laws that banditti would appear to be ideal devices. Situated outside the law, existing as part of the untamed, sublime wilderness, the bandit lair might have been used as a fantastic but credible location for romance like the feudal castle or the enclosed monastery. However, there are very few actual brigands in Gothic fiction even though banditti are popularly associated with the Gothic romance and Mario Praz somewhat misleadingly leads the reader to believe that they abound in Gothic tales.[2] Interestingly, he describes the bandit as one who 'inhabits the picturesque, Gothicized backgrounds,' implying a stage of development beyond that of 'decorative detail,' but, by locating the bandit figure in the background of the picture, he suggests that the bandit is not the focus of the action. Also, the fact that the figure inhabits this picturesque background suggests

---

[2] Praz asserts that Ann Radcliffe brought banditti to life. See *Romantic Agony*, 78.

some appropriate balance between background and figure based on a shared quality of the 'picturesque' – landscape and bandit are indivisible.[3]

The association between the bandit and the landscape he inhabits is not a simple one. The image of the carefree, daring, savage bandit, in perfect accord with dangerous surroundings and sublime landscape, depends on the author's use of sensitive, external perception. Filtered through the emotions of the heroine (or another sensitive character) and seen as part of the landscape, the bandit gang might indeed acquire some of the characteristics of the scenery they inhabit. The dominant characteristic of the bandit gang as described by a third-person narrator, however, is not carefree, not 'compellingly free from law and from conventional ethics,' which Marilyn Butler suggests was one of the bases for its popular appeal, but despairing.[4]

Comparing two different descriptions of inaccessible landscapes suitable for banditti illuminates this difference in representation. First Ann Radcliffe, who made a near-anachronistic reference to Salvator Rosa, binding landscape, painting and banditti firmly together:

> The scene of barrenness was here and there interrupted by the spreading branches of the larch and cedar, which threw their gloom over the cliff, or athwart the torrent that rolled in the vale. No living creature appeared, except the izard [sic], scrambling among the rocks, and often hanging upon points so dangerous, that fancy shrunk from the view of them. This was such a scene as *Salvator* would have chosen, had he then existed, for his canvas; St. Aubert, impressed by the romantic character of the place, almost expected to see banditti start from behind some projecting rock.[5]

Despite the stress given in the description to the absence of living things, the idea of the banditti is evoked by the picturesque nature of the landscape, and intensi-

---

[3] The picturesque does bond landscape and banditti in a particular way for Ann Radcliffe as her coupling of banditti, landscape and Salvator Rosa demonstrates. For a discussion on Ann Radcliffe and the picturesque novel see, Christopher Hussey, *The Picturesque* (1927; repr. London: Cass, 1967), 231-7. For a further discussion on the effects of Italian landscape painting on the eighteenth-century novel see Elizabeth Wheeler Manwaring, *Italian Landscape in Eighteenth Century England: A Study Chiefly of the Influence of Claude Lorrain and Salvator Rosa on English Taste 1700-1800* (1925; repr. London: Cass, 1965), 201-26.

[4] Butler, *Romantics, Rebels and Reactionaries*, 2.

[5] Radcliffe, *Mysteries*, 30.

fies its life-threatening effect. They do not appear but the expectations of the cultivated St. Aubert indicate that in such a landscape they might be expected to do so. Radcliffe also indicated the way in which such a scene should be appreciated. Although the scene is one of desolation, barrenness and gloom, St. Aubert perceives it picturesquely, as a scene that might be painted, and interprets it accordingly. Despite the fact that *The Mysteries of Udolpho* is supposedly set in the late sixteenth century, St. Aubert applies eighteenth-century attitudes to the scene on which he gazes: he is an observer who does not place himself or his party in the composition of the picture, which has a 'romantic character.'

In contrast, Shelley's description of a bandit lair in *St. Irvyne* (1811) offered a representation of landscape and banditry that could not be interpreted as romantically attractive, although it too is set in a barren landscape:

> Around their dwellings, lofty inaccessible acclivities reared their barren summits; they echoed to no sound save the wild hoot of the night-raven, or the impatient yelling of the vulture, which hovered on the blast in quest of scanty sustenance. These were the scenes without; noisy revelry and tumultuous riot reigned within. The mirth of the bandits appeared to arise independently of themselves; their hearts were void and dreary.[6]

Like Ann Radcliffe, Shelley began with the barren 'lofty inaccessible acclivities,' the mountainous landscape, and then narrowed his focus to the human dimension, moving from the bandit dwellings, to the scenes within, and finally to the hearts of the bandits themselves. Both authors similarly equate banditti and landscape, but the effect of Shelley's somewhat clichéd description is different to Ann Radcliffe's. The keynote of his passage is one of sterility rather than romantic excitement. Images of sterility and death abound, from the barrenness of the mountain peaks, to the hungry vulture hovering 'on the blast.' Shelley appears to set up a contrast between landscape and bandits by deliberately shifting from 'the scenes without' to within, from natural landscape in which the only sounds are the shriekings of birds of prey and the whistling wind to a noisy man-made interior.

---

[6] Shelley, *St. Irvyne*, 113.

Obviously, this is no true contrast because there are vultures inside and out. Shelley's emphasis, unlike that of Mrs. Radcliffe, is on the men's despair, and this is highlighted by the inhospitable environment, indicating that Shelley is going to use the bandit gang as an amplifying device for the despair and corruption of his villain-hero, Wolfstein. Both Radcliffe and Shelley use the banditti in conjunction with the landscape to create a specific physical and emotional background for the action of the plot.

The sense of despair evident in Shelley's bandits, whose 'hearts were void and dreary' is typical not only of the representation of the bandit but of the way conventional moral codes are reinforced. A familial group headed by the father in a rural society is the ideal to which all heroes and heroines aspire and which they eventually attain. The bandit, the outlaw, however, is permanently in exile outside society and can never return to it. All the qualities that would be noble and acceptable within a legal, social framework (e.g. loyalty and courage) are ignoble and doomed because the bandits have placed themselves outside and in opposition to the law. Consequently bandits are described as despairing men, as hollow as the caverns which they inhabit:

> Looking down into the abyss [the entrance to the bandit lair] I was struck with an obscure idea of the bottomless gulph of hell, from whence there is no redemption to be expected.[7]

Few reasons are given in the Gothic romance for the presence of banditti in mountains or forests. Lewis gave an explanation in *The Monk* (1796):

> His excesses drew upon him the indignation of the Police. He was obliged to fly from Strasbourg, and saw no other resource from beggary, than an union with the Banditti, who infested the neighbouring Forest, and whose Troop was chiefly composed of Young men of family in the same predicament with himself.[8]

This forms part of Marguerite's story, the tale of her lover who involved her with the 'misery inseparable from a life of pillage.' It appears to have been a socially

---

[7] Lorenz Flammenberg, *The Necromancer: or the Tale of the Black Forest*, 2 vols. trans. Peter Teuthold, (1794; repr. from 1st. ed. London: Skoob, 1989), 226.

impeccable bandit Troop, 'chiefly composed of Young men of family,' but this is unusual. The gang members described by Charlotte Dacre, Percy Shelley, and Ann Radcliffe are rarely the same social class as the bandit chief: nobility (which is both innate and genealogical) is often the source of his dominance. Banditry is advanced here as the only possible source of income for the wealthy young man rendered penniless, suggesting that there was nothing else available to the noble spendthrift. Rather than passively begging, the once-wealthy young man chooses to become a bandit preying on the society that did not sustain him.[9] A similar resentment against society is expressed by Wolf (*The Necromancer*, 1794): "'I never should have become a robber, had not the too great severity of the laws made me an enemy to the human race, and hurried me to the brink of black despair.'"[10] Shelley's banditti, too, demand to know why they should show mercy when society has:

> "compelled many of our noble fellows, who otherwise would have been ornaments to their country in peace, thunderbolts to their enemies in war, to seek precarious subsistence as Alpine bandits?"[11]

Although the bandit denies responsibility for becoming an outlaw, by suggesting that many have been 'compelled,' this is neither an admirable or justifiable defence according to the conventions of the Gothic romance. Furthermore, his claim to be in the company of 'noble fellows' is refuted when Wolfstein gains status amongst the band because he is conspicuously 'high-souled and noble.'[12] Nevertheless, this outburst is important because it creates a suitable emotional background for his hero-villain. The sense of grievance against society, of hopelessness and the daring that is a consequence of it, conveyed by the quota-

---

[8] Lewis, *Monk*, 122.

[9] Cf. Ugo's comment, which also seems to indicate that the outlaw uses the stereotype of masculine activity to justify his actions: "'This is the way to have justice done at once, without more ado. If you go to law, you must stay till the judges please, and may lose your cause, at last. Why the best way, then, is to make sure of your right, while you can, and execute justice yourself.'" Radcliffe, *Mysteries*, 404.

[10] Flammenberg, *Necromancer*, 212.

[11] Shelley, *St. Irvyne*, 111.

[12] *Ibid* 113.

tion, supplies a perfect landscape, against which Wolfstein's character will be illuminated and augmented.

The bandits themselves are of no consequence except for their reaction to Wolfstein and the effect which their company has upon his character:

> In a short space of time the high-souled and noble Wolfstein, though still high-souled and noble, became an experienced bandit. His magnanimity and courage, even whilst surrounded by the most threatening dangers, and unappalled expression of countenance with which he defied the dart of death, endeared him to the robbers; whilst with him they felt, as it were, instinctively impelled to deeds of horror and danger, which, otherwise, must have remained unattempted even by the boldest.[13]

Wolfstein's 'magnanimity and courage,' which distinguish a Gothic hero, are amplified and perverted by his contact with the banditti. Thus, by allowing Wolfstein to retain those essential qualities, Shelley reinforced the moral values of the romance formula whilst seeming to undermine them. The banditti respond to the stereotype of nobility and reflect the qualities of courage and daring, which Wolfstein displays, and these qualities are perceived as a positive force despite the 'deeds of horror and danger.' The reaction of the bandit gang is a device by which Wolfstein's potentially noble character is demonstrated and the perversion of his abilities made manifest.

The bandit chief rather than the band is the focus of attention, and is used to indicate how far a hero figure had fallen – from social to anti-social hero. This process begins when they associate themselves with the bandits in a state of self-confessed hopelessness, "'I have none,--no money--no hope--no friends; nor do I care for existence!'"[14] Anti-social despair is taken to its logical conclusion in the death of Leonardo, (*Zofloya*, 1806) who commits suicide, betrayed by a gang member. The anti-social action and perversion of the bandit chief is demonstrated by the fact that Leonardo, Wolfstein and Wolf all mark their descent towards banditry by murders:

---

[13] *Ibid* 113-14.
[14] *Ibid* 112.

"My doom was fixed, the time of repentance past, and the murder I had committed was towering behind me like a mountain shutting up for ever my return to the path of virtue."[15]

This marks a difference between the representation of the bandit and that of the monk: primary male characters become bandits through some personal choice, usually at the end of a tale, whereas the monk figure is confirmed in his role before the tale commences.

The bandit gang member displays none of the extraordinary characteristics associated with the hero – unless directly affected by him – and the dominant characteristics of ordinary banditti are cowardice and betrayal. Even the 'Troop' of noble young men described by Lewis collapsed when faced with strong military action:

> By their [the pursuing soldiers] account I found, that the Robbers had been overtaken: Guilt and true courage are incompatible; They had thrown themselves at the feet of their Pursuers, had surrendered themselves without striking a blow, had discovered their secret retreat, made known their signals by which the rest of the Gang might be seized, and in short had betrayed ever [sic] mark of cowardice and baseness.[16]

Although the bandit chief is never represented as cowardly, he does betray. Even the high-souled Wolfstein tries twice to murder his bandit chief by underhand means – poison in the goblet – in order to possess the beautiful Megalena. Betrayal (followed by murder) is the most common action performed by a bandit of any sort. Marguerite's consort, Baptiste, (*The Monk*) betrays his 'guests.' Lewis describes Baptiste through the eyes of Raymond:

> … whose appearance was calculated to inspire esteem and confidence. His countenance was open, sincere, and friendly; his manners had all the Peasant's honesty unaccompanied by his rudeness; His cheeks were broad, full, and ruddy; and in the solidity of his person He seemed to offer an ample apology for the leanness of his Wife.[17]

---

[15] Flammenberg, *Necromancer*, 226.
[16] Lewis, *Monk*, 121.
[17] *Ibid* 100.

Raymond's response is interesting because at this stage in the story he has neither met Agnes nor the Bleeding Nun, and is still young, untried, with a tendency to misread signals. In showing him as completely deceived by Baptiste's honest peasant persona, Lewis prepared the reader for Raymond's later misunderstandings with the Baroness Lindenburg and increased the shock of discovery. The banditti here are plot devices to introduce Raymond to the Baroness, and placing her under a debt of gratitude to him. They also reinforce the sense of danger lurking in the Gothic landscape, a perpetual insecurity outside the frontiers of society.

Closely associated with the landscape they inhabit, the banditti are part of the picturesque background of the world of the Gothic romance. Largely inferred from stray references, from the fears of major characters, or from the presence of the bandit chief, they provide not only a suitable pictorial but also an emotional accompaniment to the action. Wolf's unsuccessful petition to his prince (*The Necromancer*) in the closing pages of the narrative describe the bandit's position outside society as a negative life:

> "I detest life and do not fear to die, it would however be dreadful to me to die, without having lived. I wish to live, in order to repair my crimes past, and to make my peace with human society, which I have offended."[18]

The story thus concludes by stressing the importance of living within society. Wolf desires to turn from banditry to serve the state as a soldier. It is in this role that minor characters fulfil an important function within both plot and formula: the role of the faithful servant.

II. SERVANTS

Although on opposite sides of the law, the figures of the bandit and the servant have a great deal in common: both are minor characters in the orbit of a major character, both follow orders, and both are presumed to have a strong relationship with their master/leader. In the idealised world of the Gothic romance,

---

[18] Flammenberg, *Necromancer*, 231.

the nature of the relationship between bandit and chief is usually antithetical to that between master and servant, although both are superior/inferior relationships. The relationship between bandits is supposed to be based on self-interest and fear: the ideal relationship between servant and master (or mistress) is popularly supposed to be one of selfless devotion and even love. Although the character type of the major figure creates the emotional basis for these relationships (hence the difference between Charles Moor's gang in *The Robbers* and Leonardo's in *Zofloya*) the reader registers the type of relationship through the actions and speech of the minor character.

Thus, like the bandit, the figure of the servant may be used to illuminate or amplify the major character to whom he is attached. From the inception of the Gothic romance, however, interludes involving servants were specifically designed to perform other functions too. Walpole's apology for his representation of servants, in the preface to the second edition of *The Castle of Otranto*, clearly indicates that he considered the servant interludes to be important:

> My rule was nature. However grave, important, or even melancholy the sensations of princes and heroes may be, they do not stamp the same affections on their domestics: at least the latter do not, or should not be made to express their passions in the same dignified tone. In my humble opinion, the contrast between the sublime of the one, and the *naïveté* of the other, sets the pathetic of the former in a stronger light. The very impatience which a reader feels, while delayed by the coarse pleasantries of vulgar actors from arriving at the knowledge of the important catastrophe he expects, perhaps heightens, certainly proves that he has been artfully interested in, the depending event.[19]

---

[19] Horace Walpole, *The Castle of Otranto*, 8. For reactions to Walpole's characterisation of servants in *The Castle of Otranto*, see Sabor, Peter (ed.), *Horace Walpole: the Critical Heritage* (London, 1987), 71-74, 96-8. Walpole's justification was considered an adequate one by Sir Walter Scott, who commented in his introduction to *The Castle of Otranto*, (1811), that "The characters of the inferior domestics have been considered as not bearing a proportion sufficiently dignified to the rest of the story. But this is a point on which the author has pleaded his own cause fully in the original prefaces." Sabor, *Critical Heritage*, 97-8. This is not a view espoused by an early reviewer of the second edition, who indignantly accused Walpole of a lack of refined taste: "Under the same banner of singularity he attempts to defend all the *trash* of Shakespeare, and what that great genius evidently threw out as a necessary sacrifice to that idol the *caecum vulgus*, he would adopt in the worship of the true God of Poetry." *Ibid* 72.

The assumption with which Walpole began this defence, the intrinsic difference between the sensibilities of master and servant, is as basic to the Gothic romance as the precepts 'murder will out' and 'Providence vindicates the innocent.' By beginning 'My rule was nature' Walpole placed this assumption in the realm of immutable fact. The servant's inferior sensibility is constantly underlined, either by direct narratorial comment or, as in the case of Edmund, *The Old English Baron*, by the plot resolution – the noble servant proves to be noble indeed. Despite the cleverness of servants, despite occasional plots in which the hero or heroine is a servant of distinguished character, the social order in the Gothic romance is static. In his preface Walpole also supplied reasons why the ideal servant/master relationship should be fixed. Taking the opportunity to claim Shakespeare for his model, Walpole clearly saw the domestic as a useful narrative device illuminating character and contributing to the plot. Unlike the bandit, whose usage as a device depended largely on the parallels that could be drawn between the negative passions of minor and major characters, it was the contrast between master and servant that Walpole valued, 'between the sublime of the one and the *naïveté* of the other.' Walpole's intention, which may clearly be inferred from this preface, was always to emphasise the sublime. Thus, one may see that the servant, with the patterns of coarse sensibility and awkward language that became stereotypes in the world of the Gothic romance, is used as a device to heighten the stature of his aristocratic master.

Walpole's preface also indicates that the figure of the servant might be used to raise the tension generated by the prolonged uncertainties of the plot, and might even prolong those uncertainties. Unable, because of his inferior sensibility, to sift evidence or reach rational conclusions, the servant may be a witness to some action that he does not understand and cannot fully communicate. Walpole created two loquacious servants, Diego and Jacquez, in *The Castle of Otranto* whose inability to report on the supernatural phenomena that they have witnessed infuriates Manfred and the reader alike. *The Castle of Otranto* incident demonstrates both of the ways in which Walpole declared that he used the domestic. The contrast between the language and attitudes of the servants and their master emphasises Manfred's tyrannical and impatient character. At the same time the action of the plot is suspended, and tension increased, while the servants are interrogated. They simultaneously reveal character and function as plot devices.

These twin functions are characteristic of all representations of servants in the Gothic romance. What Walpole did not say in his preface, but which is evident in the characterisation and usage of servants throughout the spectrum of Gothic fiction, is that whatever the contrast in sensibility between servant and master classes, there is usually a moral correspondence between them. An idealised, hero master has an equally good, idealised servant: a villain commands other villains. A 'good' servant character, faithfully attached to his master or mistress, will inevitably share in the suffering, providing a curious counterpoint of common-sense and superstition to the elevated emotions of the major characters. A villainous servant may figure in the action of the plot, acting as the villain by proxy and intensifying the brutality to which a noble villain might not descend, before betraying his villainous master or mistress. Whether faithful or villainous, the status of the servant is another important factor for the Gothic writer because, unlike hero, heroine and villain, servants have no overt, social power and are expendable. For these reasons, the representation of the servant, and the reader's expectations about such a figure are crucial elements in the advancement of the plot.

The correspondence between the moral characters of master and servant with the consequent effects on the action of the plot can be clearly seen in George Walker's potboiler, *The Haunted Castle*, (1794). The structure of George Walker's romance depends on the importance of history, the influence of past actions (particularly past crimes) on the present action of the tale. George Walker created two major characters with corresponding servants who fit neatly into the temporal division of the story. The hero, Ignatius, who pursues his destiny through the present action of the tale has a good and faithful servant, La Moine, as a companion. The villain, Hendred, whose past actions shape Ignatius's present quest, had a servant of questionable loyalty to carry out his plans.[20] La Moine is only important as a faithful servant. He accompanies Ignatius through all the vicissitudes of his travels, fights alongside him, is captured, released, caught in a storm and terrified by supernatural phenomena. La Moine's continued faithfulness is used to construct part of Ignatius's character as hero and is expected by the reader. Thus, although his faithfulness and servitude is a device to enhance or to confirm the status of the hero, he has little to do with the plot. The evil servant, however, has a different function.

Like La Moine, Bede is the moral reflection of his villainous master, unlike La Moine, he is also his agent when, for example, Ignatius discovers a letter from Hendred to Bede confirming the plans to murder his brother and his brother's children. Bede, it later transpires, was also responsible for procuring a little, peasant girl to take the place of Manfredi's son. Thus the intentions of the villain were accomplished by the actions of the servant. There is, however, more to the usage of the servant as a plot device than simply as the convenient agent of his villainous master. When both master and servant are completely motivated by self-interest, as the villains invariably prove to be, there is the possibility of conflict, affecting both plot and characterisation. The blackmail of a villainous master by a servant in possession of his secrets is a common plot complication, and one George Walker used to get rid of both villains: Hendred is blackmailed by Bede, kills him, and, already troubled by his conscience, immures himself in a monastery. George Walker's usage of the servant/master relationship suggests several

---

[20] Interestingly, the names of both servants have religious and cultural associations: the name of Ignatius' servant, La Moine, not only links him with Catholic monasticism but also reflects Ignatius's Norman upbringing and noble background; Hendred's servant is named Bede – Old English meaning prayer. Although purely speculative, there seems to be an interesting parallel between the servant's names and their function: La Moine is a passive, subordinate figure whereas Bede is active.

important points. The past character of the villainous Hendred has been emphasised by the behaviour and character of his chosen servant, and the conflict between the two men has forced a crisis leading directly to the resolution of
Ignatius' story and the restoration of his happiness in the present. Although Ignatius's birth is revealed early in *The Haunted Castle*, that of his beloved Adelais
can only be resolved by information from the penitent Hendred (or Father Francis).

Eliza Parsons used a similar scenario in *The Mysterious Visit* (1802). Her
romance is more complex than George Walker's, but her usage of the figure of
the immoral servant and master joined in an ultimately destructive relationship is
the same. The villain, Sir William Symons, uses his servant Samuel as a confidant
and an agent in the plot against Clifford (Georgina's adoptive father). Samuel's
actions cause the papers relating to Georgina's mysterious birth and financial circumstances to be placed in Sir William's hands. Inevitably, and according to the
formula of the Gothic romance, Samuel makes demands on Sir William who responds by sending him to the Press Gang. The pattern is almost identical to that of
The Haunted Castle: a villainous master uses his servant as an agent, the servant
is then in an intolerable position of power over the master and must be removed.
Finally, the conflict between master and servant contributes to the resolution of
the plot and the vindication of the innocent. In *The Mysterious Visit* the villain is
covered in calumny and Clifford is released from the Bastille as a result of the
charges which Samuel lays against Sir William in the fourth and final volume.

Bede and Samuel are expendable. This is partly due to the nature of their
implacable masters, but also indicates that even the most cunning servant lacks
social power or influence. Unlike the priest or the heroine, who are similarly un-
influential, the servant has neither precious jewellery nor noble family name, and,
most importantly, is not a major character within the formula. Numerous servants,
good and bad, are sacrificed during the course of a Gothic romance. In *The Castle
of Wolfenbach*, (1793), several faithful servants fall victim to the villain: Margue-

rite, the companion of the suffering Countess, is found stabbed in an upstairs room and Berthe is killed when the Castle of Wolfenbach is burnt to the ground. Marguerite's death, discovered at the same time as the abduction of the Countess, is a death by proxy. The reader's fears for the safety of the Countess are engaged and heightened by the discovery of Marguerite's corpse. However, little emotion is wasted on Marguerite's behalf and she is simply emblematic of her mistress' probable fate. Berthe's death is similarly a death by proxy – the emphasis is transferred to the destruction of the castle, and the human death becomes an emblem for the destruction of the building. The servant's status reduces the reader's involvement with his/her fate because the servant is only important insofar as his/her fate reflects on the major character or on the action. The status of the servant also serves the plot because even the most well intentioned servant can only partially protect a heroine against the villain. Thus, although a journeying (or more commonly an escaping) heroine is frequently accompanied part of the way by a faithful servant, she is not safe. Matilda, *The Castle of Wolfenbach*, is accompanied by Albert, who aids her escape from the villainous Mr. Weimar, but this is not enough to protect her in Paris. Georgina, *The Mysterious Visit*, is helped to self-education by the advice of a maid, warned of Sir William's seductive intentions by another, and eventually assisted to economic independence by legacies from Lord Dunlevy's devoted steward. All this assistance, however, is very passive, confined to verbal messages and written warnings, which are the limits of a servant's activity. Even the legacies cannot help her unless she knows of them, and has the assistance of an active hero to wrest them from Sir William's grasp. A male servant is represented as less masculine, and less active, than the active hero or villain because his ability to protect the heroine is significantly less.

Servant status may add more to the intricacies of the plot than simple expendability. In several romances, the status of the servant is eventually revealed as the motivating force behind the villain. In *Clermont* (1798), the complicated plot, ostensibly centred around the fortunes and unhappy history of the de Montmorenci family, relies on the dynastic ambitions of a servant for much of its action. The abducted son of the supposedly murdered Philippe was brought up as the son of Lafroy's brother, Joseph, and Lafroy [the servant] used his knowledge of d'Alembert's villainy to blackmail d'Alembert into agreeing to a marriage between d'Alembert's daughter and Lafroy's supposed nephew. In creating this scenario, Regina Roche remained true to the formula of the Gothic Romance: Lafroy's actions are the same as those of any treacherous, self-seeking servant, although his motives are more difficult to determine. Did Mrs. Roche intend the reader to interpret Lafroy's actions as indicative of a desire to elevate his own status, or is he a character who wishes to debase others? He is represented as taking a noble child (thus acquiring status of a sort), and placing him with his brother (ensuring that the child grew up in humble circumstances). In the fixed world of the Gothic romance, however, the proposed marriage can only diminish the d'Alemberts – the Lafroy family will not be elevated. Regina Roche represented Lafroy as seeking the social debasement of a man whose moral character is no better than Lafroy's own.[21]

Yet in allying d'Alembert with an inferior, Regina Roche was emphasising the essential difference between master and servant. The master's acute sensibility, part of a noble birthright, would be grossly insulted and perpetually affronted by such a marriage. This type of class distinction is ever present in the Gothic romance, and is often explicitly stated in the text:

> This shattered pile, the record of departed greatness and the power of time, was carefully shunned by the peasant after sunset ... but though feared by superstition, it was the favourite haunt of taste and sensibility;[22]

The contrasting reactions of peasantry and nobility towards the castle on the mountainside above Clermont's rustic cottage demonstrate the gulf between the

---

[21] Cf. *The Passions*, i, 77-8, Countess Zulmer's former servant, Pietro Mondovi, writes to another servant, Catherine Glatz, about their former mistress, demonstrating a similar concern with the reduction of status, "'What is her fancied elevation? What is her rank in society? Could we not speedily topple her from her height by shewing her such as she is? ... I am always out of spirits when I am poor. The sight of the money will set us all to rights.'"

[22] Roche, *Clermont*, i, 9.

sensibilities of master and servant. Peasant and nobleman have different perceptions of the world around them. Peasants are popularly supposed to be as insensitive as the beasts they tend: 'the mind is worn down with the body, and ... a
common laborer rarely considers anything beyond those common comforts inces-
sant industry can procure him.'[23] Given this type of expectation about the peasantry, continually reinforced within the text, noble birth is a necessity for the hero
or heroine of romance, who must embody and uphold high ideals about society in
general. As the above quotation shows, master and servant differ not only in vary-
ing degrees of sensibility, but the master class is more rational, better educated,
and not given to superstitious fears.[24]

Apart from the education, these qualities are an integral part of noble
blood – as Edmund's behaviour demonstrates in *The Old English Baron* – and
cannot be assumed by a mere servant. When Sir William Symons, *The Mysterious
Visit*, realises that his servant has some power over him, the situation is intolerable:

> Samuel was ignorant, though cunning and wicked-- ... --Sir William was but
> too conscious that his servant held a rod over him; and to emancipate himself
> from a slavery so degrading to a *gentleman*, was the chief object of his wak-
> ing thoughts and dreams.[25]

The image of slavery indicates the enormity of the reversal of power in the mas-
ter/servant relationship. Sir William does not just see himself in the role of servant
to Samuel's master, but passively awaiting a beating from his social inferior. Such
a role is intolerable for the active man, particularly the active Gothic nobleman.

---

[23] Lee, *The Recess*, ii, 31. Cf. Eliza Parsons's description of the peasant gaolers in *The Mysterious Visit*, ii, 67, which also links class and sensitivity: 'From the fierce, uncouth beings who were her
guards, she had nothing to expect-- ... not one spark of hope illumined her dismal prospect, for to pity
or feeling those creatures were wholly insensible.'

[24] Although most Gothic romances show servants to be far more credulous than their masters,
there is a moment of humour attached to a consciousness of the differences in sensibility between
master and servant in *The Castle of Wolfenbach*, i. 52, when Albert (the servant) and Matilda are
about to sleep in a haunted house: 'All now retired to rest, and Albert thought himself quite safe on the
ground floor from the quality ghosts.'

[25] Parsons, *The Mysterious Visit*, ii. 73-4.

This consciousness of slavery is the first torment the guilty man has to endure, outwardly manifesting the villain's inward slavery to the passions.[26]

One of the ways in which the servant is represented and his or her status fixed for the reader is through language. The faithful servant or anyone belonging to the peasant class is unable to manipulate language, order facts, or distinguish between natural and supernatural phenomena. The first exchange between Diego, Jacquez and Manfred in *The Castle of Otranto* created a pattern that became a stereotype for the speech and thought of subsequent servants in Gothic romances. Their narrative is lengthy and inconsequential:

> My gracious lord, said Jacquez, if it please your highness to hear me; Diego and I, according to your highness's orders, went to search for the young lady; but being comprehensive [sic] that we might meet the ghost of my young lord, your highness's son, God rest his soul, as he has not received christian burial.[27]

The difference between servant and master is heavily stressed. Jacquez reminds Manfred four times of the difference of status between them as he obsequiously lards his speech with 'My gracious lord,' 'your highness,' 'your highness's orders,' and 'your highness's son.' A servant cannot think clearly, cannot distinguish between important facts and trivia, and so Jacquez tells a tangential story in his desire to provide every detail and exonerate himself. After a plea for mercy and a tacit reminder of Manfred's feudal responsibilities, 'My gracious lord,' Jacquez begins by shifting all responsibility for the news to Manfred, 'according to your highness's orders.' The description of the servants' fears serves several purposes in Jacquez's narrative: it introduces the concept of the supernatural; it justifies the servants' incoherence; and provides an explanation for the search being conducted in pairs. Including every detail of emotion, every factor that contributed to the story, indicates the fear that the servant feels for the tyrannical master

---

[26] This sensation is intensified when Sir William is eventually arraigned by Samuel, *The Mysterious Visit*, iv. "And how, it may be asked, did he feel, whilst he stood like a culprit before his quondam associate and servant?--he certainly felt all that confusion, that low-mindedness and terror which a bad heart must ever feel on a detection of guilt, and an abasement before his inferiors."

[27] Walpole, *The Castle of Otranto*, 31.

but also suggests certain limitations. Later, when Manfred demands to know what 'you saw' in the great chamber, Jacquez responds, '--I! my lord! said Jacquez, I saw nothing; I was behind Diego;--but I heard the noise.'[28] Jacquez is unable to distinguish between the general and the personal 'you.' As he had used 'comprehensive' – obviously meaning 'apprehensive' – in the previous passage quoted, it is clear that Walpole's representation of the servant type includes a basic inability to communicate effectively.[29] Such an inability suggests inferior or muddled thought processes, possibly deserving Manfred's epithet 'blockheads.'

Incoherent speech and an inability to handle or discriminate when using language became a fixed stereotype of the Gothic romance. In *The Mysterious Freebooter*, (1806), forty-two years after Walpole introduced Diego and Jacquez, Francis Lathom used precisely the same techniques in the speech of the faithful, but unintelligent, Gertrude:

> "the poor old woman, my lady, at the foot of the hill, that you pray remember broke her leg the day she was eighty, and that everybody thought must have died first."[30]

The subject under discussion is another servant's sighting of the pallid, bleeding ghost of the hero. Gertrude includes so many reference points in her narrative that, like that of Diego and Jacquez, it becomes inconsequential and parenthetic. Similarly, when Annette, Emily's servant in *the Mysteries of Udolpho*, is describing the drunken scenes inside the castle to her mistress, Ann Radcliffe used the same techniques of over-detailed, and thus inferior, narrative to emphasise the difference in status and understanding between servant and heroine. This type of exaggerated narrative allies the reader more closely with the perceptions of the hero or heroine.

---

[28] *Ibid* 32.

[29] In the notes to the O.U.P. edition of *The Castle of Otranto*, 113, Joseph W. Reed Jr. comments on Jacquez's misuse of language, "*comprehensive*: for *apprehensive*; a malapropism in anticipation of Mrs.. Malaprop, who made her first appearance in 1775." Given that Walpole claims Shakespeare as his model in the preface to the second edition, a more useful comparison is to Dogberry in *Much Ado About Nothing*.

[30] Francis Lathom, *The Mysterious Freebooter*, i. 31-2.

Thus one may see that the stereotype of the servant – inferior sensibility and judgement – is conveyed through his/her inability to communicate effectively. Ann Radcliffe demonstrated that Annette, for example, is cruder in her sensibilities than Emily when she brings news of her lover, Ludovico. Annette's grief, though perfectly genuine, is expressed in an inappropriate register and vocabulary: "'Who could have foreseen this, ma'amselle? O miserable, wretched, day--that ever I should live to see it!'"[31] Annette weeps and sobs convincing Emily (wrongly) that Ludovico is dead. Were Ludovico dead indeed, it is difficult to imagine what other, stronger words Annette might have used. In this instance, Annette's cruder sensibilities and her love affair are used as a counterpoint to Emily's refined sentiments. In *The Children of the Abbey* this lack of communication becomes part of the plot. Mrs. Edwin's dark hints to Lord Mortimer about Belgrave's persecution of Amanda, which were intended only to reinforce his good opinion of the heroine have the opposite effect. Lord Mortimer is left with the impression that Amanda is Belgrave's cast-off mistress and alters his behaviour to her accordingly. Thus, a servant's misunderstanding of nuance contributes to the first of many misunderstandings that upset the love affair and prolong the plot.[32]

Unsuccessful attempts to copy the sentiments and language of nobility – the romance of Mary and Chip the carpenter in *The Children of the Abbey* nearly founders when Mary copies Amanda's offended rejection of Lord Mortimer – suggest the servant's awareness that the master's superior discourse reflects superior sentiments and intelligence. In the master/servant relationship, as Walpole depicted it in *The Castle of Otranto*, the servants' reaction depends on the master's perception:

---

[31] Radcliffe, *The Mysteries of Udolpho*, 328.

[32] The same type of misunderstanding, based on the accepted notion that the sensibility and language of the servant or lowly born is not compatible with that of the master class, is parodied by E.S. Barrett in *The Heroine*, (1813), when his heroine, Cherry, imposes romantic language and expectations onto the romance between two peasants. The boy completely misunderstands, the engagement is broken, and the girl is rendered temporarily insane.

The tears of the assistants were suspended by wonder, rather than stopped by joy. They seemed to enquire in the eyes of their lord what they ought to feel.[33]

This passage, occurring immediately after Theodore's birthmark, exposed during the preparations for his execution, reveals him to be Father Jerome's son, demonstrates the servitude of the assistants, who cannot afford to display an unacceptable reaction, and the absolute power wielded by Manfred. Note that the servants are initially struck with amazement, rather than by more elevated feelings of sympathetic joy for the reunited father and son, showing that they are confronted with a situation outside their experience.[34] They are reliant, therefore, on Manfred.

The ties between master and faithful servant are always represented as exceedingly strong.[35] The reunion between Paulo and Vivaldi after Schedoni's death is replete with emotion:

'It is my master! it is my dear master!' cried Paulo, and, sending off a nobleman with each elbow, as he made his way between them, he hugged Vivaldi in his arms, repeating, 'O, my master! my master!' till a passion of joy and affection overcame his voice, and he fell at his master's feet and wept.

This was a moment of finer joy to Vivaldi, than he had known since the meeting with his father, and he was too much interested by his faithful servant, to have leisure to apologize to the astonished company for his rudeness.[36]

Even here the contrast between master and servant is maintained and demonstrated in the physical activity, which is the most striking thing about this scene. Paulo knocks noblemen over in his desire to reach his master, hugs Vivaldi in his arms, shouts and weeps at his feet. In contrast, the reunion of Vivaldi and Ellena is a much less physical affair, emotions rather than actions are detailed:

---

[33] Walpole, *The Castle of Otranto*, 54.

[34] It might also show the blunted feelings ascribed to the peasantry. Cf. Charlotte Dacre, *Zofloya*, i. 149: "Still having their way through, they proceeded, Victoria with a vague and indefinable feeling of hope and fear, and Catau merely with that curiosity incident to vulgar minds."

[35] Janet Todd suggests that the tie between master and servant is one of love rather than simple loyalty, and illustrates this with reference to the Vivaldi/Paulo relationship in Ann Radcliffe's *The Italian. The Sign of Angelica* (London, 1989), 260.

[36] Radcliffe, *The Italian*, 405.

In such a meeting, after the long uncertainty and terror, which each had suffered for the fate of the other, and the dangers and hardships they had really incurred, joy was exalted almost to agony. Ellena wept, and some minutes passed before she could answer to Vivaldi's few words of tender exclamation.[37]

This is a more private encounter. Ann Radcliffe did not relate whether Vivaldi swept Ellena into his arms to comfort her, and the 'words of tender exclamation' can only be imagined. Lovers commune silently, through tears and tender words unheard even by the author but Paulo's emotions are publicly displayed, represented through the excess of physical action typical of a servant. Noblemen, friends both of Vivaldi and Vivaldi's father, expressed their pleasure in Vivaldi's release by offering 'ceremonious congratulations.' Paulo observes no such ritual and his ability to convey emotion through speech is severely reduced by the strength of that emotion: he can only act. The only words that occur to Paulo at such a time are 'my master,' reaffirming their relationship.[38] Ann Radcliffe also comments on the reactions of the polite company, who witness the reunion between master and servant and are 'astonished,' indicating that this display of affection, resulting in upset snuff-boxes and affronted noble dignities, is not normal.

In fact, Paulo's noisy devotion to Vivaldi, is not typical either of Ann Radcliffe's work or of the Gothic romance as a whole. There are many devoted servants but their relationship to their master is rarely the central issue of the tale. Ann Radcliffe uses this excess of loyalty is to reinforce the reader's sense of Vivaldi's worthiness: he is a better hero simply because he can inspire (and return) such faithful devotion in his servant. The master/servant relationship indicates an embryonic family structure, a microcosm of his relationship with his family and community.[39] Thus, in protecting and caring for servants, the young

---

[37] *Ibid* 408.

[38] Paulo is similarly robbed of words during and after the marriage of Vivaldi and Ellena di Rosalba. His exultant and frequently repeated cries of '*O! giorno felice!*' ring through the last chapter as a benediction on the marriage and conclude the book.

[39] Cf. John Wesley, 'On Family Religion,' "Your servants, of whatever kind, you are to look upon as a kind of *secondary children*, these, likewise, God has committed to your charge, as one that must give an account." *Sermons on Several Occasions*, 2 vols, (London, 1825), i. 363.

hero or heroine is also exercising the same sort of responsibility that he/she will called on to display in marriage or parenthood.

Raymond's attitude to his faithful, young servant, Theodore, in *The Monk* is both paternal and loverlike. At different points in the narrative Raymond comments on his relationship with Theodore, 'rather as a Companion than as a Servant,' and 'as an adopted Child than a Domestic.'[40] Dwelling strongly on the close relationship between master and servant, Lewis devoted large sections of Raymond's narrative to descriptions of Theodore's many perfections and, like Paulo, Theodore's reciprocal attachment to his master is profound:

> He had attached himself to me most sincerely, during my stay in Strasbourg; and when I was on the point of leaving it, He besought me with tears to take him into my service: He set forth all his little talents in the most favourable colours, and tried to convince me that I should find him of infinite use to me upon the road. ... However, I could not resist the entreaties of this affectionate Youth, who in fact possessed a thousand estimable qualities.[41]

Like Paulo's joyous reunion with his master, all the activity in the relationship is undertaken by the servant. Theodore works very hard to convince Raymond that he will be indispensable – as he indeed proves to be. When Lewis described, using Raymond's narrative, the progress of the love affair and the encounter with the Bleeding Nun, he included a long paean of praise for the faithful and accomplished Theodore. Raymond's description of Theodore's person and understanding is uncomfortably akin to the description of a heroine, and suggests a love relationship:

> He had acquired much information for his Age; and united the advantages of a lively countenance and prepossessing figure to an excellent understanding, and the very best of hearts. He is now fifteen; He is still in my service, and when you see him, I am sure that He will please you. But excuse this digression: I return to the subject which I quitted.[42]

---

[40] Lewis, *Monk*, 166, 170.

[41] *Ibid* 127-8.

[42] *Ibid* 146. Interestingly, Raymond's eventual bride, Agnes, is a young woman who also has a lively countenance. Lewis included several suggestions of male/male love affairs in *The Monk*. Ambrosio's love for the supposed novice, Rosario is one such example. Also the action of Theodore's

This description of a paragon – the only thing missing from a similar description of a heroine would be the sweetness of her expression – rapidly followed by an apology for the lengthy digression suggests that Lewis was representing Raymond as aware that his affection for Theodore was evident and, perhaps, excessive.

When faithful servants and masters are bonded as strongly as Raymond and Theodore (although it is worth remarking that the servant's is the stronger attachment as it is the only attachment in his life) or Paulo and Vivaldi, the source of the bond is usually the disinterested saving of life. In other words, when a master figure proves his concern, his affection, and his duty towards his inferiors by saving their lives at the risk of his own, a bond of gratitude and affection is formed. Thus, there are emotional, moral and pragmatic reasons for the attachment – the master has simultaneously proved himself worthy of admiration and to be an able protector. Several masters and their male servants are bonded thus: Edwin (*The Children of the Abbey*) is devoted to FitzAlan because FitzAlan saved his life in battle; and Theodore (*The Monk*) is devoted to Raymond because Raymond rescued his mother and family from a life of perpetual misery with bandits. Even Hubert the surly, independent youth in (*The Mysterious Freebooter*) is devoted, despite himself, to Edward:

> there was a something, inexplicable almost to himself [Hubert], unless it could be accounted for by that reverence which a mind of discontent naturally feels for a noble and honest heart, ... and which proceeded from his sense of Edward's benevolent feelings towards him, and from gratitude for the many favours which he received at his hands.[43]

The attachment between the faithful servant and the master depends upon a fixed social order. Hubert is attached to Edward because he recognises a benevolent nature, but also because he recognises the innate superiority of that nature. Edward is worthy to be a master and Hubert's recognition of this marks him as a servant. Edward as a boy gave a chunk of bread to Hubert, a surly, dirty urchin,

---

singing around the convent is almost identical to the labour of love which Blondel performed for the imprisoned Lionheart.

[43] Lathom, *The Mysterious Freebooter*, i. 115-16.

Hubert accepted the bread but, instead of eating himself, gave it to his equally disreputable, enormous mongrel. Edward can make a benevolent gesture to someone of a lower status; Hubert, the servant, can only make the same gesture to his dog, and Edward's bounty has made Hubert's generosity possible. Thus Lathom shows the bond and the difference in status between these two characters.

If the very act of acknowledging a superior is the mark of a servant, so too is a particular attitude of mind first presented by Horace Walpole in *The Castle of Otranto*. The servant as menial and as agent is practical, and has been so represented since the 'clever slave' of Greek comedy. Theodore, for example, is indispensable in *The Monk*. Almost every action described in Raymond's narrative involves Theodore as accomplice, assistant or agent in actions like hoisting Cunegonda over the wall, creating a diversion so that Raymond can smuggle her into the inn or bribing the convent gardener so that Raymond can gain access to the convent grounds. This is not unusual: servants in the Gothic romance are invariably represented as being more practical than the hero or heroine, and are sometimes represented as possessing more common-sense than their master or mistress, whilst also being less rational and more superstitious. Bianca's comments to Matilda in *The Castle of Otranto* demonstrate both these qualities:

> No, no, madam; there is more in it than you great folks are aware of. Lopez told me, that all the servants believe this young fellow contrived my lady Isabella's escape.[44]

Bianca and the other servants have seized on a half-truth. Theodore's question about Isabella was, as the reader knows and Bianca infers, disingenuous. Furthermore, she is correct in believing that Theodore assisted Isabella's escape. But, although her conclusions are accurate, they are based on a completely false, superstitious premise – Theodore, the servants believe, must be a magician. Servants, particularly female servants, in the Gothic romance continually display these irrational prejudices which heroes and heroines refuse to countenance. The servant, however, is more adept at dealing with the physical than the metaphysical. When the Countess de Merville is stabbed in *Clermont*, servants handle all the practical details of staunching blood, moving the body etc., while the contribution of the heroine, who discovered the wounded woman, is to faint when she sees the body and to sob pathetically by the bedside. When, however, Agatha and Floretta [servants] tell tales of a haunted house, Madeleine [heroine] finds alternative explanations for the phenomena that they describe. Emily, too in *The Mysteries of Udolpho*, represses Annette's superstitious fancies and boldly confronts her own irrational fears.

Although servants are stereotyped, represented as inarticulate, credulous and expendable, Gothic writers continually remind the reader that servants too have feelings and standards of honour. In *Zofloya* (1806) for example, the servant girl, Catau, is initially introduced to the reader in unflattering terms, as 'a peasant of Switzerland, short and thick in her person, hard favoured, of rude and vacant features, ignorant and innured to labour.'[45] Catau is physically unattractive to the refined notions of the eighteenth century, her mind is indeed stamped upon her countenance 'of rude and vacant features.' Yet on the following leaf, the reader is explicitly warned not to accept this superficial assessment:

> Catau could think; and, what was more, she could *feel*--yes, infinitely beyond those who so proudly sat in judgement upon her character.[46]

The change in Charlotte Dacre's representation is partly caused by a change in her heroine's perception. Catau is on the point of becoming an ally. It also, however, reflects another tenet of the Gothic romance – the idealisation of the countryside and rural life. Just as the countryside is assumed to have all the innocence, beauty and values of an eighteenth-century Eden in striking contrast to the iniquities prevalent in urban society, so the peasant, while lacking polish, breeding and refinement, is nevertheless supposed to have all the feeling that fashionable society

---

[44] Walpole, *The Castle of Otranto*, 43.
[45] Dacre, *Zofloya*, i. 145.
[46] *Ibid* i. 146.

disdains.[47] The inarticulate Gertrude in *The Mysterious Freebooter*, who was incapable of telling a simple story, is nevertheless elevated above her social superiors by the narrator: 'the honest-hearted Gertrude, whose sentiments would have shamed the noble inhabitants of De Mowbray Castle, had they seen through any sense but that of prejudice.'[48] Similarly, Joseph, in *the Castle of Wolfenbach*, is represented as an exemplar of simple honesty and honour and set up as a standard against current social conventions:

> ...his sentiments were above his condition, and he prized his word, and kept it when pledged with much more exactness than a fine gentleman does his honour, when given to a favourite lady, or a humble tradesman.[49]

It is the simplicity of the servant, enhancing his or her good qualities that the reader is invited to admire. The idea that a servant might possess emotions that would shame the sophisticated master class is as frequently mooted in the Gothic romance as the desirability of the rural idyll.

Servants are allowed, therefore, to have some good qualities despite their innate inferiority: the good qualities that they demonstrate, however, are precisely those which make them good and faithful servants. Class boundaries are irrevocably fixed and the good and faithful servant is represented as being happy in his or her humble station. Writers of the Gothic romance, therefore, would seem to be indulging in what Janet Todd has described as 'a fantasy of service.'[50] Written in a period of considerable social unrest when food or machine riots were an annual occurrence, and the government responded by passing several parliamentary acts preventing the 'combination of working men,' the Gothic romance suggests that the working man is ideally capable of selfless and devoted service.[51] Clara

---

[47] Cf. The somewhat idealised description of the Swiss peasantry in *The Passions*, i. 12: ' The rudest mountaineer among them is not ignorant; it is nothing uncommon to see a herdman with a volume of Voltaire or Rousseau in his hand. They are universally benevolent, kind-hearted, and hospitable; their women are handsome, modest, and reserved.'

[48] Lathom, *The Mysterious Freebooter*, i. 276.

[49] Parsons, *The Castle of Wolfenbach*, i. 86.

[50] Todd, *Sign of Angelica*, 261.

[51] For Acts of Parliament passed and dates of food and machine riots see, Cook, Chris and John Stevenson, *British Historical Facts 1760-1830* (London, 1980; repr. 1991), 129-31, 147-53.

Reeve's description of the conversation between Sir Philip Harclay and the peasant in *The Old English Baron* exemplifies this view of the amicable co-existence of different classes:

> After this they conversed together on common subjects, like fellow-creatures of the same natural form and endowments, though different kinds of education had given a conscious superiority to the one, a conscious inferiority to the other; and the due respect was paid by the latter, without being exacted by the former.[52]

The correct moral values are not only upheld by the nobility, the educated and refined classes, but, in this quotation as in the Gothic romance in general, these qualities are seen and acknowledged to be superior by the contented domestic. In addition to their usefulness as narrative devices, therefore, the faithful servants also reinforce the myth of stability underpinning the Gothic romance.

III. DEMONS AND SPECTRES

Dismissed by Hazlitt in 1819 as 'the pasteboard machinery of a pantomime,' the supernatural manifestations occurring in *The Castle of Otranto* are relegated to the level of an unconvincing display of theatrical pyrotechnics.[53] The same term appears in Clara Reeve's discussion of *The Castle of Otranto*, when she claims 'the machinery is so violent,' in the Preface to the second edition of her own Gothic story.[54] Although 'pasteboard' suggests deception, a cheap sham, whereas 'violent' has more active and forceful connotations, both words indicate a similar reaction and a similar criticism: the spectres and the gigantic pieces of armour are overdrawn, out of place, and, consequently, incredible. Yet, if we are

---

[52] Reeve, *The Old English Baron*, 11.

[53] William Hazlitt, *Lectures on the English Comic Writers* (London: Taylor, 1819), 253.

[54] Reeve, *Old English Baron*, 4. 'Machinery' could be used simply as a technical term describing the supernatural elements used in literature. The tone of Pope's explanation of the word in the Dedication to *The Rape of the Lock*, (1712) is, however, as derogatory as Hazlitt's comment cited above: 'The machinery, madam, is a term invented by the critics, to signify that part which the deities, angels, or demons, are made to act in a poem: for the ancient poets are, in one respect, like many modern ladies: let an action be never so trivial in itself they always make it appear of the utmost importance.' In John Butt (ed.), *The Poems of Alexander Pope: A One Volume Edition of the Twickenham Text* (London: Routledge, 1992), 217.

to believe Walpole's letter to William Cole on the origin of his tale, it was a dream of the supernatural that was his first inspiration: 'on the uppermost bannister of a great staircase I saw a gigantic hand in armour. In the evening I sat down, and began to write, without knowing in the least what I intended to say or relate.'[55] The supernatural may thus be considered as a starting point for the Gothic romance and close examination reveals that it is an essential part of the formula.

All Gothic romances contain some supernatural (or pseudo-supernatural) event. Pseudo-supernatural events are those initially ascribed to supernatural causes by characters within the tale, evoking the same emotional and physiological reactions as genuine supernatural manifestations, and which are eventually revealed as either completely natural, but unusual, phenomena, (the effect of the blue flame on the lance in both *The Mysteries of Udolpho* and *The Three Spaniards*, for example), or man-made marvels, like the wax figure behind the black veil in *The Mysteries of Udolpho*.[56] This pseudo-supernatural is an important feature of the Gothic romance only because it temporarily creates the same effects as the supernatural itself.[57]

The supernatural (whether actual or pseudo) functions in the Gothic formula as one of the key devices by which writers created what has been generally accepted as the authentic Gothic sensation – fear. In the Preface to the second edition of *The Castle of Otranto*, Walpole declared his intention of creating a new form that would combine both ancient and modern romance forms and would lib-

---

[55] Hadley, M.A. (ed.), *Selected Letters: Horace Walpole* (1926; repr. London: Dent, 1948), 165.

[56] Scott disapproved of the pseudo-supernatural: 'we disapprove of the mode introduced by Mrs. Radcliffe, and followed by Mr. Murphy and her other imitators, by winding up their story with a solution by which all the incidents, appearing to partake of the mystic and marvellous, are resolved by very simple and natural causes.' Review of Maturin's *Fatal Revenge*, *Quarterly Review* (1810), in *Critical and Miscellaneous Essays*, 3 vols. (Philadelphia: Carey & Hart, 1841), i. 378.

[57] Colin Manlove also considers that the explained and the 'real' supernatural fulfil the same function: 'Those Gothic novels in which the supernatural is revealed to be some merely natural phenomena or a trick of the light - as in the works of Mrs. Radcliffe - are really no different in kind from those which offer no such explanation, for in both the purpose is simply to stimulate the reader's unconscious terrors.' *Modern Fantasy: Five Studies* (Cambridge: Cambridge University Press, 1975), 6.

erate the imagination by, as Sir Walter Scott recognised, the use of the supernatural:

> The influence of fear--and here we extend our observations as well to those romances which actually ground it upon supernatural prodigy as to those which attempt a subsequent explanation--is indeed a faithful and legitimate key to unlock every source of fancy and of feeling.[58]

Feeling is the keynote of Gothic fiction as Coral Ann Howells has also observed, 'feeling as the distinctive attribute of Gothic--feeling as it is explored and enacted in the fictions themselves, and feeling as the primary response elicited from the reader.'[59]

With this link established between feeling as the end, fear as the spur and the supernatural as the agent, we can see that representations of the supernatural are key devices within the Gothic formula, raising specific emotions inside the text as well as in the reader. Note, however, that the experience of fear can also be a form of entertainment and, that by raising these emotions in the reader, the supernatural is potentially playing an active part in increasing the reader's enjoyment. Friedrich Melchior Grimm commented on the relationship between fear caused by representations of the supernatural and the entertainment of the reader in a review of a French translation of *The Castle of Otranto*:

> tout cela fait férir et dresser les cheveux du sage comme d'un enfant et de sa mie, tant les sources du merveilleux sont les mêmes pour tous les hommes! Il est vrai que, quand on a lu cela, il n'en résulte pas grand'chose'; mais le but de l'auteur était de s'amuser, et si le lecteur s'est amusé avec lui, il n'a rien à lui reprocher.[60]

---

[58] Scott, *Critical and Miscellaneous Essays*, i. 379-80.

[59] Coral Ann Howells, *Love, Mystery, and Misery: Feeling in Gothic Fiction* (London: Athlone Press, 1978), 5. George Haggerty also bases his argument for the coherence of the Gothic form on the fact that Gothic fiction is primarily an affective form. See George Haggerty, *Gothic Fiction/Gothic Form* (University Park and London: Pennsylvania University Press, 1989), 4-8.

[60] 'all that made the wise man's hair stand on end just as much as the baby's and its nurse's, to such a degree are the sources of the marvellous the same for everyone! It's true that, when one read it [*Otranto*], it did not come to much; but the author's goal was to entertain, and if the reader enjoyed it, he has nothing to reproach himself with.' Friedrich Melchior Grimm, 'Sur *Le Château d'Otrante*, roman de Horace Walpole' (1767), *Correspondence Littéraire, Philosophique et Critique de Grimm et de Diderot, Depuis 1753 jusqu'en 1790*, 15 vols. (Paris: Furne, 1829), v. 321.

Grimm made three interesting points. First, that every person, of whatever age, responds in the same psychological way and to the same physiological extent when confronted with supernatural phenomena. Second, that the end result, within the text, is disappointing, and third, that the intention of the author was to amuse. The first point testifies to the power of the irrational and supports the association between the Gothic, feeling and the body. His second point is interesting when considered in the light of the third: the reader's reaction, the entertainment gained from the experience of fear, is more significant than the details of the plot.

Walpole himself, however, felt the need to justify the inclusion of the supernatural on grounds other than its entertainment value. In the preface to the first edition, when Walpole presented himself as a translator, he justified the supernatural by the antiquity of the setting and asserted that its use was a virtue in the author: 'Belief in every kind of prodigy was so established in those dark ages, that an author would not be faithful to the *manners* of the times who should omit all mention of them.'[61] Later novelists, like W.H. Ireland, whose plots abounded in ghosts, ghouls, and demons, also felt the need to justify the inclusion of overtly supernatural phenomena and commonly did so by coupling the known attraction of the supernatural with a didactic purpose. Ireland's Preface to *Gondez the Monk* (1805), for example, comments:

'Tis then we feel the glowing stamp of youth,
And seldom estimate the voice of truth;
When sound, not sense, is pleasing to the ear,
And terrors gratify, that chill with fear;
When for the marvellous we feel inclin'd,
And nought but wonders can delight the mind.[62]

Unlike Grimm, Ireland allied the attractions of 'the marvellous' with the inexperience of youth and justified its presentation as part of a didactic scheme. The reader would be more susceptible to a moral message if it were clad in the gaudy garments of Ireland's wonders.

---

[61] Walpole, *Castle of Otranto*, 4.
[62] Ireland, *Gondez the Monk*, i. ix.

This study is concerned with the representation of men, and demons are commonly represented as male. Spectres can be of either sex but are usually represented as appearing *to* male characters. Isabella does not see the ghost step down from the frame (*The Castle of Otranto*) which prevents Manfred from further pursuing his attack. It is Fernando, not his bride, who sees the ghost sitting on their marriage bed (*The Three Spaniards*). Ignatius is the only character to see the ghost of his father (*The Haunted Castle*) and Raymond is the one visited by the Bleeding Nun (*The Monk*). When female characters believe they have seen ghosts, they are usually experiencing the pseudo-supernatural.[63] The reason for this pattern is that the apparitions demand that action be taken and female characters are essentially passive, unable to further the action of the plot, unable to travel, as Ignatius does, for example, in order to find the murderer of his father.

In the presence of a spectre, every male character is described as undergoing virtually the same acute emotional and physiological reaction as the female characters:

> an indescribable thrill of horror suddenly took possession of his frame; his knees trembled, his hair stood bristling upon his brow, and the chill finger of torpor seemed to freeze the current in his youthful veins.[64]

Huberto's reaction, when confronted with the unhappy spirit of the Abbot Geronimo (*Gondez the Monk*), is entirely conventional. An encounter with a spirit is an emasculating experience for the active male, who is depicted as losing his kinetic energy to 'the chill finger of torpor' and his bodily self-control.[65] Huberto is

---

[63] Women's experiences of the pseudo-supernatural are occasionally used to create comedy: male encounters with apparitions are never as entertaining. E.g., Jacinta's reported encounter with Elvira's ghost in *The Monk*: "'But Oh me! how I shook, when I saw a great tall figure at my elbow whose head touched the ceiling! The face was Donna Elvira's, I must confess; But out of its mouth came clouds of fire, its arms were loaded with heavy chains which it rattled piteously, and every hair on its head was a Serpent as big as my arm! At this I was frightened enough, and began to say my Ave-Maria: But the Ghost interrupting me uttered three loud groans, and roared out in a terrible voice, "Oh! That Chicken's wing! My poor soul suffers for it!" As soon as She had said this, the Ground opened, the Spectre sank down, I heard a clap of thunder, and the room was filled with a smell of brimstone.'" 324.

[64] Ireland, *Gondez the Monk*, iii. 151.

[65] Cf. Ozimo's reaction to the raven: "'let the owl hoot and the bat shriek ominously; still will I disdain to bend my soul, or *debase my manhood*! [my emphasis]'" *Ibid* iv. 10. A surrender to the sen-

is literally possessed (in the demonic sense) by emotion, when 'an indescribable thrill of horror suddenly took possession of his frame.'[66] This thrill of horror acquires some of the supernatural force causing it; possessed by emotion rather than reason, Huberto's body breaks down into independent and involuntary actions. No longer in control, he is momentarily as passive as any heroine.

Lewis rendered his hero completely passive in *The Monk* when Raymond is confronted with the spectre of the Bleeding Nun:

> I gazed upon the Spectre with horror too great to be described. My blood was frozen in my veins. I would have called for aid, but the sound expired, ere it could pass my lips. My nerves were bound up in impotence, and I remained in the same attitude inanimate as a Statue.[67]

Again all the physiological functions are taken over by the sensation of horror. Similar to Huberto's encounter, Lewis also depicts his hero with an arrested life force: 'My blood was frozen in my veins.' These heroes are not simply shocked into immobility by their encounters with the unknown, they undergo physiological changes which mimic the dead condition of the spectral form. Not only is Raymond's blood frozen, but his call for aid 'expired' before it could pass his lips and he is finally described as 'inanimate as a Statue.' Ignatius (*The Haunted Castle*) is similarly described as undergoing a death-like experience:

> He trembled, he turned pale, and without being able to articulate a word, fell down at the feet of his companions.--They were alarmed at this instantaneous disorder, and hastened to bring him again to life.[68]

What Ignatius does, of course, is faint. Walker, however, eschewed the word 'faint' or 'swoon' and instead described it as an 'instantaneous disorder' producing the semblance of death as his companions are depicted as attempting 'to bring him again to life.' This representation of nervous collapse is thus rather more

---

sation of horror is only acceptable for a man when he is confronted with the actual, rather than the pseudo, supernatural.

[66] Cf. Clermont's reflection on the murder of his brother: "'horror and remorse had taken possession of me, and the spirit of the murdered Philippe continually haunted my steps.'" Roche, *Clermont*, iv. 25.

[67] Lewis, *Monk*, 160.

[68] Walker, *Haunted Castle*, ii. 72.

'masculine' and heroic than, for example, the description of Madeleine's faint as she is confronted with danger in *Clermont*: 'as she attempted to rise, her senses totally receded, and she fell, fainting, upon the outstretched arm of Lubin.'[69] Madeleine begins on her knees, in a feminine posture of supplication; there is, therefore, a gentler pattern to her collapse. She tries to rise, but collapses, an up and down movement. In contrast, Ignatius falls directly to the ground. Madeleine's senses recede (soft, progressive sound and sense) where Ignatius', by implication, are cut off. Finally, Madeleine falls 'upon the outstretched arm of Lubin.' Even if she is not actually expected to faint away, that outstretched arm suggests an anticipatory protection. There is no arm outstretched to catch Ignatius when he falls: his collapse is unexpected.

Why should these heroes react like weak women to the presence of the supernatural? One of George Walker's characters, Fernando (*The Three Spaniards*), attempted to describe and analyse the sensation:

> It is impossible to describe the sensations of the mind, at an interview with a visible yet impalpable, and supernatural being.--A being unconnected with any class of existences that are familiar to our senses; and which fills the faculty of man with so much mingled wonder and terror, that the mind becomes more bewildered, the more we attempt to reason and reflect.[70]

Walker suggested that, because the supernatural cannot be comprehended by any rational exercise of the senses, the senses and faculties of man become inoperant – the only functioning sense in this instance is sight.[71] The supernatural, the irrational with which man is confronted, is then mirrored in his own mind and sensations. It is a form of possession, unmanning the man, who gives up control of his

---

[69] Roche, *Clermont*, iii. 21-2.

[70] Walker, *Three Spaniards*, iii. 131.

[71] Cf. J.S. Forsyth, on the association between fear and the deprivation of the senses: 'The fear and caution which must be observed in the night; the opportunity it affords for ambuscades and assassinations; depriving us of society, and cutting off many pleasing trains of ideas, which objects in the light never fail to introduce, are all circumstances of terror: and perhaps, on the whole, so much of our happiness depends upon our senses that the deprivation of any one may be attended with a proportionate degree of horror and uneasiness.' 'Apparitions', *Demonologia; or Natural Knowledge Revealed* (London: Bumpus, 1827), 178.

body, and is unable to control his mind in the presence of something he can neither explain nor dominate.

When Fernando spoke of an 'interview' with a visible yet impalpable being, George Walker was emphasising the importance of the only functioning sense. These spectres are rarely described in any detail but, when any description is given, the eyes are paramount. Raymond (*The Monk*), for example, is unable to look away from the Bleeding Nun: 'Her eyes were fixed earnestly upon mine: They seemed endowed with the property of the Rattle-snake's, for I strove in vain to look off her.'[72] The Tall White Man of the Mountain (*Gondez the Monk*) is equally compelling: 'in the sockets of his eyes, two pallid flames emitted a deadly glare, freezing with horror the soul of the observer.'[73] In Percy Shelley's *St. Irvyne* this type of spectral glare has a fatal effect: 'On a sudden Ginotti's frame mouldered to a gigantic skeleton, yet two pale and ghastly flames glared in his eyeless sockets.'[74] Wolfstein promptly dies. Unable to look away, the heroes are clearly under a spell, possessed by the supernatural forces facing them. The hero who encounters the spectre is usually encountering a piece (known or, more commonly, unknown) of his past history, which must be unravelled, in order that past passions may be appeased.[75] The emphasis on eye contact and the violent surrender of the self during meetings with the spectre suggests a partial breakdown of what Kosofsky Sedgwick calls 'the barrier between self and what should belong to it.'[76] The spectre represents knowledge that the hero must acquire before a state of stability can be attained. In the formula of the Gothic romance, however, this type of buried knowledge cannot be acquired by any rational means. Hence the total collapse of the active male, whose rational faculties are suspended, whose life force

---

[72] Lewis, *Monk*, 160.

[73] Ireland, *Gondez the Monk*, ii. 224.

[74] Shelley, *St. Irvyne*, 199.

[75] Cf. The description of the function of ghosts, in Keith Thomas, *Religion and the Decline of Magic: Studies in Popular Beliefs in Sixteenth and Seventeenth Century England* (London: Wiedenfield and Nicolson, 1971), 602.

[76] Sedgwick, *Gothic Conventions*, 12-13.

is held in stasis mimicking the supernatural phenomena, in order that buried knowledge may be brought to light.

As the only possible source of important knowledge, the spectre functions primarily as a plot device. The physiological reactions provoked in characters within the text are generalised and, therefore, such reactions do not reflect on the individual character concerned. Demons, less frequently depicted than spectres, are used as devices of character rather than of plot and the appearance of a demon within the text has many specific implications for the character with whom it is associated.

In the European tradition, witchcraft is associated with perversions of Christianity and is thus a threat to the established social and political order, tailor-made to create unease in the Gothic romance.[77] Unlike spectre-sightings, raising demons had been considered a capital crime within living memory – although no actual executions for witchcraft took place in England after 1684. Familiarity with a demon implies that the human figure is certainly a sorcerer and possibly a witch.[78] The presence of the diabolic tends to suggest a potentially diabolic human nature.

The demon is a potent figure for Gothic writers. Although James I's act was repealed in 1736 (only twenty-nine years before *The Castle of Otranto* was written) and belief in witchcraft was officially dead, there were, nevertheless, several incidents throughout the eighteenth century, indicating a strong and continu-

---

[77] For a credulous Catholic viewpoint, stressing the link between witchcraft and heresy, see Montague Summers, *The History of Witchcraft and Demonology* (New York: Alfred A. Knopf, 1926). For a rational view stressing the connections between politics, legislation and the growth of witchcraft, see Wallace Notestein, *A History of Witchcraft in England from 1558 to 1718* (Washington: American Historical Association, 1911). For a more recent discussion of the relationship between religion and superstition in the sixteenth and seventeenth centuries see Keith Thomas, *Religion and the Decline of Magic*, 435-583.

[78] 'Sorcier est celuy [sic] qui par moyens Diaboliques sciemment s'efforce de paruenir [sic] à quel que chose.' [The sorcerer is one who by devilish means knowingly strives to attain something.] Jean Bodin's opening words in his *De La Demonologie des Sorciers* (Paris, 1580) cited in Summers, *History of Witchcraft*, 1.

ing undercurrent of vulgar belief.[79] The demon and attendant witch would seem to be ideal figures for the writers of the Gothic romance, simultaneously credible and incredible. Few demons, however, are represented in the Gothic romances and occasional witches are relegated to a very minor part of the setting.

Like the bandit and the servant, the demon is important only insofar as his presence reflects and underlines the diabolic passions of the human protagonist. The two romances that contain explicitly drawn demon figures, *Zofloya* and *The Monk*, both make a firm connection between demons and passion. In each case, demons are invoked in order to procure a sexual conquest for the human protagonist. Ambrosio is able to possess Antonia (*The Monk*) and Victoria to enjoy some nights of unrivalled passion with Henriques (*Zofloya*). The relationship between demon and human protagonist in these novels is also sexual and socially disturbing. Matilda and Ambrosio's relationship began as that of Abbot/Lay Brother. Victoria, too, is powerfully and reluctantly attracted to the mysterious Moor, Zofloya, in a Mistress/Servant relationship: 'yet ashamed, (for Victoria was still proud) and blushing at her feelings, when she remembered that Zofloya, however he appeared, was but a menial slave.'[80] The figure of the demon is used not only to indicate the depths of passion in the human character but also, through his supernatural agency, to exaggerate the scope of the crimes the character is capable of committing.

On their first appearances, these demons are represented as beautiful. Although Charlotte Dacre's depiction of Zofloya as a black man is a stereotypical portrait of a potential devil, his physical attractions are described in sublime terms:

---

[79] In 1780, for example, the *Morning Post* reported that two women of Bexhill were suspected of witchcraft. The mob that wanted to swim them, appealed to the local clergyman and they were rather more humanely weighed against the Bible instead. For evidence of this and other attacks in the eighteenth and nineteenth centuries, see Christina Hole, *Witchcraft in Britain* (1977; repr. London: Paladin, 1979).

[80] Dacre, *Zofloya*, iii. 130.

His form and attitude, as he sat beside her, was majestic, and solemnly beautiful--not the beauty which may be freely admired, but acknowledged with sensations awful and indescribable.[81]

Everything about Zofloya is indescribable. Victoria's opinion of him is that 'he appeared not only the superior of his race, but of a superior order of beings' and hence there is no adequate vocabulary to describe him.[82] Charlotte Dacre has shrouded her demon in the obscurity appropriate to sublime sensations. Even when describing his eyes – the most important features of the speaking countenance – she confined herself to saying that they 'sparkled with inexpressible fire.'[83] This type of representation, the idea of perfect but fatal beauty, does not come from the traditional images of the demon, and Mario Praz has argued that it is a peculiarly Romantic vision.[84] Everything is enlarged: everything is left to the imagination.

Lewis describes the manifestation of his demon (the one called by Matilda rather than Matilda herself) with a wealth of material and physical detail:

a Figure more beautiful, than Fancy's pencil ever drew. It was a Youth seemingly scarce eighteen, the perfection of whose form and face was unrivalled. He was perfectly naked: A bright Star sparkled upon his fore-head; Two crimson wings extended themselves from his shoulders; and his silken locks were confined by a band of many-coloured fires, which played round his head, formed themselves into a variety of figures, and shone with a brilliance far surpassing that of precious Stones. Circlets of Diamonds were fastened round his arms and ankles, and in his right hand He bore a silver branch, imitating Myrtle. His form shone with dazzling glory: He was surrounded by

---

[81] *Ibid* ii. 156. The Devil was frequently described as a black man in published testimonies of witchcraft trials of the sixteenth and seventeenth centuries, for full accounts see, C.H. L'Estrange Ewen, *Witch Hunting and Witch Trials* (London: Kegan Paul, 1929). Also in George Walker's *The Three Spaniards*, (1800), the enchantress is taken from Denia by the Devil in the guise of a black man.

[82] Dacre, *Zofloya*, ii. 150.

[83] *Ibid* ii. 139.

[84] A typical, traditional, non-literary image of the demon can be found in Nicolas Remy, *Demonolatry* (1595), trans. E.A. Ashwin & ed. by Montague Summers (London: John Rodker, 1930), 28: 'their features always appeared dark and obscure, and shapeless ... that their eyes were deep set, yet flashing like flames; that the opening of their mouths was wide and deep, and always gave forth a sulphurous smell; that their hands were thin and deformed with hairs and talons; their feet of horn and cloven; their stature never in proportion, but always unnaturally small or great; and that they were in all respects out of the measurement.' For the combination of beauty and death as a manifestation of Romanticism, see Praz, *Romantic Agony*, 45-64.

clouds of rose-coloured light, and at the moment that He appeared, a refreshing air breathed perfumes through the Cavern.[85]

Lewis presented this demon through Ambrosio's perception and senses in a manner very unlike Raymond's encounter with the Bleeding Nun. The demon makes a strong appeal to every physical and aesthetic sense: the intention is not to shock or to terrify but to woo. The music, the perfume, the colours and the flickering fires combine to form a sensual appeal. The demon's perfect nakedness enhances the sensual image and reinforces the link between the diabolic and bodily passion. Because Ambrosio is the one who perceives all this lushly decadent beauty, the reader believes that it is an illusion designed to appeal only to him.[86]

The devil figure that visits Ambrosio when he is imprisoned by the Inquisition is far more in accord with the traditional image of the demon. Every detail of his depiction is a dark and distorted version of the initial beauty. The essential elements of the description remain the same: huge wings, a head wreathed in continual movement and wild eyes. The figure, however, has been transformed into an androgynous figure of vengeance with Medusa-like qualities: 'his hair was supplied by living snakes,' and 'Fury glared in his eyes, which might have struck the bravest heart with terror.'[87] Instead of the silver myrtle branch, which will smooth the path towards Ambrosio's desires, he bears a parchment and an iron pen – which, if Ambrosio is willing to pay the price, will also assist him in his desire to escape. Through these two representations of the Demon, Lewis demonstrated both Ambrosio's capacity for self-deception and the darkness attendant on physical passion. Thus the demons of Lewis and Dacre are not simply devices of plot, although they are used to advance the story, but also, amplify the passions of the human protagonists and objectify the struggle between good and evil taking place within a single character.

---

[85] Lewis, *Monk*, 276-7.
[86] Just as the magic mirror showed him precisely the kind of titillating sexual image that he wanted to see – even though the whole linnet-in-the-bath sequence is incredible.
[87] Lewis, *Monk*, 433.

The passions themselves are also described as demonic and are lent a supernatural force. The inquisitor in Percy Shelley's *Zastrozzi* (1810), for example, does not fathom Matilda's true nature: 'He [the inquisitor] little thought that, under a form so celestial, so interesting, lurked a heart depraved, vicious as a demon's.'[88] Matilda, another intensely sexual and passionate woman, is consistently described in diabolic and bestial terms that de-feminise her, as the 'ferocious Matilda' gripping the helpless Julia 'with fiend-like strength' as she stabs her a thousand times, or exclaiming 'in a voice of fiend-like horror.'[89] The fury of Matilda's passion is clearly conceived as a supernatural force, and intensifies the reader's understanding of Matilda's character.

In *Frankenstein* (1818), Mary Shelley used Frankenstein's first-person narration to darken the reader's vision of the creature and his actions. There is a gradual but rapidly ascending scale of horrified denunciation, beginning in misery and culminating in devilish epithets. The unnameable monster's first appellation is 'the wretch,' a term of repugnance suggesting both misfortune and lower-class human worthlessness, when Frankenstein first beholds his creation fully alive.[90] After the necrophiliac nightmare from which he awakes to find the creature gazing down at him, Frankenstein then refers to him as 'the miserable monster,' which is swiftly intensified into 'the demoniacal corpse.'[91] Any element of pity or misfortune is now eliminated from Frankenstein's vocabulary and the creature is automatically credited with evil intent. Mary Shelley made him go further, however; after connecting the creature with the murder of young William, Frankenstein's comment is 'I thought of pursuing the devil.'[92] Frankenstein's constant references to the creature as something diabolic, something of growing and increasing evil, are qualities that he as narrator imposes on the creature. It undermines his credibility as a narrator, a reflection of the horror of his own guilt, a

---

[88] Shelley, *Zastrozzi*, 95.
[89] *Ibid* 89-90.
[90] Shelley, *Frankenstein*, 52.
[91] *Ibid* 53.
[92] *Ibid* 72.

way of avoiding his own involvement in the story by increasing the power of the evil with which he has to contend. The idea of the demon is still being used as a character device by Mary Shelley, but it is clearly a projection of the narrator's passion building towards the moment when, accepting this nomenclature, the creature describes himself as the Arch Fiend.

Both spectres and demons contribute to the sense of stability with which the Gothic romance invariably concludes in the late eighteenth and early nineteenth centuries. Elements of the irrational are introduced to advance the plot but the conclusion of the story sees the spectres, ghosts of dead passion, finally laid to rest. The temptations of demons are carried to their logical conclusions as a demon becomes a *deus ex machina*, finally and irrevocably damning the guilty. Having fed on the passions raised, the demon too retires, leaving the virtuous characters secure in a stable world. Paradoxically, the irruption of the irrational finally serves only to confirm the stereotypes of gender division and prove the efficacy of the enduring moral qualities, which support the fabric of the Gothic romance.

Conclusion

The Perfect Gentleman

Stock male figures are depicted according to fixed patterns that are repeated across the spectrum of Gothic fiction and this process of stereotyping is as much a part of the Gothic formula as are the ruined castle or abbey, set in vertiginous mountainous scenery, haunted by the spectres of undead passions and past crimes.

These fixed patterns discernible in the Gothic formula confirm gender roles that were already present in the social and cultural expectations of the reader. The dominant influence shaping all the representations of stock figures was that of the eighteenth-century 'perfect gentleman,' the pattern of idealised active masculinity indicated in contemporary conduct literature. Most primary male characters of Gothic fiction are commonly delineated through their relations with the heroine, paralleling one aspect of the definition of the male gender role – its relationship to the female – that is also found in conduct literature. The innate qualities of magnanimity, sincerity and nobility, which the conduct books ascribe to the perfect man, are demonstrated in all areas of activity and are particularly evident in a man's relations with physically weaker or dependant figures. Hero, father and villain can all be interpreted by the way in which they fulfil (or fail to fulfil) these ideals of masculine behaviour.

The perfect eighteenth-century gentleman should be a man of discernment, a man of impeccable moral standards, directing his masculine activity towards the maintenance of his society. He is also an uxorious figure, eschewing the superficial values of a fashionable society and keenly appreciative of a happy domestic existence in which he is supported by the virtues of the woman whom he has chosen.

This is the pattern which writers of Gothic romances imposed on both father and hero. The hero in Gothic fiction is a perfect gentleman in embryo: he possesses all the necessary innate qualities associated with the idealised stereotype, including the sensibility associated only with the middle and upper classes. The imposed pattern of eighteenth-century perfection, however, turns the hero into a self-reflective character who is often represented as more passive than the typical figure of the chivalric knight – the heroic image to which conduct writers referred. Heroism and masculinity are explored through the representation of the hero figure, who undergoes a learning process in the course of the tale before he can retire into a domestic existence with the heroine.

The perfect gentleman appears again in the figure of the 'good' father, establishing the paradigm at the beginning of the tales, which the hero will re-establish at their end. In the Gothic formula, the 'good' father figure and the protection he offers are quickly made absent. He is thus used as a plot device whereby the hero and/or the heroine are made vulnerable, compelled to venture forth alone and to test the moral values which the father has inculcated.

Within the formula, the 'good' absent father stereotype is made more potent by the presence of his opposite: the villain. The representation of the villain, too, is defined by the pattern of gentlemanly perfection, which he does not fulfil. Self-seeking rather than selfless, anti-social rather than social, destructive rather than constructive, the villain figure perverts the ideal of masculinity through his objective vision, malicious activity and unrestrained passion. More than one stereotype of villainy is represented in the Gothic romances: 'Grand' villains evoke the sublime and their characters and actions are interpreted aesthetically rather than morally; 'Simple' villains are repugnant rather than fascinating. The villainy of both types is commonly directed against women and measured by female perceptions within the Gothic romances. This is even the case when the villain in question is a woman – neither a perfect gentleman nor a perfect gentlewoman.

Minor male characters are also a part of the formula. They too are stereotypes indirectly influenced by the pattern of ideal masculinity. Bandits, servants, spectres and demons cannot themselves be perfect gentlemen, but, as devices either of plot or character, they enhance the effect of its presence or absence in the primary characters. In some cases they provide a background against which the action takes place.

Examining the representation of male characters in a large number of texts has provided one way of describing the Gothic formula without, however, finding a definitive answer to the question of what constitutes the 'Gothic.' Other critics have already defined the Gothic from feminist or political stances in terms of the anxieties of women or of class, which they see manifested in the texts, while men have been neglected. In attempting to redress the balance I have not defined the Gothic formula according to any *a priori* ideology but have, instead, analysed one aspect of the manifestation of the Gothic formula, that is, the representation of those neglected men. Such analysis does not define but *describes* contents and conventions. Despite being formula fiction, the 'Gothic' itself remains indefinable – and that is how it should be. All the techniques, all the devices developed by the writers of Gothic fiction were intended, as Walpole first said, to leave 'the powers of fancy at liberty to expatiate through the boundless realms of invention.'[1] One can describe the figures in the boundless realms, one can analyse the possible effects of their representation on the reader, but one cannot ever satisfactorily define them.

---

[1] Walpole, *Castle of Otranto*, 7.

BIBLIOGRAPHY

Abbreviations

ELH	*English Literary History*
MLN	*Modern Language Notes*
MLQ	*Modern Language Quarterly*
NLH	*New Literary History*
PFL	*Pelican Freud Library*
PMLA	*Publications of the Modern Language Association*
SIN	*Studies in the Novel*
SIR	*Studies in Romanticism*

I. PRIMARY SOURCES

Beckford, William, *Vathek*, ed. & intro. Roger Lonsdale (1786; repr. from corrected 3rd ed. 1816, Oxford: Oxford University Press, 1983).

Dacre, Charlotte, *Zofloya; or, The Moor: A Romance of the Fifteenth Century*, 3 vols. (London: Longman, Hurst, Rees and Orme, 1806).

...*The Passions*, 4 vols. (London: T. Cadell and W.H. Davies, 1811).

Flammenberg, Lorenz, *The Necromancer*, trans. Peter Teuthold, ed. & intro. Lucien Jenkins (1794; repr. from 1st. ed. London: Skoob, 1989).

Godwin, William, *Caleb Williams*, ed. & intro. David McCracken (first ed. published 1794 under the title *Things As They Are: Or, The Adventures of Caleb Williams*; repr. Oxford: Oxford University Press, 1982).

Ireland, William Henry, *Gondez, The Monk: A Romance of the Thirteenth Century*, 4 vols. (London: Longman, Hurst, Rees and Orme, 1805).

Lathom, Francis, *The Mysterious Freebooter, Or, The Days of Queen Bess: A Romance*, 4 vols. (London: Minerva Press, 1806).

...*The Midnight Bell*, ed. & intro. Lucien Jenkins (1798; repr. from 1st. ed. London: Skoob, 1989).

Lee, Harriet and Sophia, *The Canterbury Tales* (1797/1799; repr. London: Pandora Press, 1989).

Lee, Sophia, *The Recess, Or, A Tale of Other Times*, 3 vols. (London: Cadell, 1785).

Leland, Thomas, *Longsword, William; Third Earl of Salisbury: An Historical Romance*, 2 vols. (London: Johnston, 1762).

Lewis, Matthew, *The Monk: A Romance*, ed. & intro. Howard Anderson (1796; repr. Oxford: Oxford University Press, 1980).

Maturin, Charles, *Melmoth the Wanderer: A Tale*, ed. Douglas Grant & intro. Chris Baldick (1820; repr. Oxford: Oxford University Press, 1989).

Parsons, Eliza, *Castle of Wolfenbach; A German Story*, 2 vols. (London: Minerva Press, 1793).

...*The Mysterious Visit: A Novel, Founded on Facts*, 4 vols. (London: Hurst, Hatchard, Carpenter & Co., Didier and Tibbett, 1802).

Radcliffe, Ann, *The Romance of the Forest*, ed. & intro. Chloe Chard, (1791; repr. Oxford: Oxford University Press, 1986).

...*The Mysteries of Udolpho, A Romance*, ed. & intro. Bonamy Dobrée, (1794; repr. Oxford: Oxford University Press, 1980).

...*The Italian, Or The Confessional of the Black Penitents*, ed. & intro. Frederick Garber, (1797; repr. Oxford: Oxford University Press, 1981).

Reeve, Clara, *The Old English Baron*, ed. & intro. James Trainer (1778; repr. Oxford: Oxford University Press, 1967).

Roche, Regina Maria, *The Children of the Abbey, A Tale*, 4 vols. (1796; 2nd. ed. London: Minerva Press, 1797).

...*Clermont, A Tale*, 4 vols. (1798; repr. London: A.K. Newman & Co., 1836).

Shelley, Mary, *Frankenstein, or The Modern Prometheus*, ed. James Reiger (1818; repr. Chicago: University of Chicago Press, 1982).

Shelley, Percy Bysshe, *Zastrozzi, A Romance, and St. Irvyne, or, The Rosicrucian: A Romance*, ed. & intro. Stephen C. Behrendt, (1810, 1811; repr. Oxford: Oxford University Press, 1986).

Smith, Charlotte, *Emmeline, The Orphan of the Castle*, ed. & intro. Anne Henry Ehrenpreis, (1788; repr. from 2nd ed., Oxford: Oxford University Press, 1971).

...*The Old Manor House, A Novel*, ed. Anne Henry Ehrenpreis & intro. Julian Stanton (1783; repr. Oxford: Oxford University Press, 1989).

Walker, George, *The Haunted Castle, A Norman Romance*, 2 vols. (London: Minerva Press, 1794).

...*The Three Spaniards, A Romance*, 3 vols. (London: Walker, Hurst, 1800).

Walpole, Horace, *The Castle of Otranto, A Gothic Story*, ed. & intro. W.S. Lewis, notes, J.W. Reed Jr. (1764; repr. from 1798 text, Oxford: Oxford University Press, 1982).

II. SECONDARY SOURCES

i. Contemporary

Aikin, John, *Letters From a Father to a Son, on Various Topics Relative to Literature and the Conduct of Life*, 2 vols. (London: J. Johnson, 1793-1796).

Aikin, John and Anna L., 'On the Pleasure Derived from Objects of Terror; with Sir Bertram, a Fragment,' *Miscellaneous Pieces in Prose* (London: J. Johnson, 1773), 119-137.

A Man of The World, *Free and Impartial Remarks upon the Letters written by the Late Right Honourable Philip Dormer Stanhope, Earl of Chesterfield, to his Son, Philip Stanhope Esq.* (London: Bew, 1774).

Anon, *Memoir of the Late Henrietta Fordyce. To which is added a Sketch of the Life of James Fordyce, D.D.* (London: Hurst, Robinson & Co., 1823).

Anon, *Chesterfield Travestie; or, School for Modern Manners* (London: Tegg, 1808).

Anon, *Fordyce Delineated: A Satire Occasioned by his Sermons To Young Women* (London: Dixwell, 1767).

Barrett, Eaton Stannard, *The Heroine, or Adventures of a Fair Romance Reader*, 3 vols. (London: Henry Colburn, 1813).

Beattie, James, *Dissertations Moral and Critical*, 2 vols. (Dublin: Exshaw, Walker, Beatty, White, Byrne, Cash and M'Kenzie, 1783).

Bennett, Betty T. (ed.), *The Letters of Mary Wollstonecraft Shelley*, 3 vols. (Baltimore and London: Johns Hopkins University Press, 1980-1988).

Blair, Hugh, *Lectures on Rhetoric and Belles Lettres*, 2 vols. (London: W. Strahan, T. Cadell, 1783).

Burke, Edmund, *A Philosophical Enquiry into the Origin of our Ideas of The Sublime and Beautiful* (1757), 2nd. ed. with additions, (London: R. and J. Dodsley, 1759).

Chapone Hester, *Letters on the Improvement of the Mind*, 2 vols. 2nd. ed., (London: J. Walter, 1773).

Chesterfield, Lord, *Letters written by the Late Right Honourable Philip Dormer Stanhope, Earl of Chesterfield to his Son, Philip Stanhope Esq.* published by Mrs. Eugenia Stanhope, 2 vols. (London: J. Dodsley, 1774).
    ...A Supplement to Chesterfield's Letters (London: Dodsley, 1787).
    ...Miscellaneous Works, containing M. Maty's 'Chesterfield Memoir', 2 vols. (London: Dilly, 1777).

Cobbett, William, 'Letter to a Father,' *Advice to Young Men and (incidentally) to Young Women, In the Middle and Higher Ranks of Life* (London: published by the author, 1829).

Cole John, *Memoirs of Mrs. Chapone* (London: Simpkin, Marshall & Co., 1839).

Drake, Nathan, 'On Gothic Superstition,' 'Henry Fitzowen, a Gothic Tale,' and 'On Objects of Terror, Montmorenci, a Fragment,' *Literary Hours, or Sketches Critical and Narrative* (London: T. Cadell & W. Davies, 1798), 87-96, 97-136, and 245-260.

Elledge, Scott (ed.), *Eighteenth-Century Critical Essays*, 2 vols. (New York: Cornell University Press, 1961).

Fordyce, James, *Sermons to Young Women*, 2 vols. 3rd. ed. corrected, (London: Millar, Cadell, Dodsley, Payne, 1766).

...*The Character and Conduct of the Female Sex, and the Advantages to be Gained by Young Men from the Society of Virtuous Women* (London: Cadell, 1776).

...*Addresses to Young Men*, 2 vols. (London: Cadell, 1777).

Forsyth, J.S., *Demonologia; or, Natural Knowledge Revealed* (London: Bumpus, 1827).

Gisborne, Thomas, M.A., *An Enquiry into the Duties of the Female Sex*, 3rd. ed. corrected, (London: Cadell Jnr. & Davies, 1798).

...*An Enquiry into the Duties of Men in the Higher and Middle Classes of Society in Great Britain*, 2 vols. 2nd. ed. corrected, (London: Cadell Jnr. & Davies, 1795).

Gregory, Dr. John, *A Father's Legacy to his Daughters* (1774: repr. Ludlow: Nicholson, 1809).

Grimm, Friedrich Melchior, 'Sur *Le Château d'Otrante*, roman de Horace Walpole' (1767), *Correspondance Littéraire, Philosophique and Critique de Grimm et de Diderot, depuis 1753 jusqu'en 1790*, 15 vols. (Paris: Furne, 1829), v. 320-322.

Hadley, M.A. (ed.), *Selected Letters: Horace Walpole* (1926; repr. London: Dent, 1948).

Hawkesworth, John, *The Adventurer*, 4 vols. (1752; repr. London: for Sylvester Doig, Edinburgh, 1793).

Hazlitt, William, 'Why the Heroes of Romance are Insipid,' *Sketches and Essays* (London: Templeman, 1839), 257-274.

...*Lectures on the English Comic Writers* (London: Taylor, 1819).

Hurd, R., *Letters on Chivalry and Romance* (London: Millar, 1762).

Ireland, W.H., *The Confessions of William Henry Ireland* (London: Goddard, 1805).

Johnson, Samuel, *A Dictionary of the English Language*, 2 vols. (1755; repr. in facsimile, New York: Times Books, 1979).

Paine, Thomas, *The Rights of Man* (London: J. Johnson, 1791).

Paley, William, *Sermons on Several Subjects*, 2 vols. 3rd. ed. (London: Longman, Hurst, Rees & Orme, 1808).

Radcliffe, Ann, 'On the Supernatural in Poetry,' *The New Monthly Magazine* xvi (1826), 145-152.

Reeve, Clara, *The Progress of Romance and The History of Charoba, Queen of Egypt*, 2 vols. (1785; repr. in facsmile, New York: Facsimile Text Society, 1930).

...*Memoirs of Sir Roger de Clarendon*, 3 vols. (London: Hookham and Carpenter, 1793).

Richardson, Samuel, *The History of Sir Charles Grandison*, ed. & intro. Jocelyn Harris (1753-1754; repr. from 1st ed. in 3 vols, Oxford: Oxford University Press, 1972).

Scott, Sir Walter, *Critical and Miscellaneous Essays*, 3 vols. (Philadelphia: Carey & Hart, 1841).

Wesley, John, *The Complete English Dictionary*, 2nd. ed. with additions, (Bristol: Pine, 1764).

...*Sermons On Several Occasions*, 2 vols. Ed. T. Jackson, (London:Caxton Press, c.1825).

...*Thoughts Concerning the Origin of Power* (Bristol: Pine, 1772).

West, Mrs. J., *Letters Addressed to a Young Man On His First Entrance into Life and Adapted to the Peculiar Circumstances of the Present Times*, 3 vols. (1801; 2nd. ed., London: Longman & Rees, 1802).

Williams, Ioan (ed.), *Novel and Romance 1700-1800. A Documentary Record* (London: Routledge and Kegan Paul, 1970).

Wollstonecraft, Mary, *Vindication of the Rights of Woman* (1792; repr. from 2nd. ed. corrected, London: Penguin, 1985).

...*An Historical and Moral View of the Origin and Progress of the French Revolution*, 2 vols. (London: J. Johnson, 1794).

ii.   Other

Anderson, Howard, 'Gothic Heroes,' in Robert Folkenflik (ed.), *The English Hero, 1660-1800* (London and Toronto: Associated University Presses, 1982), 205-221.

Armstrong, Nancy and Leonard Tennenhouse (eds.), *The Ideology of Conduct: Essays on Literature and the History of Sexuality* (London: Methuen, 1987).

...*Desire and Domestic Fiction: A Political History of the Novel* (1987; repr. Oxford: Oxford University Press, 1989).

Avery, Gillian, and Angela Bull, *Nineteenth Century Children: Heroes and Heroines in English Children's Stories, 1780-1900* (London: Hodder & Stoughton, 1965).

Babcock-Abrahams, Barbara, 'The Novel and the Carnival World: An Essay in Memory of Doherty,' *MLN* lxxxix (1974), 911-937.

Bakhtin, Mikhail, *Problems of Doestoevsky's Poetics*, trans. & ed. Caryl Emerson, (Manchester: Manchester University Press, 1984).

Barthes, Roland, *Sade, Fourier, Loyola*, trans. R. Miller (London: Jonathan Cape, 1977).

Baldick, Chris, *In Frankenstein's Shadow: Myth, Monstrosity and Nineteenth Century Writing* (1987; repr. Oxford: Clarendon Press, 1990).

...(ed.), *The Oxford Book of Gothic Tales* (Oxford: Oxford University Press, 1992).

Beer, Gillian, *The Romance* (1970; London: Methuen Critical Idiom Series, repr. 1977).

...'Our Unnatural No-Voice: The Heroic Epistle, Pope and Women's Gothic,' *Yearbook of English Studies* xii (1982), 125-151.

Bettelheim, Bruno, *The Uses of Enchantment: The Meaning and Importance of Fairy Tales* (London: Thames & Hudson, 1976).

Birkhead, Edith, *The Tale of Terror: A Study of the Gothic Romance* (London: Constable, 1921).

Blakey, Dorothy, *The Minerva Press 1790-1820* (Oxford: Oxford University Press, 1939).

Bloom, Clive (ed), *Gothic Horror: A Reader's Guide from Poe to King and Beyond* (New York: St. Martin's Press, 1998).

Bordwell, David, Janet Staiger and Kristin Thompson (eds.), *The Classical Hollywood Cinema: Film Style and Mode of Production to 1960* (London: Routledge, 1985).

Botting, Fred, *Making Monstrous: Frankenstein, Criticism, Theory* (Manchester: Manchester University Press, 1991).

...*Gothic* New Critical Idiom Series (London, New York: Routledge, 1996).

Bowman, Barbara, 'Victoria Holt's Gothic Romances: A Structuralist Enquiry,' in Fleenor (ed.), *The Female Gothic*, 69-81.

Bowra, Maurice, *The Romantic Imagination* (1950; repr. Oxford: Oxford University Press, 1961).

Boyer, Abel, *The Royal Dictionary*, 2 vols. (London: R. Clavell, 1699).

Boyer, Clarence, *The Villain as Hero In Elizabethan Tragedy* (New York: Dutton, 1914).

Brissenden, R.F., *Virtue in Distress: Studies in the Novel of Sentiment from Richardson to Sade* (London: Macmillan, 1974).

Brooks, Peter, 'Virtue and Terror: *The Monk*', *ELH* xl (1973), 249-263.

...*Reading for the Plot: Design and Intention in Narrative* (1984; repr. Cambridge: Harvard University Press, 1992).

Bruhm, Steven, *Gothic Bodies: The Politics of Pain in Romantic Fiction* (Philadephia, PA: University of Pennsylvania Press, 1994).

Butler, Marilyn, *Romantics, Rebels and Reactionaries: English Literature and its Background 1760-1830* (1981; repr. Oxford: Oxford University Press, 1989).

Cawelti, John George, *Adventure, Mystery, and Romance, Formula Stories as Art and Popular Culture* (Chicago: University of Chicago Press, 1976).

Campbell, Joseph, *The Hero with a Thousand Faces* (1949; repr. London: Grafton, 1988).

...*The Power of Myth*, with Bill Moyers, (New York: Doubleday, 1989).

Carter, Margaret L., *Specter or Delusion? The Supernatural in Gothic Fiction* (Ann Arbor: UMI Research Press, 1987).

Castle, Terry, *Masquerade and Civilization: the Carnivalesque in Eighteenth-Century English Culture and Fiction* (Stanford: Stanford University Press, 1986).

Cavaliero, Glen, *The Supernatural and English Fiction* (Oxford: Oxford University Press, 1995).

Christie, Ian R., *Stress and Stability in Late Eighteenth-Century Britain* (1984; repr. Oxford: Clarendon Press, 1986).

Claridge, Laura, P., 'Parent-Child Tensions in *Frankenstein*: The Search for Communion,' *SIN* xvii (1985), 14-26.

Clery, E.J., *The Rise of Supernatural Fiction 1762-1800* (Cambridge: Cambridge University Press, 1995).

Cook, Chris and John Stevenson, *British Historical Facts 1760-1830* (1980; repr. London: Macmillan, 1991).

Cooke, Arthur, 'Some Side-lights on the Theory of Gothic Romance', *MLQ* xii (1951), 429-436.

Cornwell, Neil, *The Literary Fantastic: From Gothic to Postmodernism* (Brighton: Harvester Wheatsheaf, 1990).

Cottom, Daniel, '*Frankenstein* and the Monster of Representation,' *Sub-Stance* xxviii (1980), 60-71.

Cox, Jeffrey N. (ed.), *Seven Gothic Dramas 1769-1825* (Athens: Ohio University Press, 1992).

Curran, Stuart (ed.), *The Cambridge Companion to British Romanticism* (Cambridge: Cambridge University Press, 1993).

Danziger, Marlies K., 'Heroic Villains in Eighteenth-Century Criticism,' *Comparative Literature* xi (1959), 35-46.

Davidoff, Leonore, Catherine Hall, *Family Fortunes: Men and Women of the English Middle Class 1720-1850* (London: Hutchinson, 1987).

Davies, Rupert E., *Methodism* (1963; repr. London: Epworth Press, 1985).

De Bolla, Peter, *The Discourse of the Sublime: Readings in History, Aesthetics and the Subject* (Oxford: Blackwell, 1989).

Dowling, William, 'Burke and the Age of Chivalry,' *Yearbook of English Studies* xii (1982), 109-124.

Duncan, Ian, *Modern Romance and Transformations of the Novel: The Gothic, Scott, Dickens* (Cambridge: Cambridge University Press, 1992).

Duncan, Margaret Beaton, *Aspects of the Hero in Eighteenth Century English Literature* (Unpublished doctoral thesis, University of California, 1990).

Durant, David, 'Ann Radcliffe and the Conservative Gothic,' *Studies in English Literature, 1500-1900* xxii (1982), 519-530.

...'Aesthetic Heroism in *The Mysteries of Udolpho*', *The Eighteenth Century: Theory and Interpretation* xxii (1981), 175-188.

Dussinger, John, A., 'Kinship and guilt in Mary Shelley's *Frankenstein,*' *SIN* xiii (1976), 38-55.

Ellis, Kate Ferguson, *The Contested Castle: Gothic Novels and the Subversion of Domestic Ideology* (Urbana and Chicago: University of Illinois Press, 1989).

Ewen, C.H. L'Estrange, *Witchcraft and Demonism* (London: Heath Cranton, 1933).

...*Witch Hunting and Witch Trials* (London: Kegan Paul & Co., 1929).

Fawcett, Mary Laughlin, '*Udolpho*'s Primal Mystery', *Studies in English Literature, 1500-1900* xxiii (1983), 481-494.

Fisher, Benjamin F. IV, *The Gothic's Gothic: Study Aids to the Tradition of the Tale of Terror* (New York: Garland Publishing, 1988).

Fleenor, Juliann E. (ed.), *The Female Gothic* (Montreal/London: Eden Press, 1983).

Formani, Heather, *Men: The Darker Continent* (1990; repr. London: Mandarin, 1991).

Foster, James R., *History of the Pre-Romantic Novel in England* (New York: Modern Language Association, 1949).

Foucault, Michel, 'La Volonté de Savoir', *Histoire de La Sexualité*, 3 vols. (Paris: Gallimard, 1976), iii.

Frank, Frederick S., *Gothic Fiction: A Master List of Twentieth Century Criticism and Research* (Westport and London: Meckler, 1988).

Franz, Marie Louise von, *The Pyschological Meaning of Redemption Motifs in Fairytales* (1956; repr. Toronto: Inner City Books, 1980).

Freud, Sigmund, 'Totem and Taboo' (1913), trans. James Strachey 1953, *On the Origins of Religion*, *PFL* xiii (1985; repr. London: Penguin, 1990), 43-224.

...'The Uncanny' (1919), trans. Alix Strachey 1955, *Art and Literature*, *PFL* xiv (1985; repr. London, Penguin, 1988), 335-376.

...'Family Romances' (1909), trans. James Strachey 1959, *PFL* vii (1977; repr. London: Penguin, 1984), 217-225.

Frye, Northrop, *The Secular Scripture: A Study of the Structure of Romance* (Cambridge: Harvard University Press, 1976).

...'The Archetypes of Literature,' *Myth and Literature: Contemporary Theory and Practice*, John B. Vickery (ed.), (Lincoln, NE: University of Nebraska Press, 1966), 87-97.

Garber, Frederick, 'Meaning and Mode in Gothic Fiction,' in Harold Pagliaro (ed.), *Studies in Eighteenth-Century Culture*, 3 vols. (Cleveland: Case Western Reserve University Press, 1973), iii. 155-169.

Geary, Robert F., 'From Providence to Terror: The Supernatural in Gothic Fiction,' in Donald E. Morse (ed.), *The Fantastic in World Literature and the Arts: Selected Essays from the Fifth International Conference on the Fantastic in the Arts*, (New York: Greenwood Press, 1987), 7-18.

Gilbreth, Frank, Jr., *How to be a Father* (1958; repr. London: Heinemann, 1959).

Gorer, Geoffrey, *The Life and Ideas of the Marquis de Sade* (London: Panther Books, 1964).

Graham, John, 'Character Description and Meaning in the Romantic Novel,' *SIR* v (1966), 208-18.

Grixti, Joseph, *Terrors of Uncertainty: The Cultural Contexts of Horror Fiction* (London: Routledge, 1989).

Guazzo, Francesco Maria, *The Compendium Maleficarum* (1608), trans. E.A. Ashwin, (1929; repr. New York: Dover Publications, 1988).

Haggerty, George E., 'Fact and Fancy in the Gothic Novel,' *Nineteenth-Century Fiction* xxxix (1985), 379-391.

...*Gothic Fiction/Gothic Form* (University Park and London: Pennsylvania State University Press, 1989).

Hart, Francis, Russell, 'The Experience of Character in the English Gothic Novel,' *Experience in the Novel: Selected Papers from The English Institute*, Roy Harvey Pearce (ed.), (New York: Columbia University Press, 1968), 83-105.

...'Limits of the Gothic: The Scottish Example,' in Harold Pagliaro (ed.), *Studies in Eighteenth-Century Culture*, iii. 137-153.

Hill-Miller, Katherine C., *"My Hideous Progeny: Mary Shelley, William Godwin and the Father-Daughter Relationship* (Newark, London: Associated University Presses, 1995).

Hirsch, Gordon, D., 'The Monster was a Lady: On the Psychology of Mary Shelley's *Frankenstein,' Hartford Studies in Literature* vii (1975), 116-153.

Hole, Christina, *Witchcraft in Britain* (1977; repr. London: Paladin, 1979).

Holland, Norman H., Leona F. Sherman, 'Gothic Possibilities,' in Elizabeth A. Flynn and Patrocino P. Schweickart (eds.), *Gender and Reading: Essays On Readers, Texts and Contexts* (Baltimore and London: Johns Hopkins University Press, 1986), 215-233.

Howells, Coral Ann, *Love, Mystery, and Misery: Feeling in Gothic Fiction* (London: Athlone Press, 1978).

Hume, Robert D., 'Gothic Versus Romantic: A Revaluation of the Gothic Novel,' *PLMA* lxxxiv (1969), 282-290.

Hume, Kathryn, *Fantasy and Mimesis: Responses to Reality in Western Literature* (London: Methuen, 1984).

Hunt, John Dixon, *The Figure in the Landscape: Poetry, Painting, and Gardening during the Eighteenth Century* (Baltimore and London: Johns Hopkins University Press, 1976).

Hussey, Christopher, *The Picturesque: Studies in a Point of View* (1927; repr. London: Cass, 1967).

Ingham, Patricia, 'Dr. Johnson's Elegance,' *The Review of English Studies* xix (1968), 271-277.

Jackson, Rosemary, *Fantasy: the Literature of Subversion* (1981; repr. London: Routledge, 1988).

James I, *Daemonologie* (1597; repr. London according to Edinburgh text: Aspley and Cotton, 1603).

Jones, Vivien (ed.), *Women in the Eighteenth Century: Constructions of Femininity* (London: Routledge, 1990).

Joseph, Gerhard, 'Frankenstein's Dream: The Child as Father of the Monster,' *Hartford Studies in Literature* vii (1975), 97-115.

Jung, C.G., *Aspects of the Masculine*, trans. R.F.C. Hull, John Beebe (ed.), (London: Ark Paperbacks, 1989).

...*The Spirit in Man, Art and Literature*, trans. R.F.C. Hull (1984; repr. London: Ark Paperbacks, 1989).

...*Four Archetypes*, trans. R.F.C. Hull (1972; repr. London: Ark Paperbacks, 1986-1988).

Kaplan, Morton, and Robert Kloss, ' Fantasy of Paternity and the Doppelgänger: Mary Shelley's *Frankenstein,*' in *The Unspoken Motive: A Guide to Psychoanalytic Literary Criticism* (New York: Free Press, 1973), 119-145.

Kiely, Robert, *The Romantic Novel in England* (Cambridge: Harvard University Press, 1972).

Kilgour, Maggie, *The Rise of the Gothic Novel* (London, New York: Routledge, 1995).

King, Stephen, *Danse Macabre* (London: Futura, 1988).

Kooiman-Van Middendorp, Gerada Maria, *The Hero in the Feminine Novel* (New York: Haskell House, 1966).

Lacan, Jacques, *Ecrits: A Selection* (1966), trans. Alan Sheridan, (1977; repr. London: Routledge, 1989).

Levine, George, 'Translating the Monstrous: *Northanger Abbey*', *Nineteenth-Century Fiction* xxx (1975), 335-50.

...'*Frankenstein* and the Tradition of Realism', *SIN* vii (1973), 14-30.

Lévi-Strauss, Claude, 'The Structural Study of Myth', in Thomas A. Sebeok (ed.), *Myth: A Symposium*, (Bloomington and London: Indiana University Press, 1965), 81-106.

Lévy, Maurice, *Le Roman "Gothique" Anglais, 1764-1824* (Toulouse: Association des publications de la faculté des lettres et des sciences humaines de Toulouse, 1968).

Lewis, Charlie, *Reassessing Fatherhood: New Observations on Fathers and the Modern Family* (London: Sage Publications, 1987).

Longueil, Alfred, 'The word "Gothic" in Eighteenth Century Criticism,' *MLN* xxxviii (1923), 453-60.

MacAndrew, Elizabeth, *The Gothic Tradition in Fiction* (New York: Columbia University Press, 1979).

MacDonald, Gordon, *The Effective Father* (Crowborough [E. Sussex]: Highland Books, 1989).

MacKenzie, Alan, *Certain Lively Episodes: The Articulation of the Passions in Eighteenth Century Prose* (Athens and London: The University of Georgia Press, 1990).

Manlove, Colin, *Literature and Reality, 1600-1800* (London: Macmillan, 1978).

...*Modern Fantasy: Five Studies* (Cambridge: Cambridge University Press, 1975).

Manwaring, Elizabeth Wheeler, *Italian Landscape in Eighteenth Century England: A Study chiefly of the Influence of Claude Lorrain and Salvator Rosa on English Taste 1700-1800* (1925; repr. London: Cass, 1965).

Massé, Michelle, 'Gothic Repetitions: Husband, Horrors, and Things that Go Bump In The Night,' *Signs* xv (1990), 679-889.

...*In the Name of Love: Women, Masochism and the Gothic* (Ithaca and London: Cornell University Press, 1992).

Massey, Irving, *The Gaping Pig: Literature and Metamorphosis* (Berkeley: University of California Press, 1976).

McNutt, D.J., *The Eighteenth-Century Gothic Novel* (Folkestone: Dawson, 1975).

Milbank, Alison, *Daughters of the House: Modes of the Gothic in Victorian Fiction* (London: Macmillan, 1992).

Miles, Robert, *Gothic Writing 1750-1820: A Genealogy* (London, New York: Routledge, 1993).

Miles, Rosalind, *The Rites of Man: Love, Sex and Death in the Making of the Male* (London: Grafton, 1991).

Miller, D.A., '*Cage aux Folles*: Sensation and Gender in Wilkie Collins's *The Woman In White*,' in Jeremy Hawthorn (ed.), *The Nineteenth-Century British Novel*, (London: Edward Arnold, 1986), 95-124.

Miller, Jane, *Women Writing about Men* (London: Virago, 1986).

Miyoshi, Masao, *The Divided Self: A Perspective on the Literature of the Victorians* (New York: New York University Press, 1969).

Modleski, Tania, *Loving with a Vengeance: Mass-produced Fantasies for Women* (London: Methuen, 1984).

Moers, Ellen, *Literary Women* (1977; repr. London: The Women's Press, 1986).

Monk, S.H., *The Sublime: A Study of Critical Theories in XVIII-Century England* (1935; repr. Ann Arbor: University of Michigan Press, 1960).

Moorman, John R.H., *A History of the Church in England*, 3rd. ed. (1973; repr. London: A & C Black, 1986).

Moretti, Franco, 'The Dialectic of Fear: *Dracula* and *Frankenstein*,' *New Left Review* cxxxvi (1982), 67-86.

Morris, David B., 'Gothic Sublimity,' *NLH* xvi (1985), 299-319.

Mussell, Kay J., 'But Why Do They Read Those Things?: The Female Audience and the Gothic Novel,' in Fleenor (ed.), *The Female Gothic*, 57-68.

Napier, Elizabeth R., *The Failure of Gothic: Problems of Disjunction in an Eighteenth-Century Literary Form* (Oxford: Clarendon Press, 1987).

Neuberg, Victor E., *Popular Literature: A History and Guide* (Middlesex: Pelican, 1977).

Nichols, Nina da Vinci, 'Place and Eros in Radcliffe, Lewis and Brontë,' in Fleenor (ed.), *The Female Gothic*, 187-206.

Nicolson, M., *Mountain Gloom and Mountain Glory: the Development of the Aesthetics of the Infinite* (New York: Cornell University Press, 1959).

Notestein, Wallace, *A History of Witchcraft in England from 1558 to 1718* (Washington: American Historical Association, 1911).

Pagliaro, Harold (ed.), *Studies in Eighteenth-Century Culture*, 3 vols. (Cleveland: Case Western Reserve University Press, 1973).

Paulson, Ronald, 'Gothic Fiction and the French Revolution,' *ELH* xlviii (1981), 532-54.

Platzner, Robert L., 'Gothic versus Romantic: A Rejoinder,' *PLMA* lxxxvi (1971), 266-74.

Pointon, Marcia, *Milton & English Art* (Manchester: Manchester University Press, 1970).

Poovey, Mary, *The Proper Lady and the Woman Writer: Ideology as Style in the Works of Mary Wollstonecraft, Mary Shelley and Jane Austen* (Chicago: University of Chicago Press, 1984).

Praz, Mario, *The Romantic Agony* (1933; repr. London: Fontana, 1960).

Punter, David, *The Literature of Terror: A History of Gothic Fictions from 1765 to the Present Day* (London: Longman, 1980).

Raglan, Lord, *The Hero: A Study in Tradition, Myth and Drama* (London: Methuen, 1936).

Railo, Eino, *The Haunted Castle: A Study of the Elements of English Romanticism* (London: Routledge, 1927).

Rank, Otto, *The Myth of the Birth of the Hero and Other Writings*, Philip Freund (ed.) (New York: Vintage Books, 1964).

Reed, Toni, *Demon-Lovers and Their Victims In British Fiction* (Lexington: University Press of Kentucky, 1988).

Reed, Walter L., *Meditations on the Hero: A Study of the Romantic Hero in Nineteenth-Century Fiction* (New Haven: Yale University Press, 1974).

Remy, Nicolas, *Demonolatry*, trans. E.A. Ashwin, Montague Summers (ed.) (London: John Rodker, 1930).

Richter, David H., *The Progress of Romance: Literary Historiography and the Gothic Novel* (Columbus, OH: Ohio State University Press, 1996).

Robert, Marthe, *Origins of the Novel* (1972), trans. Sacha Rabinovitch, (Brighton: Harvester Press, 1980).

Roberts, Bette, B., *The Gothic Romance: Its Appeal to Women Writers and Readers in Late Eighteenth-Century England* (New York: Arno Press, 1980).

Ronald, Ann, 'Terror-Gothic: Nightmare and Dream,' in Fleenor (ed.), *The Female Gothic*, 176-86.

Rubenstein, Marc, A., '"My Accursed Origin": The Search for the Mother in *Frankenstein,*' *SIR* xv (1976), 165-194.

Russ Joanna, 'Someone's Trying To Kill Me and I Think Its My Husband: The Modern Gothic,' in Fleenor (ed.), *The Female Gothic*, 31-56.

Saagpakk, Paul F., 'A Survey of Psychopathology in British Literature from Shakespeare to Hardy,' *Literature and Psychology* xviii (1968), 135-65.

Sabor, Peter (ed.), *Horace Walpole: The Critical Heritage*, (London: Routledge, 1987).

Sade, Marquis de, 'Idée sur les romans', *Les Crimes de l'Amour*, (1800; repr. Paris: Gallimard, 1987), 27-51.

...*The Gothic Tales of the Marquis de Sade*, trans. Margaret Crossland, (London: Peter Owen, 1990).

...*Selected Letters*, trans. W.J. Strachan, ed. Gilbert Lely (London: Peter Owen, 1965).

Schlaffer, Heinz, *The Bourgeois as Hero* (1973), trans. James Lynn, (Cambridge: Polity Press, 1989).

Schmitt, Cannon, *Alien Nation: Nineteenth-Century Gothic Fictions and English Nationality* (Philadephia, PA: University of Pennsylvania Press, 1997).

Schofield, Mary Anne, Cecilia Macheski (eds.) *Fetter'd or Free, British Women Novelists 1670-1815* (Athens: Ohio University Press, 1986).

Schroeder, Natalie, '*The Mysteries of Udolpho* and *Clermont*: The Radcliffean Encroachment on the Art of Regina Maria Roche,' *SIN* xii (1980), 131-143.

Sedgwick, Eve Kosofsky, *The Coherence of Gothic Conventions* (1980; repr. London: Methuen, 1986).

Showalter, Elaine, *A Literature of Their Own* (1979; repr. London: Virago, 1988).

Simpson, David, 'Romanticism, criticism and theory', in Stuart Curran (ed.), *The Cambridge Companion to British Romanticism*, 1-24.

Sinistrari, Ludovico Maria, *Demoniality* (1875), trans. Montague Summers (1927; repr. New York: Dover, 1989).

Skilton, David, 'Gothic, Romantic, and Heroic,' *The English Novel: Defoe to the Victorians* (Newton Abbott and London: David & Charles, 1977), 59-79.

Spender, Dale, *Mothers of the Novel* (London: Pandora Press, 1986).

Stevenson, John, *Popular Disturbances in England 1700-1870* (London: Longman, 1979).

Stone, Lawrence, *The Family, Sex and Marriage in England 1500-1800* (London: Weidenfield and Nicholson, 1977).

Summers, Montague, *The Gothic Bibliography* (London: Fortune Press, 1941).

...*The Gothic Quest: A History of the Gothic Novel* (London: Fortune Press, 1938).

...*The History of Witchcraft and Demonology* (New York: Alfred A. Knopf, 1926).

Tarr, Sr. Mary Muriel, *Catholicism in Gothic Fiction: A Study of the Nature and Function of Catholic Materials in Gothic Fiction in England (1762-1820)* (Washingon: Catholic University of America Press, 1946).

Thomas, Keith, *Religion and the Decline of Magic: Studies in Popular Beliefs in Sixteenth and Seventeenth Century England* (London: Wiedenfield and Nicolson, 1971).

Thompson, Gary, ed. *The Gothic Imagination: Essays in Dark Romanticism* (Washington: Washington University Press, 1974).

Thompson, Leslie M., John R. Ahrens, 'Criticism of English Fiction 1780-1810: The Mysterious Powers of the Pleading Preface,' *Yearbook of English Studies* i (1971), 125-34.

Thorslev, Peter, L., *The Byronic Hero: Types and Prototypes* (Minneapolis: University of Minnesota Press, 1962).

Todd, Janet, *The Sign of Angellica: Women Writing and Fiction 1660-1800* (London: Virago, 1989).

Todorov, Tzvetan, *Introduction à la Littérature Fantastique* (Paris: Editions du Seuil, 1970).

Tompkins, J.M.S., *The Popular Novel in England 1770-1800* (London: Constable, 1932).

Varma, Devendra, P. *The Gothic Flame: being a History of the Gothic Novel in England: its Origins. its Efflorescence, Disintegration, and Residuary Influences* (London: A. Barker,1957).

Veeder, William, *Mary Shelley and Frankenstein: The Fate of Androgyny* (1986; repr. Chicago: Chicago University Press, 1988).

Watkins, Daniel P., 'Social Hierarchy in Matthew Lewis's *The Monk*,' *SIN* xviii (1986), 115-124.

White, R.S., *Innocent Victims: Poetic Injustice in Shakespearean Tragedy* (1982; repr. London: Athlone Press, 1986).

Willey, Basil, *The Eighteenth Century Background* (1940; repr. London: Ark Paperbacks, 1986).

Williams, Raymond, *Culture and Society 1780-1950* (1958; repr. London: Penguin, 1961).

Index

STUDIES IN BRITISH LITERATURE